HONEST BROKER

PEDRO LATOEIRO
FILIPE DOMINGUES

Honest Broker

A Biography of António Guterres

Translated by
KEVIN ROSE

HURST & COMPANY, LONDON

Book supported within the scope of the Open Call for
Translation of Literary Works by the Luso-American
Development Foundation

First published in the United Kingdom in 2022 by
C. Hurst & Co. (Publishers) Ltd.,
New Wing, Somerset House, Strand, London, WC2R 1LA
© Pedro Latoeiro and Filipe Domingues, 2022
All rights reserved.

Printed in Great Britain by Bell and Bain Ltd, Glasgow

Distributed in the United States, Canada and Latin America by
Oxford University Press, 198 Madison Avenue, New York, NY 10016,
United States of America.

The right of Pedro Latoeiro and Filipe Domingues to be identified as the
authors of this publication is asserted by them in accordance with the
Copyright, Designs and Patents Act, 1988.

A Cataloguing-in-Publication data record for this book
is available from the British Library.

ISBN: 9781787387126

This book is printed using paper from registered sustainable
and managed sources.

www.hurstpublishers.com

Dedicated to our sons,
Francisco and António

CONTENTS

vii

CONTENTS

LIST OF ILLUSTRATIONS

Part I

1. Guterres with his first wife, Luísa, during a trip with friends to Southern Europe in 1978. (Guterres' private archive)

2. In the early days of Portuguese democracy, Guterres worked on expanding the Socialist Party across the country. (Guterres' private archive)

3. Guterres' speech to the III Congress of the Portuguese Socialist Party, held in Lisbon in 1979. (© Portuguese Socialist Party)

4. At the constituent summit of the CPLP (Community of the Portuguese-Speaking Countries), one of Guterres' many links with Africa. (Guterres' private archive)

5. With Jacques Chirac, Boris Yeltsin and the NATO Secretary-General Javier Solana at the signing of the Founding Act with Russia. (Guterres' private archive)

6. António Vitorino, the current Director General of the International Organization for Migration, was Guterres' Minister of Defence. (Guterres' private archive)

7. Guterres' close friendship with Hillary Clinton began in the early 1990s. (Guterres' private archive)

8. The conservative José María Aznar, who served as Prime Minister of Spain, became one of Guterres' best friends. (Guterres' private archive)

LIST OF ILLUSTRATIONS

LIST OF ILLUSTRATIONS

LIST OF ILLUSTRATIONS

PREFACE

TAKE OFF

— Mr. Guterres, I believe I already know what your answer is going to be... but a couple of days ago two former journalists came to me. They want to write your biography and they would like to interview you.

— I'm not interested.

— Yes, I know, but think about it this way: you have just been elected UN Secretary-General, this is an international project to be published in English and there is no book whatsoever that tells your story...

— Yes, right, thank you very much, but I don't have time for this.

This was how António Guterres reacted to our first approach, in October 2016, while travelling in South America.

The flight between Colombia and Brazil would last almost ten hours. That was more than enough time for David Damião, former press officer for Guterres at the time when he was the Prime Minister, to become the informal godfather of this work.

For having believed from the off in two unknown writers, without a published book between them, these acknowledgements must start with Damião. And, of course, with the biographical subject.

Only after a year of work did Guterres agree to meet us. In his New York office, we explained our premise, which was, having followed his 2016 campaign for the post of UN Secretary-General, we had found that his political thinking was not well known internationally. We also outlined our motivations for writing this book, which were to promote the irreplaceable role of the United Nations and the ideas defended by the man who would lead the organisation in an uncertain global environment.

We reasoned, on that same occasion, that the work would end the moment he assumed office, since it would be extemporaneous to try to cover that mandate. We guaranteed that we had no hidden agenda, that we were not aligned with a political party, that it was an original idea and a truly independent project without funding from any individual or institution safe from the translation grant. We promised to be impartial and objective. With the exception of the publication deadline, which ended up slipping from three to five years, we were true to our word.

Guterres gave us four exclusive face-to-face interviews, in which we were able to ask whatever we wanted. We were never obliged to announce in advance the subjects we were going to discuss. In fact, these were more free-flowing conversations than interviews, during which Guterres responded to all of our questions.

In this book, every excerpt and quote from these interviews is introduced in the present tense, as are quotes from other interviewees. All of those introduced in the past tense are either public statements or third-party interviews properly identified in the endnotes.

Additionally, Guterres granted us access to his personal photographic archive and was also, at our request, the first to read this book.

As this is not a commissioned work, it is therefore of the utmost importance to recognise that this biography could not have been written with the same rigour or in the same depth without the invaluable contributions of the Secretary-General of the UN.

Guterres' participation becomes even more relevant when we acknowledge that he had no prior relationship with us. Indeed, with the exception of a very brief meeting in the months of the 2016 campaign, he had never met us.

In order to write this biography, we also interviewed 121 other individuals: former heads of state and members of governments,

PREFACE

diplomats and artists, business and religious leaders, academics and humanitarians, senior officials of the United Nations and people from all over the world. To each and every one of you, and to the countless friends who lent a hand—or two—and helped to arrange contact with interviewees, our most sincere thanks. It would be exhausting to list them one by one, but it would also be ungrateful not to mention a few: Ana Gomes, Anna Bergström, António Luiz Cotrim, Athar Sultan-Kahn, Carlos Lopes, Jaime Moro Agud, Jean-François Blarel, João Lima Pimentel, Wilhelm Hofmeister. Thanks to them, we had the opportunity to go in search of lost stories in Madrid and Paris, in New York and in Geneva, as well as in a refugee camp built just a few kilometres from Syria.

At the United Nations High Commissioner for Refugees, we have to thank Marwa Hashem, who guided us through the narrow paths of Za'atari, Jordan, and who introduced us to refugee homes and families, all with personal names and individual histories, people who only a short time ago had lives similar to ours.

It is also essential to thank the extraordinary and visionary team working at Hurst Publishers: our editor Lara Weisweiller-Wu, and Michael Dwyer, as well as our lawyer and dinner companion Diana Domingues, our translator Kevin Rose, Marta Ceia for her thorough revision and helpful comments, and our friend Paulo Neves. We must also express our gratitude to the Luso-American Development Foundation (FLAD) in Portugal for the translation grant.

Finally, we must thank the two people who have accompanied us the most throughout this journey, the two women who have so often watched us go to bed late and wake up at 5 am: Sandra Simões and Maria Luísa Santos.

Thank you and happy reading,

Pedro Latoeiro
Filipe Domingues

INTRODUCTION

François Delattre, the French Ambassador to the United Nations, was a busy man in those days. The dark rings under his eyes had turned permanent as he grew increasingly pale. On his desk, five enormous reams of paper impatiently awaited his attention.

At the intersection of 47th Street and Second Avenue in New York, the forty-fourth floor provided Delattre with a sweeping panorama of the UN headquarters. That month, it was his turn to preside over the organisation's most powerful forum—the Security Council.

In most sessions, the Council's chamber has no view of the outside world. Its windows have the curtains drawn so as not to spotlight some participants and leave others in the shadows. Likewise, the circular seating of the diplomats, around a horseshoe-shaped table, is an attempt to camouflage the asymmetry of power among the countries represented. There are fifteen chairs, each associated with a single vote, but only China, the United States, France, the United Kingdom and Russia hold permanent seats and the right to veto. This permanent group of members is known as the P5.

The declared victors of World War II are the ones who effectively select the Secretary-General of the United Nations, in that very room. It is a rather peculiar election as the winner is not always the candidate with the most votes. The determining factor for success is the opinion of the P5. It takes just one of these members to end a candidate's aspirations.

1

The same applies when the Secretary-General runs for a second term. In Boutros-Ghali's case, all the countries on the Security Council supported his bid to renew his mandate. All except, that is, the United States—enough to force the Egyptian to cede his place to another African.

Kofi Annan followed in his place, only to clash with Washington as well. After him came the South Korean Ban Ki-moon, whose mandate in the United Nations ended in the same year that Barack Obama left the White House.

Thus, in 2016, the arduous task of electing a new UN Secretary-General was back on the table, and the instructions received by Ambassador Delattre from Paris were categorical: "We supported António Guterres' candidacy from the moment he announced his intentions. We were no doubt the first P5 country to do so. His proven competence and leadership, his vision of the world and political weight, his solidly anchored values, the genuine interest he has always shown for the most vulnerable, the fact that he speaks French so well—he was in our view the perfect candidate."

PART I

THE PARABLE OF THE TALENTS

1

SOCIAL ENGINEER

The piercing sound of the bell announced that the break was over and it was time to return to the classroom. Seated in alphabetical order at individual wooden school desks, geometrically aligned in front of an enormous slate blackboard, the students, all boys, all wearing ties, all sitting in silence, awaited their French exam grades—then the predominant foreign language spoken in Portugal.

A published poet, the intellectually demanding teacher hardly hurried through his commentaries on the tests. He began enumerating each and every error so the whole class could hear their classmates' mistakes. "You got the wrong word here, this verb is not correct, this sentence is poorly written." If not for his dangerous and incurable communist convictions, long known to the Portuguese political police,[1] the professor would certainly have had a university audience sitting before him—instead of 12-year-old children.

Overbearing, phlegmatic in tone, the schoolteacher handed back the exams, starting with the lowest grades. He took note of the mediocre, moving slowly on to the better tests before finally reaching the ones with the higher grades. Guterres was among the last to receive their exams.

"He was excellent in all his subjects. He would always beat us all on the important stuff," recalls António Sá da Costa, now a renewable energy expert who was in the same class as Guterres at Camões

High School. "We had our revenge in physical education because he wasn't very agile. He couldn't do somersaults, couldn't climb a rope and it seemed like the ball burnt his hands playing handball—he'd pass it as soon as he could so no one would rush him."

Guterres' arrival at Camões had coincided with the school's 50th anniversary, a solemn event meriting the visit of its three most illustrious pupils: the Minister of Education, the Minister of the Presidency, and Professor Marcelo Caetano, the former Minister of the Colonies. They had been ceremonially received by the rector, an austere pedagogue nominated by the government, who lived on the upper floor of the high school and was rarely seen out of the regime's uniform—a dark, three-piece, straight-cut suit.

He always carried a large key. Its clinking was a constant accompaniment to his regular inspections to all corners of the school. "Young man, you go back home right now and get your tie." The rector knew all the boys by name and saw an example in the impeccable conduct of Guterres. "He was as obedient as possible to all of the rules and the school's code of behaviour," another former classmate relates, the playwright Luís Miguel Cintra. "It was as though he'd come to conquer the bourgeois life of the capital, which initially he didn't belong to, and he probably saw as yet another challenge."

In fact, Guterres spent long periods of time far from Lisbon. During the school holidays, he took the train back to the countryside, to his grandfather's village. In Donas, Guterres stayed in a white house that had sheltered three generations of his family. The first was born during the monarchy; the second during the Republic; and the third, António and his sister, Teresa, during the dictatorship.

Located at one of the oldest intersections in the village, the Guterres home was three storeys high. On the other side of the street, just a few steps away, sat the old Santa Maria Church, a community meeting place and a natural haven for a child raised as a Christian.

"Little Toni", as he was known to the villagers, was on friendly terms with his front neighbour. He helped the priest during mass, read the Epistles without hesitations and attended baptisms. Free to play outside and having the run of the town, the time spent in the rural world brought him into close contact with poverty: "I was very lucky and I started to be aware of this at a young age. While my friends in Donas went around barefoot, I wore shoes. While I went back to Lisbon to study, they stayed there and worked in the fields or became mechanics at a young age."

At Camões High School, the best students earned the right to have the best teachers so that the rector was able to locate the most suitable students when required. "Who speaks English well?" Responding to the query, the class' teacher pointed to Guterres and two other boys. "Very well, they're going to visit an American ship." The classmates broke into smiles, but soon their joy began to fade when the rector added, "They're expected to wear their Youth uniforms."

A clumsy imitation of the Hitler Youth, the Portuguese Youth took up the boys' Wednesday and Saturday afternoons. Between the plane trees that flanked the schoolyard, the pupils would fall in and march in uniform before attending lectures on the country's magnanimous achievements. Membership was mandatory up to the age of fourteen, but after that, many students distanced themselves from such tiresome activities.

Already in their teens, Guterres and his friends were having trouble fitting into their uniforms. They could barely slip the dark green shirtsleeves over their shoulders, the brown shorts strangled their legs, and the belt, with its buckle sporting an excessively disproportionate metal S in honour of Salazar—the finance specialist who had ruled Portugal as an authoritarian corporate state for the past three decades—was running out of holes.

So it was that, in January 1964, the 14-year-old Guterres put on his uniform to visit the cruiser USS *Springfield*, witnessed the passage of the United States Sixth Fleet flagship, carrying more than a thousand men onboard, and the greetings exchanged between the two commanding officers, all in line with the courtesies due to fellow NATO allies.

However, this alliance between Portugal and the United States had recently been turned inside out as a result of John F. Kennedy's election—a president who Salazar, twenty-eight years his senior, referred to as a "kid" when no one was listening.

The root of the problem was the White House's engagement with the African independence movements, which clashed with Portugal's colonial interests.[2]

Camões High School was baptised in honour of the poet Luís Vaz de Camões. In his masterpiece *Os Lusíadas*, the sixteenth-century writer glorifies the founding of the Portuguese empire that would stretch across four continents and contain territories that today belong to more than fifty countries, including Brazil.

When Guterres first started high school, in 1959, Portugal still possessed colonies: it administered Macau, in China, and it exerted power over regions that would eventually go to war and fight on until winning independence. Such was the case with Angola, Mozambique and Guinea-Bissau in Africa, as well as East Timor, the small island adjoining the Indonesian archipelago.

African countries had been gaining independence since the end of World War II, and by the early 1960s, Portugal seemed behind the trend. The entire map of Africa was changing, with major colonies now liberated following the British recognition of Kenya and the French acceptance of Algeria's independence. Salazar continued to resist the wave of decolonisation as best he could, even against pressure from the United Nations, which Portugal had finally joined in 1955 after a first attempt was vetoed by the Soviet Union.[3]

However, these were not subjects discussed in school textbooks, and so they were beyond the concerns of young Guterres as he set about his meticulous study habits. After twenty-five minutes poring over his books, he would pause briefly in order to refocus. During these breaks, he put a record on and listened to classical music before getting straight back to work.

Such discipline enabled him to appear, time and again, on the school's honour roll. His grades were particularly good in mathematics and physics, subjects whose interest was influenced by his father Virgílio, who worked for a natural gas company and had a life-long dream of becoming an engineer. "Physics was maybe my biggest intellectual passion and what I most liked to study, above all the theory of relativity," Guterres stresses today. "I find those attempts to understand the world that go beyond our normal daily intuitions fascinating."

Guterres finished high school determined to pursue a university career in physics. However, at times, the path one chooses is altered by the whims of history.

10002

Guterres was no enthusiast for watching the sun rise, but on this special day he made an effort to wake up early. The Instituto Superior Técnico was even closer than Camões High School to the apartment where he lived with his parents and sister. At Técnico, a school for engineers, not politicians, numbers took precedence over letters. On the day of enrolment, in the summer of 1966, Guterres wanted to be number one. He felt the need to be the first in line, but ended up being beaten by an even more determined freshman. This unexpected failure sentenced him to second place, to number 10002.

Técnico was already renowned as a prestigious and demanding school, where many dropped out after their first maths test. There were those who, on finishing their degree, decorated their business cards with the epithet "IST Engineer", adding the university's initials to their degree as though, in a country where a quarter of the population was illiterate,[4] being a graduate wasn't already impressive enough.

Indeed, Guterres was not immediately able to reaffirm his reputation as a top student. In his first test, mechanical drawing, his grade was 8 out of 20. Nevertheless, his perfect class attendance record and assiduous note-taking were soon reflected in his results.

Rational Mechanics: 19
Atomic Physics: 19
Infinitesimal Analysis: 19

"I only came to realise the impact Guterres had on me," asserts José Tribolet, an undergraduate classmate of Guterres and now a professor at Técnico, "when I did my doctorate at MIT and I understood several different kinds of intelligence exist. Even in complex problems of quantum mechanics, it was amazing how quickly he came up with solutions, while the rest of us needed to hammer away at equations for two or three hours to get to the same place."

As Guterres enrolled at Técnico, Portugal was already fighting on the three fronts of the Colonial War: first Angola, then Guinea-Bissau, quickly followed by Mozambique. University attendance was a justifiable means to defer the draft, but students still lived in terror of being called to war. The conflicts in Africa were one of the political worries simmering among youth circles, such as Técnico's Student Association.

Led by communist and Maoist sympathisers, the Association boasted its own facilities, a proper budget and a structure worthy of a large company. The printing shop produced the bound class notes, which many depended on to get through the school year. Its tourism agency chartered dozens of aeroplanes a year and staged internships abroad. The cultural department organised concerts, conferences and exhibitions on campus, which meant that, at times, they managed to avoid the censor's "blue pencil". However, and despite their importance to academic life, Guterres never took part in these student activities.

"He didn't see himself in this spirit nor in the leftist political actions of the Student Association," recalls António Andrade Tavares, now a business director and formerly a Técnico classmate. "He had his democratic and social concerns, but I'd have called him more Christian-Democratic."

Despite the social turmoil of those years, powered by events happening beyond Portugal's borders, including the war in Vietnam, the assassination of Martin Luther King and the May 1968 protests in France, Guterres did not join the student movement that defied the Portuguese dictatorship.

He did not attend the Association's demonstrations that were inevitably marked by run-ins with police dogs and baton-wielding officers; nor did he risk expulsion from the university, which would have forced him into the army: two common punishments the regime reserved for the rebellious youth.

He did not join the ranks chanting against the Colonial War and calling for the end of the dictatorship that had seen hundreds of students from his generation dragged off to the cells of the political police.

However, a club he did join was the Catholic University Youth. JUC, as it was familiarly known among students (for Juventude Universitária Católica), was dedicated to the Catholic apostolate. At Técnico, they had a room in the central campus building where young people gathered to reflect on the contents of the encyclicals and texts of the French Catholic Left. The group had neither the means nor the political audacity of the Student Association, but rather functioned as a network of Christians spread across Lisbon's different universities. It served as a platform for meetings that took place after masses, in colloquia, or even in members' houses. It was at one meeting that Guterres met his first wife. "Zizas was studying medicine. We became very good friends and then we started dating, then we got married. This was a fundamental relationship I had in my life, later associated with a very dramatic tragedy."

The Lisbon Floods

The rain that fell lightly throughout the afternoon was typical of an autumn Saturday. However, on the night of 25 November 1967, people awoke to chaos. Some had to cope with floodwaters bursting into their homes, others with shouts for help that came from nearby ceilings. In the darkness, and in the midst of the deluge, no help came.

Early that morning, the Minister of the Interior assured the press that "aid had been effective."[5] However, the reality in the Lisbon suburbs utterly contradicted his words. The torrent carried away houses, destroyed villages and coated the streets in thick mud. As the sun rose, destroyed furniture and rubble could be seen everywhere, next to the muddied cadavers of humans and animals.

Guterres learned of the extent of the tragedy when he arrived at Técnico. Faced with the state's incapacities and the urgent need for help, students rallied to respond to the population's needs. Such efforts brought together student associations from different universities (including the Catholic University Youth) into a unified front.

Técnico was the operational headquarters where thousands of humanities, economics, medicine and engineering students organised themselves into brigades and went in trucks to the zones worst hit by the storm. Despite the close proximity to campus, many students were facing the poverty of Lisbon's outskirts for the very first time.

For weeks, they distributed clothing and meals, helped clear streets and attended to medical needs, administering medicine and anti-typhoid vaccines.

"I did what I could," recalls Guterres, "but I don't remember having done that much because after just an hour of shovelling mud by spade, one gets absolutely exhausted. That episode did help radicalise the students, that's for sure."

Government propaganda spread the narrative that, when nature unleashes itself in all its fury, leaving automobiles floating like canoes, halting train traffic and downing electricity and communication lines, nothing can be done but let the storm pass. "But how could that be?" students asked in their publications. The floods had hit Estoril too, a coastal area sheltering bankers and exiled European monarchs, and where the meteorological reports recorded the most rainfall. So why had the majority of deaths occurred in the poorest areas?

Having waded through mud, having faced such misery and poverty, and having gained an unfiltered insight into the ineffective workings of public services, the students reached their own conclusions. For the young Catholics, it became increasingly difficult to reconcile the insensitivity of the Portuguese state with the teachings of the Church.

A Very Heavy Moment

"Either we go in now, or it's over!" Glued to the telephone, Guterres was trying to put together a rapid response team. Two years after the devastating flood, he had taken over JUC's leadership and was trying to save a volunteer centre that had succumbed to acute financial crisis. Finding other students ready to help him would not be too difficult, especially as the centre, while functioning within the orbit of the Catholic University Youth, was also open to non-believers.

However, what his predecessors had left him amounted to very little. CASU (The University Centre for Social Action) had no active members, no budget, and not even the funds to pay its debts. After a few telephone calls, and having brought on board a few more contacts, Guterres chaired his first meeting in a dim, third-floor back room in central Lisbon.

"António's talent for leadership," writes Rafael Prata, a friend from Camões High School who took on the intricate job as the group's treasurer, "was clear from the beginning: the perfection in the group's numbers, the ratio of women in management positions, the cooperation that he created between Catholics and non-Catholics, or between smokers and abstainers."[6]

Luísa Melo, or Zizas as she was known, was also part of the board. They divided the different functions between them and put together a programme of activities, set deadlines for carrying them out, and even visited the Cardinal of Lisbon to pay their respects.

This was not Guterres' first contact with the centre. Some years earlier, on the request of one of his Técnico friends, he started visiting the suburbs to tutor mathematics to underprivileged children. And even then, while running CASU, he continued to volunteer his time.

"He asked me to organise classes in those neighbourhoods," says Diogo Lucena, another Técnico alumnus, "for kids of 10 and 11 years old, in mathematics or whatever else was needed, which was almost everything. I got a lot of people. He was the brains behind all that, the motor. Once I was late for one of the activities and he started reprimanding me right there."

As the crew of volunteers grew, so did CASU's accounts, courtesy of donations made during mass and contributions from institutions such as Lisbon Town Hall.

The transformation was such that, in its first year, CASU was able to set up a summer camp for children from three social projects. During that summer of 1969, a public bus packed with tents carried excited children to one of the many beaches surrounding Lisbon. During the 20-minute trip from the city to the seaside, Guterres paid close attention to the troublemakers in the group. However, he knew the hard part would come after they arrived, so he drafted a preventive strategy. The first step was to get the kids to accept him. Then, once they reached the sand, he would tire them out with games, sports and activities, so that, without realising it, they would use up all their energy and have no strength left to get into trouble later on. However, there was just one small detail Guterres had failed to anticipate. Just as soon as the bus stopped, the agitators blasted through the doors and, still dressed and without even a backwards glance, sprinted straight towards the sea and threw themselves into the water.

— *What's gotten into you?! Why did you do that?*
— *It's that... we've never seen the ocean!*

"It was at that moment that I... I mean, there are moments like that. It was a very heavy moment," Guterres recalls. "It was a shock. When I was in the Catholic University Youth and later at CASU I was confronted with such social injustices that made me want to dedicate myself to politics."

Pacem in Terris

Diplomacy is a game. It is said to have been a favourite game of John F. Kennedy and Henry Kissinger.

But *Diplomacy* is also a board game. It starts out on the eve of World War I and each player represents one of the early twentieth-century powers: Germany, the Austro-Hungarian Empire, France, Italy, the Ottoman Empire, Great Britain and Russia.

Diplomacy, the board game, was the favourite of young Guterres and his friends, a pastime that kept them busy long into the night.

Diplomacy, above all, requires patience and precise planning, navigation in troubled waters, and anticipating one's adversary. There is no place for luck in this game, which might explain the absence of dice. There are only pieces that can be moved over a coloured map of Europe after careful decision-making, according to both the negotiations forged out loud and in plain sight, and also to the secret strategies of each player. Every decision, every victory and every defeat are a result of these agreements. As such, *Diplomacy* is a game where time is mostly spent negotiating. Yet, on the way to victory, alliances and compromises can be honoured, but can also be broken.

"António had one principle: to follow through on the promises he'd made," recalls Francisco Motta Veiga. "That is exactly how it is. And he was able to win the game. The last move might come as a surprise, but that was the way it was: he'd agree to something and then do it. It was always strategically thought out and then executed. The game's rules alone filled this huge manual and sometimes we'd play from one week to the next, only wrapping up the damn game on the following Sunday. We played it a lot and the game certainly heralded what was to come."

A friend since the 1970s, and later best man at his wedding, Francisco was part of the small group that Guterres gathered in his laboratory of diplomatic manoeuvres. What brought them together was a shared set of values, organised under the same hierarchy; and what kept them together all these years was a mentor.

Father Vítor Melícias is eleven years older than Guterres. Since the beginning of their friendship in the late 1960s, Melícias has been a source of inspiration and surprise. It was rare for a Portuguese priest to participate in a demonstration against the war in Vietnam outside the US Embassy in Lisbon. It was also rare to find one open to criticism against the Church and still agree to engage in dialogue.

"He was central to many things which were decisive in my life," Guterres explains. "His worldview is closer to the Gospels than it is to the more concrete and practical aspects of Church life today. We would go there with the idea of protesting and he would say, 'Yes, fine, you are right.' So, if the Church can be that way, then I'm there, I don't need to leave it."

As in other places around the world, the complicity between Church and dictatorship led many young Portuguese to distance themselves from Catholicism. Nevertheless, this Franciscan was able to unify and mobilise dozens of young men and women disillusioned with the direction the country and the Church were taking. Furthermore, he understood their discontent and encouraged them to engage in the struggle against inequality and injustice.

They soon started to meet on a regular basis, in Melícias' eccle-siastical residence: the Luz Seminary—hence the name "Luz Group" that the press would give them years later. On Tuesday nights after dinner, the same austere room, its walls decorated with just a few discreet religious images, awaited them. Sitting in a circle around a table, in order to avoid any hierarchical distinc-tion, they alternated between discussing the topics agreed upon the week before and a period set aside for celebrating mass.

As Melícias explains, the Luz Group began as "a meeting of Christians at the top of the intellectual chain who were highly involved in social work. I quickly became friends with António Guterres. After mass, we would speak about the social projects we were involved in and the problems the country was facing: pov-erty, emigration, the Colonial War, censorship, while finding a context for reflection on the texts of the Second Vatican Council."

Guterres and Melícias' first meeting took place in 1966, on Lisbon's Avenida de Roma. This was Fate's jesting, perhaps, since Melícias had just returned from the Italian capital where his diplo-matic skills had granted him access to the four-year conference often known as Vatican II. Melícias witnessed first-hand the discus-sions of this pivotal moment in the history of the Catholic Church, learning with those who were updating its doctrine for the first time in nearly 2,000 years. This new liberalising paradigm would allow for a repositioning of the institution among the faithful, not only due to the spiritual openness it proclaimed, but also through reforms in the rituals. Masses, for example, would no longer be celebrated in Latin, but rather in each country's own language, so that everyone could understand them.

For Guterres, the most important message of this theological revolution, and one that could hardly be more appropriate for his future professional endeavours, can be found in the encyclical *Pacem in Terris*, or "Peace on Earth". From his perspective, whether in terms of social thinking or as a theoretical basis for international politics, this is the most interesting religious text of the Council, especially due to its contemporaneity and relevance.

Published during the fiery aftermath of the erection of the Berlin Wall and the Cuban missile crisis, the Letter placed as much

importance on the defence of values and rights as today's movements do—from women's positions in public life to the rights of
migrants and the treatment of minorities and refugees. It also
speaks of the role of multilateral organisations in helping solve the
problems of humanity and defends the idea that supporting the
common good is the *raison d'être* of public institutions.

The Council issued a call to action to all Catholics to help establish a great social and human project. The only problem was that,
living under Portugal's repressive regime—a regime that stood
against the winds of change blowing in from beyond its borders,
where Coca-Cola was banned and women were forbidden from
leaving the country without the permission of their husbands—such
a summons would only reach a small and attentive intellectual elite.

The Luz Group kept meeting, and Guterres did not lose faith in
the open-minded Christianity Melícias represented. For various
members of the Luz Group, the priest's influence was so decisive
that they would eventually ask him to celebrate the most important
rituals in their personal lives. When he married Zizas, on
21 December 1972, one year after graduating from university,
Guterres asked Melícias to preside over the ceremony at the church
of Nossa Senhora da Luz, just 100 metres from the seminary.

The wedding ceremony was simple and few friends were
invited. The bride and groom did not dress accordingly for the
occasion and the typical princely banquet did not follow the religious ceremony. They took the liberty to adapt the inside of the
church so that the ceremony would unfold in the same familiar
manner as the Group's masses: the church pews, typically running
in parallel lines facing the altar, were re-arranged in a circle with
the bride and groom in the middle. Around them sat no more than
thirty guests.

Zizas, a child psychiatrist, shared her husband's sensibilities,
including his political ideas and philosophy, and was frequently
praised by their friends for her ability to encourage him in
moments of hesitation and advise him in periods of doubt. She was
the one who introduced him to opera, which would become a
lifelong passion. And from their marriage, two children were
born: Pedro and Mariana.

17

Talents

On one of the few occasions when Guterres made remarks to journalists during his campaign to become UN Secretary-General, he was questioned about why he was running for "the most impossible job on this earth".[7] The response was as quick as it was trenchant, "because of the Parable of the Talents."[8]

Despite the perception that the regime under which Guterres lived during his early years was not considered as brutal as other contemporary totalitarian governments, persecution and torture at the hands of the political police, media censure and the general lack of freedom galvanised the will of several young Catholics to intervene socially, especially after the tragic floods of 1967. In Guterres' case, such motivation had deeper roots in "The Parable of the Talents", from the Gospel of Matthew (25:14–30).

In this account from the New Testament, a wealthy lord sets off on a journey and entrusts talents—a monetary denomination—to three of his servants in the hope they will apply them in a way that will bring him future profits. Upon his return, he finds that two of the servants have invested their capital and have seen returns on the money, while the third has decided to save the talents for himself, and has therefore contributed nothing to his master's work. He is, in turn, criticised and punished, while the first two are invited to sit at their lord's table and are promised more talents.

"The fundamental question," says Guterres, "is as follows: am I doing the thing that has the best odds to deliver returns proportionate to the talents I was given? We are given talents and so we have to repay what we get. In my life, I had this extraordinary thing, which was opportunity opening before me. It might have been different, I was incredibly lucky, but this comes with a responsibility."

In spite of this conviction, the Luz Group never took public positions against the dictatorship. While maintaining contact with more liberal members of parliament and dissident members of the clergy, they still found it useful to cultivate relationships with important figures in the establishment. At the age of 21, Guterres taught a course for the Portuguese Youth, but as the first classes unfolded, he expressed dissonant opinions and was not invited back.[9]

In fact, the first beneficiary of the young engineer's talents was the regime itself. Shortly after graduating in 1971, Guterres became a member of a body coordinated directly by President Marcelo Caetano—who had taken office following Salazar's withdrawal from government in 1968—that brought together some of Portugal's best economists. Similar to what in other countries was named a "think tank", the Technical Secretariat of the President of the Council of Ministers was set the task of preparing strategic plans for national economic development.

Meanwhile, Guterres took every opportunity to participate in projects that only cracks in the wall of a dying dictatorship could make possible, such as the launch of a Consumer Defence Association, of which Guterres was a founding member; he became one of the first small shareholders of a new weekly newspaper, *Expresso*, inspired by Britain's *The Sunday Times* and *The Observer*; and he also helped in founding the Association for Economic and Social Development (SEDES), a proto-political party operating as a civic association that comprised of people from all political backgrounds who shared a common desire to link economic development to the betterment of living conditions.

In the Luz Group, the only occasion its members adopted a coordinated approach to take a political stance was when they sent a letter of support to the Bishop of Porto. Upon his return to the country after ten years in exile for having expressed positions against the regime, the bishop continued to be openly and blatantly critical of the government and its leaders. In January 1974, he received a letter with the signatures of Guterres, Zizas and Melícias:

We are a group of young Catholics striving to find a way to live intense and truly religious lives. [...]

The great difficulties that we feel in our attempt to apply the word of Christ to our daily lives, and the lack, or timidity, of clear and up-to-date guidance on the part of most Portuguese bishops, including in the Diocese to which we belong, has led us to enthusiastically seek clearer directives from other pastors about the Gospel for our times. [...] This group has wanted to write to you for a long time now [...] to tell you, "We are with you!"

Guterres still sees "The Parable of the Talents" as his guiding light, orienting his most important decisions. It represents a connection between Catholic morals and his political action. Indeed, Melícias recalls how the discussions in the Luz Group were always about more than just religion: "For us, Sweden's social-democrat Prime Minister, Olof Palme,[10] was a model and we began to develop a certain sympathy for the socialist self-management of Yugoslavia.[11] We found it a very interesting model, a unique kind of social democracy."

The group's members were nearly all university students from the middle or upper classes who held no illusions about the extremist drift of the far right or the far left. This was also the worldview taught at the household in which Guterres grew up: "My father was a democrat, he always was, and my grandfather as well. So, I always considered democracy as the best model." Despite this, and contrary to many young people of his generation, Guterres never engaged in direct opposition to the dictatorship and his name never made it into the records of the political police.

Even before graduating, he was hired as an assistant professor at Técnico—despite the fact that it was against university regulations, since he was officially still an undergraduate—setting him on the way for a tenure as a physics researcher. That was his first job, his intellectual passion. However, the moral imperative to apply his talents to the service of others, supported by the confidence he already had in his own abilities, continued to lure him away from his academic goals.

"It didn't take me long to realise he wasn't going to be an engineer, that he'd find his way into politics and spend very little time with engineering," explains Luís Mira Amaral, one of Guterres' professors at Técnico, who many years later would face him as a political adversary. "It felt like he'd already discovered his knack for politics, with a great skill for persuasion, for selling his product, yet without arousing animosity and antipathy. He wasn't the kind of guy who seemed arrogant, not like some yuppie from an investment bank. He would go on to find that common ground between religion and socialism in its widest sense." Amaral even heard a rather prophetic ambition slip from Guterres himself: "I once told him all of this and he said I was right. He told me he was going to become a social engineer."

Indeed, his experience in social work, mostly through CASU, had shown Guterres a reality that theory books did not mirror, leading him to conclude that solutions for his country's problems would have to be political: "Physics is a beautiful thing but, I mean, a Portuguese in physics... what are you going to do? Are you going to discover the fifth degree of some electrical wave? And what about those guys living in the slums?"

In the early 1970s, the hope for a democratic society, which was born after Salazar's withdrawal from the political stage, proved to be a disappointment. As the Colonial War continued to take the lives of sons, brothers and friends, the Portuguese families and the armed forces were becoming increasingly impatient with the conflict in Africa. An estimated one million men served overseas between 1960 and 1974, of which more than 8,000 servicemen had perished in combat. It was becoming starkly apparent that the regime, which ruled over one of the poorest countries in western Europe while spending 45 per cent of its national budget on the war, was no longer able to reform itself.

Hence, without any idea when Portugal would swirl onto the path of democracy, the young Guterres, who had finished his course in Electrotechnical Engineering with an average of 19 out of 20, decided, once and for all, to give up academic life and dedicate himself exclusively to politics.

At home, this announcement caused mixed reactions: "When I began to get more political," Guterres recalls, "we were still under the old regime, and my mother became quite worried. My father, on the contrary, was greatly impressed."

Even contrary to the opinions of some of his fellow members in the Luz Group, Guterres made his decision. Melícias believes this was "not out of any greedy obsession for politics or seeking power, it was out of the desire to be useful, out of the desire to serve." However, for his childhood friend Carlos Santos Ferreira, another member of the Luz Group, this desire was already drawing on a political ambition under a well-thought-out plan: "When somebody with that capacity rejects a university position in favour of politics, they can only be thinking of what is the most important thing they can do. This means being party leader first, and then Prime Minister."

La Promesa

A brutal explosion rocked the very heart of the city. The first flames rose, and black ash and smoke the colour of gunpowder mixed together in the stunned morning sky. The forces commanded by General Augusto Pinochet bombarded the presidential palace La Moneda, announcing to the world at large that the country's socialist experience was over. In a little less than an hour, the deafening rounds from the tanks in the capital's streets, the indiscriminate shooting by the army and the ceaseless bombing by the air force's Hawker Hunter jets were over. Salvador Allende lay dead, assassinated along with Chile's democratic process.

The military radio station confirmed the fateful outcome of the victory: "Mission accomplished. La Moneda taken. President dead."

The news of the 1973 Chilean coup reached Guterres and Zizas in the middle of the Austrian Alps. Even though they were on their honeymoon, the couple was travelling with a friend from their CASU years. Zizas was the one who noticed a growing crowd and increasing apprehension on everyone's faces. They were all leaning over a battery-operated radio. Rafael Prata recalls: "We also joined the group, thinking there'd been some accident. That was when we heard through the static on the radio a voice speaking in Spanish with a sweet accent, and the sound of jets in the background along with the explosions of air-to-surface missiles, and the rat-tat-tat of heavy machine guns. [...] It wasn't direct sound, but its force coming through the radio was like getting punched in the stomach."[12]

A few days earlier, in Venice, Guterres and Prata had decided to grow their moustaches, just for the sake of it. But what started out as an innocent joke that was intended to last only a handful of days, turned into a serious promise inspired by Salvador Allende's own look. "We made a promise: we keep our moustaches not only during the holidays, but until there has been decisive change in Portuguese society," says Prata.

The assassination of the Chilean President and the resulting imposition of one of the bloodiest military dictatorships in Latin America transformed Guterres' moustache into a kind of subliminal message: it was in homage to a political martyr, but also to all those who dreamed of democracy.

Guterres would only shave off his moustache years later, despite the changes that he had so longed for within Portuguese society arriving the following year, on 25 April.

Tanks were again on the streets, just as in Santiago, but this time with flowers instead of bullets.

A WATCHMAKER'S WORK

"I remember I had my G3 at my side and António Guterres was stunned by this. And what's more, I had four grenades clipped to my belt."

On 25 April 1974, the military unit led by António Reis stormed the country's only television station. Five days later, Reis explains, Guterres decided to visit him, as he was one of the first members of the Portuguese Socialist Party (PS). "Right after the PS was founded, in Germany,[1] I ran into António in Lisbon. Even then he was interested. In the meantime, the news spread across Portugal and he wanted to know more."

So when he arrived at the headquarters of the national broadcaster service RTP to speak with Reis, Guterres had some news of his own to share: on that very day, 30 April 1974, his 25th birthday, he would join the Socialist Party.

Many of his friends thought he was more suited to conservative parties on the right of the emerging political spectrum. However, Guterres explains, "My personal shock with social inequalities is closer to socialist ideology. I didn't move to the extreme because that's not in my nature. So, I stayed on the side of what in socialism is called democratic, or social democracy. And still today that's where I fit, that hasn't changed over the years. It was quite linear."

The week before he went to see Reis, Guterres had been warned by telephone that a coup was under way. During the night, someone called him at home with the update: soldiers were already on their way to Lisbon to bring an end to the dictatorship.

Not very much was known. An imprecise number of officers had left their barracks and would reach the capital within a few hours. Guterres hurried to the *Expresso* newsroom, where it was hardly likely he would encounter rebellious mobs, but almost certain he could receive all the latest information.

In the heat of the Cold War, the left-wing inspired revolution beckoned international attention and raised mixed feelings among world leaders. The socialists and communists behind the 25 April liberation were committed to re-establishing relations with the USSR, which of course sent alarm bells ringing in the United States.

Time magazine even dedicated its cover to Portugal. For the 11 August 1975 edition, three austere individuals with menacing looks were set against a blood-red background. On the left, a soldier stood at the ready, in uniform and with a slanting beret. On the right, came the oldest of the three, with a broad forehead and neatly combed-back hair. In the middle, rose the Manichaean appearance of a man boasting only two colours: white shirt, black suit and tie. They represented an officer from the army responsible for the revolution, the President of the Republic of Portugal and the Prime Minister[2] with close ties to the Portuguese Communist Party. The three men were authoritatively framed by a hammer and sickle rendered in yellow, just like those on the flag of the USSR, with the headline: "Red Threat in Portugal".

Frank Carlucci, US Ambassador to Portugal and a former CIA deputy director, had few doubts about the best strategy to defend US interests: "The only logical group to work with was the non-communist left. Working with them both in the military and in the Socialist Party, working through NATO, and working with the Church, seemed to be the best opportunity."[3]

Indeed, PS would prove the most important ally to the United States in constructing an anti-communist dam, especially through its growing ability to challenge the communists in what had hitherto been their exclusive domain: the ability to take people to the streets. This was exactly the area in which Guterres would become an expert.

"I don't know if I've already told you how to pull together a spontaneous protest …" begins Guterres more than forty years later. "At five in the afternoon, when everyone is leaving their offices, we would gather in front of a central train station. So, people are leaving the ministries to catch the train or the subway, we cordon everything off, pick up our megaphones and shout, 'The government wants to ruin… whatever, we all have to go to the Presidential Palace!' Or to Parliament. And all of a sudden, we'd have ten or twenty thousand people joining the protest march. I'm not kidding, that's how it was."

After being admitted into the party ranks, many socialists viewed Guterres—a Catholic and a conservative, with no history of opposition to the dictatorship—with open suspicion. After all, the PS was made up of many enemies of the former dictatorship, political prisoners carrying the scars of torture, Marxist-Leninists, Trotskyites, and many other large-moustachioed, long-haired rebels.

However, Guterres soon won the trust of the first PS leader, the charismatic and internationally well-connected Mário Soares who, in the summer of 1975, tasked him with organising in Lisbon the largest mass demonstration in the history of Portugal—or, at least, that was how it was billed.

One of the witnesses to the rise of Guterres inside the party was António Vitorino, the same man who, many years later, in 2018, would capitalise on the United States' negligence of multilateralism to become the first non-American since the 1960s to be elected Director-General of the International Organization for Migration. "António has a fabulous memory," states Vitorino. "Right away he knew everyone by their first name, and knew exactly who he should call to deliver on every task. He had a huge list of people that he would personally talk to, so when we planned a demonstration or a meeting, he would telephone the ones responsible and ask whether they'd spoken to A, to B, to C, which then had a multiplying effect."

The Luminous Fountain rally—as the demonstration became known—was designed to send out an unequivocal message that it was possible to steer the country away from the Soviet model that the revolution seemed to be imposing following 25 April, such as nation-wide expropriations, land invasions, the nationalisation of banks and the self-exile of wealthy families. The rally succeeded then in posing a political challenge to the extreme left, whose legitimacy relied mostly on their public demonstrations.

Guterres never set foot on the lawn in front of the fountain. Coordinating the protest by telephone from party headquarters, he was able to bring together a deafening crowd of nearly 300,000 people who brought posters, cried slogans, waved flags, chanted songs, displayed banners and joined in the applause.

Nevertheless, this victory was not simply derived from the talents of a young party official, or even the party's ability to draw in the masses. Melícias explains the role the Church played in its organisation: "Mário Soares spoke with the Cardinal-Patriarch in secret and what he said was, 'We're in a very difficult situation and we need the Church's help,' and the cardinal responded right away: 'Certainly.' From then on, the Church started to play an active role in the mobilisation for the demonstration."

The rally succeeded in sending that unequivocal message and, after less than a year, in 1976, the Socialist Party won the first democratic election in Portugal. The moderate parties obtained 75 per cent of the votes and the Communists were reduced to parliamentary irrelevance.

According to American historian Samuel Huntington, the events in Portugal went beyond domestic politics, inaugurating a new global paradigm. The first wave of democratisation had its origins in the United States and lasted until 1820; the second arose from the allied victory in the Second World War; the third was starting to take place in Portugal and Spain. According to the Harvard professor, this was a Catholic-inspired movement which "swept through six South American and three Central American countries, moved on to the Philippines, doubled back to Mexico and Chile, and then burst through in the two Catholic countries of Eastern Europe, Poland and Hungary."[4]

These elections also led to the emergence of a group of moderate young politicians who challenged the resistance of the party hardliners. This new generation was naturally on the radar of

American diplomatic services, as demonstrated in the following dispatch to Washington:

> The PS leaders now rising to the fore tend to be more pragmatic and less ideological. [...] The technicians group, led by Antonio Guterres [...] is distinguished by technical competence in economic matters and by close relations with many social democrats.[5]

Guide Bleu

Guterres likes to say, ironically, that should he one day change career, he would become a travel agent. Vitorino frequently accuses him of getting more satisfaction from planning trips than actually going on them.

More than half a century before Airbnb, Google Maps or Tripadvisor, Guterres used to read travel guides and history books in detail to prepare for his journeys. "That's the easy part", he says. "I'm a history fanatic and I read all the guides." Of all the guidebooks he used, his favourites were the French-language Guide Bleu—first published in the nineteenth century, and still produced today in their original style: a few photographs, a lot of text.

It was thanks to his first job in government, as chief of staff to the Secretary of State of Industry, that he was able to come into contact with a specific reality he had only studied in books. The government had decided to negotiate a political deal with the Brezhnev administration for the treatment of uranium, similar to the one Portugal already had with the United States. This was Guterres' first visit to the USSR.

The official agenda included a stay in Moscow, where meetings would follow the signing of the agreement, a visit to the Kremlin and the Tretyakov Gallery. They would then go to Leningrad to visit a factory and the Winter Palace of the Tsars. What the young chief of staff saw was "an unattractive society, it was a harsh dictatorship. It was a closed Soviet regime and consumption was limited; we were in the 1970s, still a long way from *perestroika*. You could see it was a fossilised society, and the heroic phase of socialism and expansion was over. This was the phase in which all of that was no longer functioning."

HONEST BROKER

Shortly after visiting Moscow, Guterres had the opportunity to study the Guide Bleu for another superpower. He was part of a small group of young people, between 20 and 30 years of age, from a variety of countries, who had been selected for a programme run by the US State Department to take part in a month-long visit to the United States.

The only obligatory stop was Washington D.C., in order to see the most important institutions in the capital. Other than that, their schedule was fully open. "The purpose of these programmes is to show off American society," says Guterres, "out of the conviction that theirs is the best in the world. So, if they show their country, everyone will realise just how great they are. And for me it was a very pleasant experience."

In 1976, at the age of 27, Guterres was elected Member of the Portuguese Parliament and soon after he took up his first international position as chair of a European Parliamentary Commission working on demography, migration and refugees. That allowed him to cross the Iron Curtain once again.

"Most of the meetings were in the north of Europe, so I took some weekends off to visit Poland, the Czech Republic, Hungary and the like. I caught Poland still in the Jaruzelski dictatorship, a heavy atmosphere, a time of martial law. And, at the same time, the churches were full, there seemed to be two Polands. Prague was also depressing and oppressive, but not Budapest. You could see that communism there was already more relaxed. I travelled by train and went wherever I wanted, no one bothered me about anything, I didn't feel any oppression there at all."

Increasingly engaged in international cooperation projects, in 1985 Guterres also travelled to sub-Saharan Africa for the first time. As soon as he landed in newly independent Guinea-Bissau, a former Portuguese colony, everything seemed to stick to his perspiring skin: clothes, mosquitoes, the dust raised by the anarchic traffic of trucks, carts, motorcycles, jeeps and pack animals.

The sovereign authorities in Guinea-Bissau were hosting a mission of four Portuguese specialists brought there to analyse the country's education system and to advise the government on how best to reform its institutions, including how to write applications for World Bank financing. Guterres, an engineer fond of economics, was in charge of the budgetary considerations, financial questions and international aid. There was also an architect to work on infrastructure, plus two education experts.

Since Bissau's independence in 1974, the Soviet-style political party that ruled the country had succeeded in abolishing the private sector, prohibiting small shops and closing warehouses. The economy had been completely nationalised, freedoms curtailed, plurality of ideas eradicated. Any dissident who dared oppose the state was persecuted, thrown into prison or executed. Public spaces and infrastructure fell into disrepair and this, combined with the scarcity of materials, bestowed an air of abandonment and decay on the country—especially on its schools.

Even the main hotel in Bissau, where Guterres and his companions were staying, suffered daily blackouts and cuts in water supply. Rubbish accumulated on the roadsides and the sight of huge black vultures picking over bags of rubbish in the streets was commonplace in the capital. Disease loomed in the background, and one of Guterres and his Portuguese colleagues' biggest fears was the poor quality of the water.

On one occasion, when they had driven out of the capital for a lunch in the field, the heat was so intense that none of the clean water they had loaded in the jeep lasted the trip. They arrived at their destination with nothing more than a series of empty bottles.

"What kind of water are they going to give us to drink?"

While trying to appear relaxed, conversing with their hosts, the four Portuguese shot glances back and forth until, with typical Guinean hospitality, pitchers of water were brought to the table. They then remembered the box of strong chlorine water purification tablets brought from the hotel for just such an emergency.

"Let's just slip over there without anyone noticing and drop the tablets in the pitchers."

However, the disinfection dose must have been excessive and, just as soon as they sat down to eat, one of the locals, worried about his guests' health, promptly declared:

"This water is bad!"

Guterres quickly rose to the occasion:

"No, no, the water is wonderful! It might taste funny… but it's an excellent water!"

"It had an unbearable taste of chlorine!" recalls one of the team members, Eduardo Marçal Grilo. "I don't know how, but he convinced them that it was all good."

The research mission resulted in a report entitled "Education in the Democratic Republic of Guinea-Bissau." This is a work Hélder Vaz Lopes, former Guinean Minister of Economy, USAID consultant and ambassador, continues to praise: "For me, it's still today the best tool for analysing the Guinea-Bissau education system. This document provides an understanding about how it works, what it is and what are the constraints to build a system that is truly workable for the country."

The architect Luís Lamas, one of the report's authors, considers the most important lesson for everyone was "understanding the role of poverty and the difficulties that African children in general, and Guineans in particular, experience. It is dramatic to grasp their very limited future prospects. We were there in those schools with dozens of happy children, smiling, who wanted to learn, and we witnessed how limited the path forward was for them because of a lack of means, of support and aid."

The late 1970s and 1980s saw Guterres continue the same kind of global-facing work as a member of parliament, travelling to difficult-to-access locations. In 1991, an invitation came from the Inter-Parliamentary Union, which brought together members of parliament from almost 200 legislative houses.

The organisation's 85th conference was to be held in North Korea, where Guterres was disturbed by the robotic levels of conformity and obedience demanded by the Kim regime: "I still have a DVD they gave me of a gymnastic performance en masse of 15,000 children performing a gymnastic routine in a stadium, doing the most beautiful things you can imagine, using feathers and creating maps and everything. And what strikes you is that you are watching this for over an hour, 15,000 children… and there is not a false move. So you're sort of enchanted and then you end up depressed, thinking about those poor kids."

What impressed him most about the country was the isolation in which more than twenty million North Koreans lived: "These guys had no idea what was happening in the outside world, and I imagine they still don't.[6] There were only two TV channels that just showed beautiful things in North Korea and then you could watch black-and-white reports from South Korea of police beating students."

Ironically, it was in North Korea where Guterres decided to modernise his own image. His wife could not stand his moustache any more. So, on his first night in Pyongyang, Guterres decided to shave it off once and for all. He had been wearing it for twenty years.

Comrades

In the late 1980s, lunchtime was the occasion for all four vice presidents of the PS to meet with their new leader. They didn't sit, however, at the table of a fancy restaurant, but inside their own office in Parliament. A spartan platter of sandwiches guaranteed the minimum nutritional requirement as Guterres and his team planned their next attack on the centre-right government.

"He draws on a piece of paper, scribbles, writes a few words down," recalls Edite Estrela, then the only woman in the party leadership, "and then after two hours, all of us talking and taking notes, he sums up everything said. Not only what was argued, but the most important lines of thinking and the direction which should be taken."

To become the leader of the parliamentary group, his role since 1988, Guterres had had to overcome two divisions with comrades and mentors. The first was with Soares, the all-powerful leader of the party and the Prime Minister who had signed the Portuguese accession to the European project in 1985. Guterres' internal rebellion had been unable to topple the Secretary-General, despite having mobilised some of the most promising names in the whole PS structure for late-night conspiring, whom he had hosted in the attic of his own house in 1984. Following his failed coup against Soares, Guterres spent two years in political exile before being called back into the party's inner chambers.

But while the Socialists quarrelled in internal dispute, their rivals in the Social Democratic Party (PSD) had been able to form a government, and with a majority since 1987. Having no need to negotiate with the opposition, the PSD government either ignored or rode roughshod over the opposition, so when Guterres was chosen to command the PS action in Parliament, he opted for a strategy that differed in both style and content. Vitorino stresses how personal attacks were immediately vetoed: "It happened several times. We discussed using certain arguments against our opponents and he would say, 'No, don't even think about that, never, that would set a precedent that would let them do the same thing to us later... no, no.' Nowadays no one cares about these things, but he never gave into this temptation. He said that if we made the first move towards demagogy, then we'd be legitimising any and all demagogies."

Vitorino also recalls how even Guterres' friends and closest advisers were constantly scrutinised by their leader: "At a meeting between us senior MPs, he told me to do something. The meeting ended at 2 pm and by 3.30 I got the first phone call: 'Did you do it?'... Then at 4.30, another call—which meant that I still hadn't done it—and I told him not to worry, that it would be done by the end of the day. Then later, around 7.30, he called me again: 'It's just to tell you that it's already the end of the day.'"

Guterres' second and most painful rupture had come as soon as he was summoned back into favour, in 1986. He was then forced to choose one of two Socialist Party presidential candidates: Mário Soares or Francisco Salgado Zenha, a former Minister of Justice, a lawyer to political prisoners and "the great political and moral reference at the beginning of my own public activity,"[7] as Guterres once wrote. This time, Guterres chose to align himself with the party, and supported Soares. But the friendship and intellectual admiration Guterres felt for his mentor was so deep that even his wife had taken Zenha's side, against her husband's own position. "Had he decided to support Zenha, he would have had to leave the Socialist Party," says Jorge Coelho, then a young former Marxist, with a bushy beard and a powerful voice, who had just joined the Socialists and would become one of Guterres' most loyal allies. "If he left, then he would be leaving behind everything that was his future political prospects."

Soares ended up winning that year's elections to become President of the Republic, leaving PS' leadership open for the first time. In Portugal's semi-presidential system—in which the President is officially the head of state, but the one holding executive power is the Prime Minister—the President must not be a party leader. Therefore, Soares, Secretary-General of the Socialist Party ever since the April 1974 revolution, had to step aside in order to take up the presidency.

With Guterres in charge of parliamentary issues, party leadership had been won by Lisbon Mayor Jorge Sampaio, who would be the Socialists' candidate for Prime Minister in the 1991 legislative elections. The bid, however, turned out to be a disaster. Portuguese voters handed the centre-right its second absolute majority, condemning the Socialist Party to yet another four years in opposition, taking their absence from power up to at least ten years.

"I'm in a state of shock,"[8] Guterres said immediately after the defeat. Conscious of the internal disillusionment with Sampaio's leadership, he saw an opportunity to advance his own ambitions. This declaration of war was the beginning of one of the most contentious internecine conflicts in the history of the party.

Guterres maintains that he tried to avoid a division with Sampaio, offering him the senior ceremonial position of Party President—a platform that could launch Sampaio towards a future presidential bid, while leaving the political stage open for Guterres. But Sampaio was not interested, so the internal fight for the party's leadership began. Of the cascade of insults Sampaio's allies let loose on Guterres, the nicest ran from "cynic" to "opportunist", all the way to accusations of being a "Secretary-General backstabber".

Guterres kicked off his internal campaign with a promise to speak to the Portuguese people in a manner they would understand; and he was not shy to denounce Sampaio's alliance with the Communist Party that had enabled his rise to Mayor of Lisbon, an alliance many had interpreted as a betrayal of the Socialist Party's own democratic identity.

When taking the stage at these party rallies, Guterres proved able to galvanise and win over the audience, putting into practice the oratory skills he was able to perfect during fifteen years in Parliament.

He had learned to choose the exact term for every situation, to shape his words according to different audiences, and to master public speaking. One time, during a parliamentary session, he exploited a seemingly invisible flaw in an adversary's remark to make the whole Parliament burst into laughter, only to wreak complete havoc inside their minds the very next instant: "Mr. President, let me just say that I already suspected that the level of teaching of mathematics in engineering courses was much higher than the one in economics courses ... (*laughter*). In fact, my colleague has just confused two different equations. He intends to say that in our project x plus y plus z is equal to zero. But that is wrong, because it is delta x—in this case a negative increase in the subsidy provided for in the Organic Law—plus y plus z which is equal to zero, that is, y plus z must equal the negative increment of the Organic Law, so that everything can stay the same."[9]

Both in parliamentary debates and party rallies, Guterres trained himself to speak without even looking at his talking points, hand-written by himself on some almost pocket-sized paper cards. But as Coelho recalls, these improvisations required a lot of work: "I went on all trips with him and he kept fine-tuning his speeches all the time as we drove, rehearsing them out loud, gesticulating with his hands even as we listened to opera the whole time. What's more, some people can campaign, but it's clear it's a sacrifice for them. Getting in their station wagons on weekends and travelling 500 kilometres, then another 300... it's a lovely thing for a couple of months, but doing it for years takes its toll. This is a life that is only for those who really like human contact and António really had that in him. He really was connected to people—this is what gave him the strength no one else had in the Socialist Party."

The 10th Socialist Party Conference in 1992 confirmed what the press had been predicting over the previous months, and what was being carefully planned behind closed doors and whispered in corridors: Guterres was able to defeat Sampaio in seventeen of the eighteen districts.

He was Secretary-General of the Socialist Party, and a candidate to become Prime Minister.

3

ESTATES-GENERAL

Any empty office in Washington, as small as it might be, was enough to hoist a flag and set up an embassy. The budget might be tight and the dollar exchange unforgiving, but at least they had found a place. Not a mansion with luxurious gardens on Massachusetts Avenue, the preferred location for foreign representations, but at least now the United States formally recognised them.

For Armenia, Ukraine and other young states eager to integrate into the diplomatic community at the beginning of the 1990s, the only thing that really mattered was renouncing their contract with number 11245, 16th Street, the address of the former embassy of the USSR.

The day the Berlin Wall fell, Moscow immediately understood that the implosion of the system was irreversible. Mikhail Gorbachev's own foreign policy adviser wrote in his diary: "This entire era in the history of the socialist system is over."[1]

After his resignation, Gorbachev had the opportunity to observe first-hand just how left-wing leaders of the world were adapting to this new reality in September 1992, during the Congress of the Socialist International.[2] All the appeals for disarmament and for the revitalisation of the United Nations that would have been out of place during his years in the Kremlin were now, at the beginning of this new period, perfectly aligned with their efforts to demonstrate that the ashes of communism did not represent the triumph of capitalism and that the right way forward was democratic socialism.

The Congress, the first since the end of the Cold War, and the first during Guterres' leadership of the Portuguese Socialist Party, took place at the German Bundestag in Berlin, and elected the Portuguese leader as one of the organisation's twenty-five vice presidents.

"My involvement in the Socialist International opened several doors and allowed me to create a network of relationships that is really helpful, even today," Guterres recognises. "Later down the line, at the UNHCR, I created a new network that went beyond ideologically socialist contexts and that was extremely useful in my candidacy for UN Secretary-General."

Socialist comradeship brought him to the Middle East to meet with Yitzhak Rabin, another one of the International's vice presidents. Apart from membership in the same political family, the common ground between these men was rather slim. On one side, there was a military leader with weak connections to religion, who had been elected Prime Minister of Israel for the second time, in July 1992. On the other, a young Catholic who had never even been in the army and who was still in the process of making his governmental debut.

"Rabin had impressive inner strength," Guterres recalls. "But what he told me didn't make sense, that the Palestinians didn't matter and the important thing was to make peace with the Syrians. That same afternoon, I had a meeting in Tel Aviv with Shimon Peres, who was his Foreign Minister, who said the Syrian question wasn't the most relevant. That's when I understood that such deep differences inside the same party leadership did not just exist in Portugal, but were a reality everywhere."

A few months later, Guterres and Peres met again in Lisbon, for a meeting of the Socialist International. Sixty-two countries were hosted by Guterres in the Ritz Hotel, but there was one name that stole the spotlight. "We had been in contact with Nelson Mandela since his release," remembers Luís Ayala, the Chilean Secretary-General of the Socialist International since 1989, "and we would have liked to have him in one of our meetings, which was not easy in those days, but we managed to do it with António." Two years after the South African's release from prison, and with talks under-way to design the post-apartheid system, "Mandela's presence was filled with symbolism, and after that, Guterres and I met with him again many times."

For his staff at home in Portugal, the benefits these connections brought Guterres were evident: his involvement with international figures made him a more credible candidate to become Prime Minister. However, political winds in Portugal were still not pull-ing in his direction. The government had full control of Parliament and Prime Minister Cavaco Silva, a conservative of austere demean-our with a haughty gait, and with whom Guterres was not on the best of terms, could still seek another mandate.

A Civilised Opposition

"My idea was always that the opposition doesn't win elections," says Guterres, "rather it's the government that loses them, and that the opposition needs to be there when that happens and be able to count on people's trust. We had a clear opposition strategy, but it was, at the same time, civilised. If you maintain an unbridled pos-ture, you lose the people's trust. So, the opposition should be consistent, serious and serene at the same time."

He was very much aware of the ten-point lead the government had and how unpopular he seemed to be in the polls. He seemed far, very far, too far some of his colleagues murmured, from his main adversary. Nevertheless, winning the party's leadership in 1992, right at the beginning of the parliamentary term, offered him some time to unify the party and build a proper political alternative that could be accepted by the people.

"Guterres imposed a different style to his predecessors, less strident and capable of creating bridges between us,"[3] points out Luís Marques Mendes, then a deputy minister.

Now in his early forties, Guterres, the young socialist leader, was looking for a new synthesis in thinking, a left-of-centre policy programme update that no longer tried to "guarantee everything to everyone."[4] He had seen how Bill Clinton's presidential campaign had been ideologically reinvigorating and was looking to do the same in Portugal by finding a meeting point "between traditional European social democratic values and those of the liberal left that the United States championed."[5]

For months he launched countless theme-based panels, regional debates, meetings between coordinators from various sectors and, lastly, dialogue—a lot of dialogue, on the present and the future of the nation. The Socialists dubbed the initiative the "Estates-General for a New Majority", an allusion to the assemblies once convened by the French monarchy that brought together representatives of the different social classes, each with their own agendas and lists of complaints.

Complaints, in the Portuguese case, generated a "legislative contract", a pre-electoral programme based on contributions from all those—from universities to sports, from artists to economists, from Catholics to communist dissidents—the Estates-General had attracted into the socialist orbit to begin forming the desired "New Electoral Majority".

The document, first signed by Guterres, covered the main areas of governance, including foreign relations. This also extended to the United Nations, proposing "the division of the Security Council into one body for matters of political security and another for the development and defence of human rights around the world."[6] As for the decision-making process, it recommended "the replacement of the veto with a qualified majority system."[7] It also included explicit support for Brazil to become a permanent member and a more active role for the Secretary-General in conflict prevention and the coordination of peacekeeping operations, as part of necessary reforms that should be "set in motion at the centre of the system before working its way outwards to the periphery."[8]

The end of the Cold War also required changes to the architecture of European security. The Portuguese socialists understood that the former Soviet republics viewed NATO as a barrier the Kremlin would respect, but they also foresaw that any immediate integration into the military alliance would threaten "the security guarantees of countries such as Russia and Ukraine,"[9] and raise "more problems than it would solve."[10]

One area flagged as needing serious initiative was "deepening the Euro-African dialogue,"[11] particularly through "a greater effort to provide development aid."[12]

Guterres' voice was ubiquitous in Portuguese society. Through radio stations he spoke about domestic issues and world affairs. His speeches spread out from the grandstand of the Estates-General and from the Socialist parliamentary bench. All this combined with his constant appearances in the studios of the newly launched television stations granted him the nickname of the "Talking Pickaxe".

Do the Math

It was still early morning when Guterres arrived at Coimbra, home to one of Europe's oldest universities. It was May 1995, the Estates-General was up and running and the Socialist Party leader was on the campaign trail, touring the country on board what he called the "New Majority Caravan".

Inspired by Bill Clinton and Al Gore's campaign bus, the caravan seemed to appeal even to older voters distrustful of the uncertainty caused by Prime Minister Silva's decision not to run again.

Reporters following the nationwide roadshow had grown used to Guterres' cautious choice of words, either to address different voters' sensibilities, or to respond to difficult questions the media threw his way. Whatever the enquiry, the socialist seemed to have a convincing answer on the tip of his tongue. But not even the journalists' keenest noses for misfortune could imagine the magnitude of the mistake about to be made.

Health. This was the subject of the day and the reason for visiting a public hospital. Wearing a white smock worn over his dark suit, just like the doctors accompanying him, Guterres toured the various departments. Walking slowly, he began in the paediatric wing and moved on to the infectious disease wing where he met AIDS patients. In the last ward, he lingered to talk to, and question, the surgeon who had performed the first liver transplant in Portugal.

When the visit was over, the press was waiting outside.

"How much will the health budget increase?" asked one journalist, before holding his microphone up to Guterres.

"We should be able to reach, in the shortest possible timeframe, something in the order of 6 per cent of gross domestic product in terms of health spending," he promptly replied.

"And how much money is that?"

Guterres looked away, glanced up, before gazing to the right, as though searching for the answer. It was a simple, basic calculation, especially for a renowned engineer. The problem was that he could not remember the figure for gross domestic product. A Socialist Party staff member tried to whisper him the numbers, but the harm had been done—and recorded.

"Ah, it's... the gross domestic product is around 3 billion, so... well... 6 per cent... that's... ah... 6 per cent of 3 billion... that's... one would have to do the math," Guterres stuttered, reducing the Portuguese economy to a fifth of its real value.[13]

The reaction from the governing party was as harsh as it was swift: "How is it possible that a candidate for Prime Minister does not know his own country's GDP?"

Unknown to all was the fact that Guterres' wife was ill, the prognosis poor, and that she potentially required a liver transplant.

Zizas, like their children, rarely took part in the campaign. Guterres did everything possible to spare his family from the public exposure his political ambitions demanded of him. This is a principle he maintains today: "When I see these guys parading their wives and their children... the next day some problem comes up and the press buries them all. But if you keep them safe and out of view, you protect them from these things."

The GDP incident changed the tone over the last days of the caravan. So Guterres, as an attempt to end the campaign on a high note, came up with the idea to walk to the summit of the highest mountain in Portugal, Pico, in the Azores. Three thousand, three hundred and fifty-one metres is not an easy task, especially for someone with more intellectual than physical prowess. Nevertheless, Guterres prepared for the journey by dieting and avoiding chocolates for a few weeks.

To the journalists present, this media stunt was well known: of course the candidate would not climb to the top... that had never happened before! The bus would take all to the summit, then they would climb the last 200 metres, take a few photos, a small speech would be given, and then they would drive back down.

However, the next morning, Guterres was ready to conquer the summit. Most of his colleagues, and journalists, unprepared for the occasion, did not join the long and arduous hike.

Hours later, carrying only some water, an apple and a little bread to keep them going, they finally reached the top. Guterres planted a Portuguese flag, and made a small speech that the only cameraman who had accompanied him throughout the climb—ready to capture the moment when the candidate would give up—was able to capture before the battery died. But there was still time for Guterres to pick up the camera himself and film the intrepid reporter who had shared this trip with him.

The Confederate Diet

They used to gather late at night, always on weekdays, always far away from the Socialist Party's headquarters. By gathering in a private apartment, the *petit comité* of Portuguese diplomats avoided the risk of being spotted together entering an evident political partisan meeting.

Throughout the evening, they turned over ideas, took notes and scribbled down commentaries that would become the foreign policy agenda of the 1995 socialist manifesto. Among those present was the Director of European Services from the Ministry of Foreign Affairs, João Lima Pimentel, a man educated in the elitist German private school in Lisbon, a long-time friend of Guterres, dating back to the times of the Luz Group, and whose day-to-day work required regular contact with embassies. It was during one of those exchanges that a German diplomat came to him with an unexpected proposal.

"We were talking in a restaurant," recalls Pimentel, "and he started explaining that it was common practice in Europe for Chancellor Kohl to receive opposition leaders who were interested in explaining their policies to him, not least because they might one day become heads of government. And then he asked me, 'Why don't we set up a meeting with your friend [Guterres]? It will only take a half hour. In Germany. Yes, in Bonn.'"

43

Guterres travelled to the city that had been the capital of West Germany during the Cold War and where Kohl still kept the government's headquarters. "He was a very interesting figure and the last Chancellor to truly experience the war and, therefore, someone who wanted to see Germany integrated into Europe," Guterres emphasises. "A young socialist who, suddenly, right before the election campaign, gets an invitation from Kohl… it's an unforgettable favour, don't you think? I believe that Kohl wanted to send a signal that, as a Christian Democrat, he wouldn't take it badly if a young socialist were elected in Portugal."

Chancellor Kohl (6 feet 3 inches tall, with a PhD in history, and the architect of Germany's reunification, a nation he had led for thirteen years) displayed a stately appearance that must have seemed most opulent to the two short Portuguese men visiting him. Guterres had taken Vitorino along. The conversation took place in the Federal Chancellery on the banks of the Rhine.

After the formal introductions and the discussion of European issues, Guterres played his trump card.

"At a certain point," recalls Vitorino, "he started talking about the difference between German unification under the Frankfurt Diet[14] and unification under the Prussian aegis, and from there they engaged in a conversation about history that prolonged the meeting for an hour and a half. Guterres prepared this conversation thoroughly and Kohl acknowledged it. I think it was one of the most notable exercises I ever witnessed in terms of the capacity to bring up a subject and draw it out in conversation."

A smiling handshake between Guterres and Kohl found its way into the Portuguese media. The elections were only five weeks away.

The Name of the Rose

The clenched left fist, a symbol of resistance against the dictatorship, now appeared more rounded. While still presented against a red backdrop, the skin seemed rejuvenated: softer and with the veins, formerly so protuberant, now hidden. A rose was also added, which looked, as one party elder sarcastically lamented, like a cabbage. Modernising the party's image and aligning it with the change already undertaken by European peers, including Britain's Labour Party, constituted another of the changes Guterres set in motion as Secretary-General. Nevertheless, there was one area in which his efforts appeared fruitless: increasing the participation of women.

"I am personally dissatisfied with the number of women in the Socialist Party's lists,"[15] he said, responding to an indignant journalist who had confronted him on television about the male-dominated leadership roles of the lists. Furthermore, women only comprised 17 per cent of those on the lists, the interviewer insisted. "I haven't gone as far as I wanted,"[16] and "I'm much more about parity than the party is,"[17] Guterres conceded, explaining that, as Secretary-General, he only got to select a third of the seats. Nevertheless, even with his personal quota of 25 per cent women, parity was still a mirage.

With election day looming, the campaigns stepped up their intensity. Street billboards still played a key role in political communication strategies, and the project presented that morning by a Brazilian advertiser raised doubts among the socialists. It was an arduous task to define candidate Guterres in a couple of words. There were those who immediately thought the proposal was brilliant, but others wrinkled their noses and thought it too risky. So, Coelho called Guterres. Their conversation was brief and ended with a smile. "So, when are we going public?" asked Guterres.

"Guterres. Mind and Heart." "Mind" came first to invoke the rigour of his training as an engineer and his mastery of the many ministries he critiqued. This was the *ethos*. It spoke of a calm and responsible change, based on knowledge, without ideological whims that could frighten the electorate. "Heart" conveyed his human face, his concern for social issues and his willingness to engage in dialogue that many electors no longer saw in the current government. This was the *pathos*.

The slogan went up in large letters in public squares, on the side of the road, near traffic lights and anywhere else there was a high traffic of people. By election day, 1 October 1995, there was nothing more to do other than await the results. Guterres lunched at home with his family and went to vote arm in arm with his wife. At dusk, he made his way to the party's traditional election-night headquarters.

On the twelfth floor of the Altis Hotel, right next to Lisbon's most famous boulevard, socialists roamed about in three adjoining rooms: the data room, in permanent contact with local party structures, the meeting room, and the suite with its televisions and buffet.

Guterres was restless. He wanted information on the most out-of-the-way localities. He questioned the polling technicians. He consulted the state of voting once, twice, three times, four times, five times. He went through the numbers and kept staring at the screens.

One hour before the television stations were able to go public with the results, Guterres was already certain that he was Portugal's next Prime Minister.

Comrades jumped into each other's arms while, in the back, every telephone kept ringing off the hook. The winner kicked off election-night celebrations with his first words to the country and then the party carried on, all pink and exuberant, along the capital's avenues.

At dawn, Guterres took his friends and party colleagues back to his house for another round of greetings, toasts and congratulations. It was a family-like atmosphere and happiness abounded. However, this did not prevent his Mind, at least in that moment, in the midst of his outpouring of words, from speaking louder than his Heart.

"Celebrate today because, starting tomorrow, it's all downhill."

4

ORDER AND PROGRESS

After an entire decade sheltered from the public eye, its luscious gardens hiding and safeguarding the closed privacy of its former tenant, the São Bento estate was now on display to the public. Waiting at the door was the Prime Minister, eager to welcome the hundreds of citizens wishing to take this chance to explore his official residence.

"That's when we suggested something that would have been impossible before," says Luís Patrão, Guterres' first chief of staff, "that once a year, on the anniversary of the April Revolution, anyone could visit the palace as if it were a normal thing." According to Patrão, this decision was one of the most emblematic of the desired spirit for the relationship between the Prime Minister and the country: "It was highly symbolic to have over a thousand people there, wandering about the gardens of the official residence without any restrictions."

"What happened was a breath of fresh air," explains Francisco Motta Veiga, a friend from the Luz Group, who had been called on to serve as the Prime Minister's cultural adviser. "There were so many things that needed lightening up and the changes we made in São Bento aimed to reflect this sense of openness that was also felt across the country. We made everything a lot more contemporary and that enabled the creation of the right kind of environment."

Contrary to his predecessor, Guterres decided not to use the palace as his residence and continued to live in the same rented apartment with his wife and two children. Once in office, the new Prime Minister sought to break with the inherited relationship between citizens and politicians, taking advantage of the media as a priority means with which to affirm his concept of dialogue. The same privilege was extended to the international correspondents in Lisbon, who were regularly invited for dinner with time set aside at the end of the meal for Q&As with both on- and off-the-record comments.

Patrão maintains that, after a decade of conservative rule, "people felt repressed and had a desire for openness, wishing to get closer to power. In those early years, even António Guterres was surprised because we would go somewhere and there would be a thousand people who had turned up just to see the Prime Minister."

In practice, the dialogue Guterres advocated was also a political necessity given that his was a minority government. Furthermore, the new leader of the opposition was an old companion from the Luz Group with whom he had shared so many political discussions: Marcelo Rebelo de Sousa.

Thus, Guterres took advantage of this juncture to launch one of his most challenging democratic initiatives: he promised to appear regularly before Parliament in order to answer questions from MPs.

No Jobs for the Boys

Despite having twenty-four more seats in Parliament than the main opposition party, the PS were still four MPs away from a majority. As such, any new legislation still required tactical negotiations to pass. Since many ministers had entered the government through the Estates-General initiative, they were independent outsiders with no previous political experience. And so, the permanent talks with the opposition involved coordinating all public communications, while also keeping party expectations under control.

As the tiring and urgent details of governing began to accumulate, Guterres still had to maintain his deep personal relationships with the countless Socialist Party national structures. He was certainly seeking a professionalised party, but above all his leadership stemmed from the close contacts he kept with the comrades. That was the source of his political power; that was how he established the foundations of his leadership.

To this end, he anticipated a negative, if moderate, reaction to the announcement he was about to make. He trusted the loyalty of the victorious troops and, in effect, he was fulfilling a campaign promise.

At the first internal meeting following the national elections, which brought together the entire structure of the party at the national level, the Secretary-General shattered the aspirations of many who were counting on him as the only means of gaining a decent position in the state apparatus. With five chilling words, quoted from his British peer Tony Blair, Guterres told his supporters straight: "No. Jobs. For. The. Boys."

His first government promised—and at the beginning even strove to comply with—to raise the moral standards of the state, opting for recruitment tenders on the basis of merit, rather than politically motivated nominations, as the means of filling key roles in the state structure. Perhaps with excessive idealism, especially as this task could never be under the direct control of the Prime Minister, this aimed to depoliticise public organisms by guaranteeing senior civil service positions were not filled due to party affiliation, nor were they performed by those whose political loyalties compensated for their lack of qualifications. This was just part of the job and it had to be done.

"The international themes on which the Prime Minister had a say were always a matter of personal and political pleasure for him," recalls the then Secretary of State for Foreign Affairs, Luís Amado. "I remember him telling the Minister of Foreign Affairs, 'You have the best job in government. That is a good position; not being Prime Minister. I end up with all the hassles.'"

Portugal maintained good relations with the leading stakeholders in the international community, but the interpretation the Prime Minister had of his country's role in the world defined new priorities for Lisbon's external agenda.

Without overlooking the European Union or the bonds with the United States and NATO, the government sought to implement a vision that involved "broadening the concept of trans-Atlantic relations to the South Atlantic." According to Pimentel, the friend who had facilitated the unforgettable meeting with Helmut Kohl, and was subsequently invited to become a diplomatic adviser, "in addition to the United States and Canada, on that side of the ocean there were a series of countries colonised by Portugal and Spain, displaying a certain facet of Iberian culture, and with which we did not have major relations, perhaps with the exception of Brazil. And then came Fernando Henrique Cardoso, with whom António Guterres got along marvellously well."

Brazilians Are Not Foreigners

Swept away by the optimistic international landscape that the unipolar world order cast over the 1990s, Guterres climbed the steep stairs leading to the entrance of the Palácio do Planalto. There he would find a warm and welcoming embrace from Brazil's social democrat leader, President Fernando Henrique Cardoso.

This was his first official visit as Portugal's head of government. Despite the common language and five centuries of shared history, which included a period when the Portuguese capital was transferred to Rio de Janeiro,[1] the two Atlantic neighbours had previously shown little mutual interest. Their economic links were negligible, while migration from Brazil to Portugal was becoming a problematic bilateral issue.

Aware of the prevailing discomfort, Guterres' government transformed this first trip into an expression of political goodwill and sent an official delegation of almost forty people. In addition to the several dozen large companies that accepted the Prime Minister's invitation, travelling with Guterres were, among others: five ministers, three Secretaries of State, five Foreign Affairs Ministry representatives, and sixteen advisers from different government departments.

"We got over the phase of cordial words and poorly disguised bad feelings and replaced those for a mature relationship between two countries," claims Cardoso. The Brazilian President recalls how "Guterres did in fact know Brazil and felt at ease among us."

Guterres explains how the commitment to this country provided solutions to two problems Portugal faced: demography and economy: "I had this idea that we needed more immigration. What workforce can be better than that from a country where the people already have a certain level of education, who speak Portuguese, who do not experience any kind of cultural shock and who easily integrate into our society?"

In the seminars held in São Paulo and Rio de Janeiro, Guterres deployed all of his arguments to convince major local businesses to believe in the political will of his government. He took to the stage to pitch his country, presenting national economy statistics, explaining his government's strategy, burying the divisions of the past and beautifying the more technical aspects of the presentation with affective sentences such as "Brazilians are not foreigners."

The political scope and the overall ambition of the visit was such that the joint declaration that Guterres and Cardoso signed at the end of their official meeting stated, "Stipulating, on Portugal's initiative, the reiteration of support from Portugal for the participation of Brazil as a permanent member of a restructured UN Security Council."[2]

In his speech during the official banquet, the host referred to another project that was emerging and that would provide a bridge for both countries to expand their relationship: "We want the community of language and culture that we share with five developing countries in Africa to serve our joint actions at the international level and the development of our own sphere of cooperation and development."[3]

The Most Spoken Language in the Southern Hemisphere

Carlos Lopes raised an eyebrow.

In the 1990s, many African countries were still experimenting in their first decades of independence and undergoing constant political reinvention. So, when the plan was formed to establish—in Lisbon, of all places—a Community of the Portuguese-Speaking

Countries (CPLP), to bring African countries closer to their former coloniser and the colossal Brazil, Lopes was filled with suspicion. Subsequent decades would see this young economist from Guinea-Bissau become an adviser to Kofi Annan, then Executive Secretary of the UN Economic Commission for Africa, and a personal friend of Guterres. But at this time, when he was still a low-profile pan-Africanist academic, he perceived the proposal as a flagrant attempt to resuscitate imperialist fantasies: "The idea seemed terrible. We thought the CPLP was entirely neo-colonial and, above all, we thought this would undo the cooperation that was already ongoing between our five African countries, which was based on solidarity. Our leading figures all knew each other from the liberation period, as young men having very strong political and ideological affinities, and many of us believed in pan-Africanism. This had nothing to do either with Portugal or with Brazil."

In contrast, for Pedro Comissário, the Mozambique Ambassador to Lisbon in 1996, the institution did not hold any hidden agenda, and even the proposal for Lisbon to host the headquarters did not reflect any veiled desires: "The neo-colonialist temptation never truly existed. Our project was different to those of the Francophonie or the Commonwealth. There was no parallelism between our institutions. They were always totally different conceptions."

Part of CPLP's strategic value stemmed directly from the cross-referencing of political support among its member states, in keeping with their respective sub-regions and areas of influence. While, to African states, Lisbon was the gateway into the European Union, for Portugal, these diplomatic interactions were a contact point with Africa, the largest regional group in the UN General Assembly.

Over time, Lopes' reservations about the CPLP faded and he now recognises how the community found its own space. On the one hand, its importance derived from representing the most spoken language in the Southern Hemisphere and, on the other hand, from its founding leaders: "It also helped that the Portuguese left was in charge of the CPLP and these were people who seemed very much involved, in a way that I considered very genuine."

Indeed, by the time he took office as Prime Minister, Guterres had already built a reputation among African leaders due to his activities in the Socialist International. Regarding the CPLP, he happened to be in the right place at the right time to cut the ribbon on a project that had already been under construction for some years before his time.

On 17 July 1996, Guterres, only ten months in government, commemorated the official launch of the community. He set to work with a political tool that first and foremost enabled him to strengthen his political network in Africa and, secondly, put into practice his geostrategic vision on the need to find a counterbalance to the European axis of Portuguese foreign policy.

At that time, the African CPLP member states were converging their diplomatic alignments. With the collapse of the Soviet Union and the end of the Cold War, the great reference point that had provided ideological, financial and military support to African independence movements was no longer available. Consequently, their leaders were open to diversifying the contexts of their international relationships.

Macau, Not Hong Kong

At the main banquet table, Guterres couldn't stop laughing. The high representative sent by the Chinese government, who travelled specially from Beijing, was practically in tears. The laughter of the Governor of Chongqing echoed around the room.

Sat at some distance, Ministers Pina Moura, Jorge Coelho and Mariano Gago, who were accompanying Guterres on this first official visit to China, in April 1998, exchanged some startled looks.

"What the heck...?"

Having complied with local gastronomic protocol that stipulates guests and hosts pair their food with liberal amounts of mao-tai, a rice-based spirit with 60 per cent alcohol, Guterres had decided to share stories from his ministers' political pasts. He started with the Minister of Economy, the "Cardinal" Pina Moura.

"Right, that one over there, he used to be on the Central Committee of the Communist Party! Soviet! Hold on, there's more... Jorge, come here! This friend was an activist in the Maoist Party in Portugal. And over there is Mariano, he's the

53

Science… that one was the leader of, imagine this, the Marxist-Leninist Youth!"

Coelho recalls, "The Chinese were speechless, they could not understand how all those people there were representing the government of Portugal, as ministers! Ministers! It was highly amusing, especially because António Guterres is not one for big jokes at formal events, but the ambience there was made very favourable!"

Guterres was the first foreign head of government to visit Chongqing, a municipality in the south-west of China, home to thirty million people. However, aside from the commercial opportunities that this region already offered to the small and peripheral Portuguese economy, the core purpose for the visit was political: the transfer of the Portuguese colony of Macau to the Chinese state. Hence, the visit also included a stopover in this territory of some 20 square kilometres, formerly used by the Portuguese Empire as a post for trading and disseminating Catholicism in the Far East.

To properly welcome the Prime Minister of Portugal, the main avenues in Macau were decorated with photographs of Guterres and Portuguese flags. This visit sought to convey to China a strong guarantee about the calm acceptance in Lisbon regarding the imminent transfer process, which dated back to the re-establishment of diplomatic relations between the two countries in 1979.

Macau would be integrated according to the principle of "one country, two systems" and become an autonomous region of China for a period of no less than five decades—as had happened with the British handover of Hong Kong in 1997. The hardships of that process inevitably influenced the Portuguese negotiations even though the two territories were very different. Macau's population was fifteen times smaller than Hong Kong's, and the majority of the inhabitants were immigrants who had been born in mainland China. Furthermore, Macau, which was on its way to becoming the world's casino capital, outstripping even Las Vegas in turnover, did not have the connections with the West that Hong Kong had, with its international deepwater port and financial centre. There was also another factor that could not be ignored: Portugal had not taken Macau by force, unlike the United Kingdom, which had seized Hong Kong during the Opium Wars. The trading post had been leased to the Portuguese by the Ming dynasty centuries ago, and the political takeover had been without violence.

"The Chinese did not want the troubles they had—and continue to have—with Hong Kong," explains Coelho (who, like many other Portuguese socialists, spent time serving in the government of Macau), "and, from our perspective, Macau was the last part of a colonial empire" for which Portugal bore moral responsibility and which could serve as an important diplomatic door to Beijing. "It needed to be well looked after" in its transfer to Chinese authority.

At stake was not only the future of the bilateral relationship between Portugal and China, but also the file registered by the Chinese authorities of one Guterres.

"The Macau talks went very well," recalls Guterres. "It was Prime Minister Zhu Rongji who welcomed me to China, and their treatment was very good. For the Chinese, Portugal represented the opposite of the United Kingdom, and Macau the opposite of Hong Kong—and the Chinese have elephant memories and do not forget these things."

The meeting with Zhu Rongji, a fellow electronic engineer, took place in the Great Hall of the People, in Tiananmen Square. According to one of Guterres' media advisers, the metaphors that the pair used in their exchanges helped to overcome the expected cultural barriers and lower the guard of the deeply rooted Asian formalism. "The Prime Minister of the People's Republic of China looked through the window and began talking about the light of that spring day, about what that meant for the growth in bilateral relations," recalls David Damião, then press adviser to the Prime Minister. "Then Mr. Guterres, who had put in a lot of preparation for the meeting, applied the same type of language in order to anticipate the flourishing of contacts between the two peoples."

A few years after that meeting, the Special Autonomous Region of Macau was created. After almost 500 years, the Portuguese flag flew for the last time over the governor's residence in Macau, under the watchful eye of Prime Minister Guterres.

5

A NATO-RUSSIA ALLIANCE?

Boutros Boutros-Ghali was apprehensive. The Egyptian knew that the 1996 UN General Assembly would probably be his last given his unpopularity in Washington and the predicament in which the end of the Cold War had put the Secretary-General: his overdependence on the only superpower left within the now unipolar world.

Even while recognising that "the first priority of a Secretary-General has to be the relationship between the United States and the United Nations,"[1] and even after having placed so many Americans in key roles throughout the organisation, Boutros-Ghali was never able to get himself into the White House's good books.

In fact, soon after re-election, the Clinton administration confirmed its intention to replace the UN Secretary-General. US media speculated that this rejection stemmed from failures, such as the the 1994 Rwanda genocide and 1995 Srebrenica massacre, while also covering the growing admonishments of Boutros-Ghali—who was publicly insisting the United States pay what it owed to the UN—that had infuriated both Republicans and Democrats.

The reasons for the Washington veto—which were confirmed eventually—only became clearer years later with the publication of the memoirs of Secretary of State Madeleine Albright. These reasons may be read as a set of rules that any UN Secretary-General should abide by:

- Rule no. 1—It is not advisable to criticise the United States in public: "Boutros-Ghali became more and more critical of America, which may have earned points for him elsewhere but made it even harder for me to garner support for the UN on Capitol Hill," wrote Albright.
- Rule no. 2—Featuring as a campaign theme may prove fatal— "Republican candidate Bob Dole's most reliable applause lines made fun of the UN leader."
- Rule no. 3—In Washington's view, the UN Secretary-General should appear humble and discreet: "Boutros-Ghali was hyper status-conscious and seemed to believe that administrative tasks were beneath him."
- Rule no. 4—The White House is sensitive to the management capabilities of the Secretary-General: "He is not committed to, or capable of, achieving our urgent reform goals."
- Rule no. 5—The Security Council always prevails over the Secretary-General: "We began with one big advantage. If we didn't vote for him, he could not win."[2]

Despite the impending sentence, Boutros-Ghali still had scheduled commitments, and on the morning of 9 September these included his participation in the congress of a political organisation he had been a part of before his international mandate. On this occasion, the Egyptian would not have before him the usual member state representatives, but a crowd of comrades.

The Secretary-General exchanged greetings and shook warm hands as he arrived at the venue. In one of the corridors, he greeted the leader of the Portuguese Socialists with a friendly smile. Guterres was also in New York to speak at the same conference—the 20th Socialist International Congress, held at the UN headquarters.

Even after becoming Prime Minister, Guterres continued to attend meetings, pass on contacts, collaborate on reports... and accumulate responsibilities. In addition to the groups' vice presidency, he also chaired the Economic Policy Committee and he co-chaired, alongside the President of Senegal, Abdou Diouf, the Africa Committee.

In the General Assembly Hall, Boutros-Ghali took his place on the stage while Guterres sat in the same audience where some 700 delegates listened to triumphal speeches praising the recent successes of the Socialist International: of the fifteen European Union countries, eleven had affiliated members in power. Furthermore, the organisation had just accepted a record number of thirty-three new members.

Building critical mass, however, was not enough. For the world to head in the desired direction, "A New System of Collective Responsibility" was required. That was the title of the report drafted by the economic committee chaired by Guterres, an authentic anti-neoliberal manifesto that called for changes in institutions such as the World Bank and the International Monetary Fund (IMF). To present its key proposals, Guterres climbed for the first time the four steps leading up to the pulpit of the UN General Assembly:

> Olof Palme was right. We need to place solidarity and equity as the priority themes on our political agenda. [...] Poverty and social exclusion are the soil in which anti-democratic trends set their roots. [...] We need better mechanisms for international coordination. These might take shape as an Economic Security Council, an expanded G-7, within the framework of the United Nations.[3]

A Great Victory

Having fulfilled his duties towards socialist comrades of the world, Guterres returned to Lisbon, missing the opening of the UN General Assembly. Representing the Portuguese government on this occasion was the Minister of Foreign Affairs, whose mission that year went far beyond the usual formalities on the diplomatic calendar.

Within a few weeks, that same UN body would be electing the non-permanent members of the Security Council for the 1997/98 term—and Portugal was running as a candidate. Lisbon was up against Sweden and Australia for one of the two places allocated to the Western European and Other States group.[4]

Jaime Gama, the Minister of Foreign Affairs, took advantage of this opportunity to campaign, intensify contacts and consolidate support. Each state represented one vote and the group with the most members was Africa, to which Portugal was now formally linked through the CPLP. A candidacy to the Security Council is a test of a country's capacity for dialogue with every region worldwide and, in effect, measures the influence they are able, or unable, to wield throughout different diplomatic networks. For a small Catholic country like Portugal, member of the European Union and a founder of NATO, this tested the strength of the bonds with both the Global North and the Global South.

On election day, and with no surprises, Sweden was elected in the first round. There were two candidates left for a single seat. All would be decided on the second ballot.

Even though Portugal was not a favourite from the outset, and with the diplomats still managing their low expectations, the informal polls after behind-the-scenes conversations and guarantees of support suggested victory was possible. At the same time, Australia was doing the same exercise and reckoned they also had the numbers to be elected. This could only mean that some member states were promising their loyalty to both suitors…

Nerves were peaking as the ballot papers were gathered once again. The session was suspended for twenty-five minutes to count the votes. At 12.35 on 21 October, the President of the General Assembly announced:

> The result of the voting for the election of two non-permanent members of the Security Council is as follows:
>
> Number of valid ballots: 181
> Required two-thirds majority: 121
> Abstentions: 0
> Portugal—124
> Australia—57
>
> I congratulate the states which have been elected.[5]

In Lisbon, Guterres greeted the media waiting for his press conference with a large smile of contentment. "A great victory,"[6] emphasised the Prime Minister, who witnessed first-hand the way in which diplomatic networks were able to transform modest candidacies into global victories.

Despite the secrecy of the proceedings, it was not long before it was known how the states had voted. The Portuguese Minister of Foreign Affairs concluded that "very important and significant was the support from three of the permanent members of the Security Council: France, China and Russia. [...] The African continent voted almost as a bloc for the Portuguese candidacy. The same may be said of the Arab world. [...] There was strong support from states in Latin America,"[7] highlighting the efforts undertaken by Brazil.

Therefore, it had been among the European states—in Guterres' own backyard—that Portugal's candidacy was received with less enthusiasm.

A Walk in the Rose Garden

Seven months after his New York trip, in April 1997, Guterres was back in the United States. There was no need to book a hotel in Washington D.C., since he would be staying in Blair House, the residence next to the White House that accommodates the President's special guests.

The visit had been prepared by Bill Clinton's National Security Adviser who justified hosting the Portuguese delegation in the following terms.[8]

PURPOSE	Guterres has been Prime Minister since last fall. There are a number of important issues to discuss with them as leaders of a NATO country. A meeting would be well received by Congress and the Portuguese-American community.
BACKGROUND	We enjoy excellent cooperation with Portugal, including access to the important Lajes airbase. Portuguese support on our Bosnia and NATO initiatives is important to their success.
PREVIOUS PARTICIPATION	The President has not met Guterres.

DATE AND TIME	August or September, date and time open.
FIRST LADY'S ATTENDANCE	Not required.

In the briefing documents handed to President Clinton was a recommendation to discuss the expansion of NATO as a topic of high priority. Following the collapse of the USSR, the military alliance sought to advance eastwards on two different fronts: establishing a new relationship with Russia, and incorporating former members of the Warsaw Pact into the organisation.

To avoid provoking Moscow, both Ukraine and the Baltic states would be left out of the expansion plans, at least for the time being. Regarding the rest of the strategy, however, the member states could not reach an agreement: should this geopolitical movement extend only to Poland, the Czech Republic and Hungary, or should the organisation send out a more robust show of support to the democracies emerging in Eastern Europe and open NATO up to Romania and Slovenia?

The best means of approaching Russia also elicited internal dispute. Should the Alliance seek only to establish mechanisms for military consultation? Or should attempts be made to use the diplomatic momentum in order to reach a broader political commitment? In this case, would it make sense to study the possibility of Russia joining NATO?

There were still several issues outstanding, but many believed the enemies during the Cold War could sign a partnership agreement by the end of May 1997. This was also a reason to bring forward the US President's meeting with Guterres, which ended up happening, not in August or September as initially proposed, but on 3 April—the day Portugal was to take its position on the UN Security Council.

Arriving at the Diplomatic Reception Room, Guterres was greeted by the leader of the free world on crutches, after a fall in the mansion of a golfing friend. They sat on the yellow armchairs by the fireplace in the Oval Office. By his side, Guterres had Minister Gama and the Portuguese Ambassador to Washington, while Clinton was accompanied by Vice President Al Gore and his new Secretary of State, Madeleine Albright.

Before the meeting could start, protocol allowed in some photographers and journalists. Clinton expressed his welcome to his Portuguese counterpart and handed over to Guterres, who took up the opportunity to respond to some questions from the American media.

"Are you also in favor of expansion of NATO, and what kind of an agreement, charter are you going to have with Russia?"[9]

"I once heard Vice President Al Gore telling me that he looked at the enlargement of NATO and relations with Russia like the coupling of two spaceships, and the need to put them in the same orbit. I think this is a very good idea. [...] I hope that one day in the future NATO and Russia can be allies, defending the values of enlightenment against all the irrational behaviours based on extreme naturalism, religious fundamentalism, and all other things that should not exist in a modern world,"[10] Guterres responded. In other words, Russia and the West should certainly, and would need to, move closer together; but Russia should remain outside NATO itself.

Following the scheduled meeting, Bill Clinton and Guterres took a short walk alone in the Rose Garden. The Portuguese had two subjects prepared, with one inevitably relating to the North Atlantic Alliance.

"There was this concept I tried to sell, but it never got very far," explains Guterres. "We should build a security ring from Bering to Bering, with a triangular relationship between NATO, Russia and the Ukraine in a super alliance that would ensure the avoidance of ruptures like the one we are having at the moment," referring to the rising tensions between the West and Moscow since Putin's annexation of Crimea. "I had a vision—and I still do today, even if it's ever more compromised—that in order to bring about international balance, it is fundamental that the USA and Russia maintain an operational relationship, independent of whatever divergences there may be."

Following their walk, Clinton and Guterres joined their delegations in the Red Room. The diplomatic adviser to Guterres was
anxious to learn how the one-to-one had gone. "António told
Clinton that if Russia were to progress in the direction of a
European democracy, the partnership with NATO should also
evolve—and then came the fundamental expression—'towards an
alliance'," explains Pimentel. "And he expressed his willingness to
set out this position at the speech he would make at this scheduled
ceremony in Paris. He told me exactly what Clinton's response
was: 'António, if I said such a thing, Congress would crucify me.
But you go ahead and say it.' That then happened and it profoundly
marked his relationship with Russia."

Lunch served in the State Dining Room brought the White
House reception to a close, but the Prime Minister's trip to the US
was not over yet. The visit had been planned to last seven days,
including stopovers in Chicago and San Francisco.

However, as Guterres kept notching up political triumphs, his
personal life was painful. The drama surrounding the unexpected
GDP verbal slip during the election campaign was only worsening.
And in San Francisco, these two dimensions of his life collided.

Guterres was arriving at a meeting when his wife called him.
Zizas was in London, in the hospital undergoing another battery of
treatments. A liver transplant had taken place a month earlier and
the risk now was that the new organ could be rejected.

His wife's health continued to deteriorate and the Prime
Minister, with two school-age children, was unable to hang up. He
asked the driver to slow down and the car began going around in
circles. Five, ten, fifteen silent circuits of the same roundabout,
with the concern of his team rising with every turn.

Guterres suffered in silence. He especially did not want the issue
to be leaked to the press, but inside his government Zizas' situation
had long since been common knowledge. "We knew of the risks
associated with the transplant, we always knew," explains Vitorino.
"But the thing is, she was a transcendental person, she was always
very present and very important to the balance of António
Guterres. The energy she emanated managed to disperse some of
the anguish around the evolution in her health, but it was known
that that was a progressive, degenerative disease."

After returning to Portugal, and as the months passed, Zizas showed some signs of improvement. In the second half of 1997, she was even able to appear at occasional ceremonies, such as when she hosted a very special visitor: the First Lady of the United States.

On the first of the five days spent in Lisbon, Hillary Clinton and her daughter Chelsea were received by Zizas and Guterres in São Bento Palace. They met privately and had a relaxed lunch with some guests and friends of the couple, such as Melícias.

The US Ambassador to Portugal, Elizabeth Bagley, also present, noted, through the fluid flow of conversation coupled with the convergence in their points of view, how Hillary and Guterres "got along really very well." When lunch was over, Bagley reveals that "she told me exactly that she had been very impressed with him, and I am sure she shared that with her husband."

On her return to Washington D.C., the First Lady wrote to Guterres and Zizas:[11]

Dear Mr. Prime Minister and Mrs. Guterres:

Thank you for the exquisite silver boxes. They are a lovely reminder of my visit to Portugal and the warm welcome I received from the Portuguese people. Your generosity and hospitality made this a memorable visit for me.

With best wishes, I am Sincerely yours,

Hillary Rodham Clinton

6

THE BRUSSELS JOB

It appeared to be nothing more than a small sheaf of unbound, handwritten papers. Not more than ten pages, A5 in size. Despite having been written in the distant past on the night of 13 November 1997, only half a dozen or so people had ever seen these notes or even imagined they existed.

The Alpha Plan, as it was entitled, complied with three basic principles. It was simple, it was secret, and it reflected an unprecedented level of ambition on the part of a Portuguese government.

The small pages, which had been scribbled on from top to bottom, progressed from the macro to the micro, beginning with an international perspective, taking into special account the calendar for the rotating Presidencies of the European Union.

Every six months, an EU member state holds the Presidency and gains the opportunity to shape the bloc's medium- and long-term agenda, while proposing issues that invariably correspond to their own executive priorities.

Hence, and as the schedule for these *pro tempore* presidential terms was known in advance, the Plan's steps were designed to match the interests of each member state holding the Presidency.

"This should take into account that the German Presidency takes place in the first half of 1999."

Next came the identification of different governments' support that needed to be won over: the Chirac-Jospin duo, referring to the French President and Prime Minister; British Prime Minister Blair; Spanish Prime Minister José María Aznar, who should receive a subtle show of support over the Gibraltar issue;[1] as well as the head of the Luxembourg government, Jean-Claude Juncker.

The Plan's implementation phase aimed to incorporate a clear message of support for the European Union's eastward expansion—the desired geopolitical shift that, in parallel with the expansion of NATO, sought to bring countries formerly under Soviet dominance into the Western sphere, including Hungary, Poland, Bulgaria and the Czech Republic.

Zooming in at the domestic level, the Alpha Plan recommended, "We need to take into consideration that, during this period, the pre-campaign phase of the Portuguese elections begins." Hence the imperative to ensure an "inevitable" Socialist Party victory "with an absolute majority in the 1999 legislative elections." Planning for a change in national leadership would be equally important, but it should be done "naturally and without undue drama."

The original draft of the Alpha Plan was written in a riverside restaurant in Lisbon. The diplomatic adviser to the Prime Minister had invited only two people for dinner: the Secretary of State for European Affairs, Francisco Seixas da Costa, and the Minister of Economy, the "Cardinal" Joaquim Pina Moura.

"All this should take into account that we are still one year off a decisive period for the maturing of the Alpha Plan. I would urge the outlining of a strategy to be refined over the forthcoming months."

To Get Something You Have to Give Something

The large, heavy and cumbersome folder Guterres was carrying onto the aeroplane explained in detail each of the points on the agenda. The imminent meeting of the leaders of the fifteen European Union member states intended to take decisive steps towards the organisation's growth, and Portugal had several interests to defend.

Representing the highest level of decision-making, these European Councils brought together all government leaders four times every year—each country holding the rotating Presidency would organise two summits—to manage the ongoing themes of relevance to the bloc and resolve the inevitable conflicts arising from the competing ambitions of its members.

Even in this golden era of multilateralism, when all the winds were blowing in favour of European integration, the collective path of the states was framed by the views and expectations of the electorates that would ultimately hold their respective leaders accountable on their return home.

Hence, if all countries at these Council meetings were theoretically equal, in reality some were more equal than others. Governments were ultimately responsible for gathering as many victories as they could, trumpeting each and every disputed and difficult triumph to their voters back home.

In fact, discussions among leaders were becoming monopolised by the division of EU resources, especially against the backdrop of the largest expansion in the Union's history. In one fell swoop, ten new members would be joining from the east and the reunification of the continent brought an obvious problem to those already there: the budgetary cake was growing, but not enough so to feed all mouths.

The Portuguese case was particularly delicate given that, in addition to the predictable loss of funding, all the analysis pointed to a simultaneous loss of competitiveness towards these new countries with their cheaper workforce engaging in direct competition with the country's textiles, agribusiness and manufacturing industries.

However, Guterres remained favourable to the enlargement. Francisco Seixas da Costa explains the political thinking behind this position: "He would say one thing that was ethically irrefutable, 'We cannot have the nerve of having spent decades showing to the other side of the Wall a certain model of development and democracy and then, suddenly, when the Wall falls, we tell them, you know what, on second thoughts, you can't be part of this right now.'"

In practice, the Eastern enlargement confirmed some of the worst Portuguese fears. After returning to Lisbon, during a government cabinet meeting, Guterres received a phone call from the chief of staff to Portugal's European Commissioner.

With its headquarters in Brussels, the Commission is the executive branch of the European Union. Under scrutiny from the European Parliament—whose members are directly elected by each country's citizens—the Commission is composed of one representative (a commissioner) from, and appointed by, each member state. It acts according to the political orientations handed down by the European Council meetings, on which sit the member states' heads of government and is the only European institution with authority to take government-like decisions. Its organisational structure is divided into commissions handling different sectors, similar to ministries.

During the phone call, rooted through a speaker for the benefit of everyone in the cabinet meeting, the Portuguese Commissioner announced that the financing plans for Lisbon were practically settled and they were disastrous.

Guterres asked Seixas da Costa for a detailed survey of the internal priorities of each EU member state. The strategy was to gather allies, to conciliate the ambitions of other governments with his own, to wrap everything in the same package and to present it publicly as a collective European interest, making sure Portugal was benefitted.

The Secretary of State and his team set about discovering what Sweden, for example, wanted. Was the country seeking finance to launch a Northern Dimension policy?[2] Then, a detailed dossier on the topic would be written, followed by an immediate visit to Stockholm.

The Swedes were used to receiving all kinds of requests and complaints from smaller economies, especially during periods of financial negotiations, but what they heard from Guterres was different.

"I want to tell you right away: we entirely agree with your Nordic dimension plans and I wanted to assure you that Portugal shall support you until the end."

As a newcomer, Guterres defended the need for lengthy individual talks, face-to-face, with each head of government. He wanted to establish bonds of personal trust and empathy to boost the probability that, when push came to shove, his interlocutors would keep the promises they had made.

The 1996 roadshow around European capitals took Guterres to unfamiliar governments and peers he had yet to win over. But it also created opportunities to visit old acquaintances who received him with open arms.

"I welcomed António to the Palais de Bourgogne so many times," jokes Juncker, then the Luxembourg Prime Minister, "that we almost had a spare front door key cut out for him!"

Problem-solving

Educated in the university triangle of Oxford, Cambridge and London, the disciplined advisers swelled the delegation led by Tony Blair. At a distance, the British team certainly had over twenty impeccable bureaucrats, specialists in guaranteeing that the United Kingdom's positions were duly defended and that the relationship of eternal distrust with Europe would continue to benefit their country. As the old saying goes, "The United Kingdom does not have friends, it has interests," and in order to pursue these at decisive European Council meetings, Her Majesty's Government deployed whatever means necessary.

On the other side of the corridor, there stood the imposing Portuguese armada led by the Prime Minister and made up of no more than... one adviser.

"I had a fabulous guy with me," recalls Guterres, "and, in the negotiations about money, he was there with a computer on the other side of the door doing the sums with a model that he had created and we would immediately see the impact of the proposals. But I was otherwise alone. We were just a pair and it was only with him that I would test our proposals. He would send me the data and I would say, 'No, no, do it this way,' and so we managed."

By the time he started these expeditions into the European arena, tensions were indeed mounting. The deadlocks at each Council dragged onto the next, and the financial talks were becoming increasingly bogged down. Until, on the fringes of the European Council in Cologne, Chancellor Gerhard Schröder took Guterres to one side.

With the deadline for the negotiations looming, and faced with prevailing intransigence from different actors, the German leader informally invited his Portuguese peer to be the spokesperson for the small countries: "The two of us have to find a solution here."

In effect, the majority of leaders from that period recognise the role played by Guterres in concerting the European states. Beginning with Schröder: "António Guterres, who had a good network of contacts, naturally canvassed other European Union partners to glean support for his position. And I, too, understood that the plans were difficult to swallow for a country like Portugal. Concessions indeed had to be made on both sides and António Guterres was highly instrumental in bringing these about, as he defended his positions very clearly, but also built bridges, paving the way for joint decisions. He once said that self-interest stands in the way of the European project, and that we either solve problems together, or not at all. He is right."

José María Aznar, the Spanish conservative who became one of Guterres' best friends among the heads of government: "He is not a negotiator who puts forward impossible things, and he always moves towards the terrain that is also possible for him, with some minimum and maximum limits that he protects very well. António always had a very clear idea of what he wanted in negotiations and would mark out his red lines from which he would not move."

In just a few years, Guterres managed to affirm himself as a problem-solver who could be trusted. Pimentel, the Prime Minister's diplomatic adviser, attributes this rising prestige to "the structured way he talked, in various languages, and how he would find solutions nobody had thought of. And his passion for negotiation, for the European game, was quite overt."

A slender figure, with a Germanic education and aristocratic pose, Pimentel was responsible for the Plan, seeking to get the Prime Minister of Portugal into the most powerful position in European politics.

The Alpha Plan

Guterres had completed half of his term when his old friend and international relations adviser entered his office. He was not there to raise a point of the government's agenda, nor a set of bilateral issues to deal with, but rather with a product to sell.

Pimentel argued that the name "Guterres" was gaining an undebatable reputation among European leaders. He declared the political environment was favourable, thanks to centre-left parties serving in the majority of European governments. He then concluded that Guterres met every condition for becoming the next President of the European Commission, a position elected by the heads of government in the European Council.

"One day, I decided to ask the question openly," Pimentel explains. "And in one of those António-style answers, he said something like, 'I would not say that could never happen.'"

The response was enough for the diplomat to start working the field. The first step, on which all others depended, was to ensure support from the largest economy and the main driver of the European Union. Indeed, his education in the German School of Lisbon, mastery of the language and a long list of contacts across the Germanic world, meant Pimentel was able to gain swift access to the Chancellor's inner circle.

"I can only tell you that there is openness. But this, as you know, is always a personal question and a decision for the boss," Pimentel would hear at the end of some calls.

Involved ever since that first riverside dinner, the Secretary of State for European Affairs joined Pimentel's efforts, taking advantage of his travels to sow the name of Guterres, consistently working it into his talks and discussions with journalists, diplomats and government officials. Along the corridors of Brussels, Seixas da Costa would murmur:

"You know, if there is something that does not even cross the mind of Guterres… it's being the next President of the European Commission…"

"Your Prime Minister? No, really?"

"No, no, don't even think about it…"

Meanwhile, the arguments in Pimentel's telephone campaign were beginning to make advances, breaking through the first layer of German resistance. "I know, João, I know, you don't need to go any further. And perhaps the Chancellor will be even more favourable to that idea than myself…"

However, the small team, which never exchanged any written correspondence, needed a clear answer, a green light that left no doubts about the German position.

The verdict arrived a few weeks later, still in early 1998, in good German fashion: telegraphic and without any room for misinterpretation. "João, you can count on us. Obviously."

A Pointed Star

Pimentel grasped that, for the first time, he was standing on solid ground. It was time to trigger the rest of the plan laid out on the small set of A5 sheets.

Driven by the personal chemistry between Aznar and Guterres, support from the Spanish was not long in coming. This was followed by the French and even the British, facilitated by his personal friendship with Blair and the ideological alignment with the Labour Party.

The Luxembourg leader Juncker confirms that, "given his talents, his collegiate approach and the strength of his personality, António was a natural candidate for President of the European Commission. It is true that he had many admirers, the first amongst them was me!"

Initially sceptical about the chances of Guterres, Seixas da Costa details that, "We began to understand how there was an objective appreciation and, at a certain time, I began believing. I recall going to Blair and he told us, 'He has to be the Commission's President.' And then the Dutch and Swedish were also saying the same. Suddenly this thing was starting to gain an unstoppable momentum."

The Alpha Plan also contemplated sounding out two states that did not belong to the EU, but which had always wielded influence over issues of global magnitude.

The first stop was a sumptuous three-storey palace flanked by centuries-old trees in the north-east of Rome. The Portuguese Ambassador to the Vatican received his briefing from Pimentel. He was informed of the progress thus far, the various tasks completed and the international support already guaranteed. Now, the Ambassador needed to make his moves in the corridors of the Holy See.

"Given António is who he is," says his former diplomatic adviser, "it was important to get the Vatican to put into motion all the organisations and their mechanisms over which the Church has influence, in the different countries, to provide him with their support. Similarly, there were also those who worked to guarantee there were no opposition groups or masonic resistance to António."

Indeed, the due diligence carried out with the Vatican did not take long to produce results. Pimentel's telephone was once again ringing to convey the result: "We are going to create something here. The eyes of the Archbishop glowed, seemingly celestial."

Only when the process was properly underway at the European level was it worth considering the other side of the Atlantic. This involved taking into consideration the perspective of the Democrat administration and attempting to ensure that the United States did not issue any contrary signal or that no senior American figure would make any comments susceptible to eliciting doubts.

According to Guterres' diplomatic adviser, the message was planted not in the Department of State, but rather directly in the White House among the President's team of advisers, so that it would be directly conveyed to Bill Clinton: "A conversation of this type is of relevance to the top. And the top could not have been more open because, still today, the relationships between António and Bill, and with Hillary, are really good."

The one individual who was never personally involved in the plan was Guterres himself. He did not campaign or make telephone calls; he did not write to anybody and did not even cross the street to gather support. Despite being the target and the beneficiary of the Plan, he was never personally engaged with it.

The focal point of the operation was thus Pimentel who, in the meanwhile, was nominated Ambassador and sent to Vienna, where the machine continued to operate: "Everything was done under António's authority, even though in the first conversations, people knew about things through me. For that kind of thing, it was necessary to have an expression of authorisation from him, but there was very little conversation with António. And it all worked, as they say in the language of communications, like a pointed star."

In just a few months, the Alpha Plan managed to reach almost complete maturity.

The only thing that was missing was the ability of the Prime Minister to leave the country.

The Loss

By 1997, Zizas' health was so fragile and the visits were so frequent and for such long periods, that Guterres had rented a flat in North London, a five-minute walk from the Royal Free Hospital, where his wife was receiving treatment.

However, even during the most critical periods, with weekly visits to London, he refused to make any alterations to his official agenda and doubled-down on meeting all the commitments of office.

On certain occasions, Guterres left Lisbon late in the afternoon on Fridays, knowing that he would have to return to Portugal the following morning. However, in order to spend yet another night close to his wife, he would buy another ticket to return to London on that same Saturday before making his return to Portugal again on Sunday.

"I do not think our country was appropriately fair with its Prime Minister, who remained in the position full-time undertaking all of his obligations; every one of them," explains Luís Patrão, Guterres' chief of staff at that time. "There was never any sense of victimisation, without even an external perception that there was this problem throughout the final two years of his wife's life… That was a superhuman effort."

Zizas' return to Lisbon had been perceived by his closest colleagues as a sign of hope for the Prime Minister, the Secretary-General of the Socialist Party, the husband and the father.

However, while the small group of Guterres' friends and confidants were fully engaged in the European manoeuvres that sought to take him out of the country and begin an international career, Zizas relapsed and had to be hospitalised again. Her body was rejecting the liver transplanted several months earlier and the only possible and inevitable solution, according to the British medical team, was further surgery. With the outlook nevertheless uncertain, the delicate operation went ahead with the prognosis remaining extremely poor.

In early 1998, Guterres received a group of Timorese resistance leaders in his official São Bento residence. The dramatic struggle for the freedom of this former Portuguese colony occupied by Indonesia had for years represented a cornerstone of Portuguese foreign policy and drew the personal attention of the head of government.

With the meeting already underway, Guterres' secretary interrupted and approached the Prime Minister in order to deliver a handwritten note. Guterres flew immediately to London where Zizas was already in a critical state.

A few days later, on 28 January 1998, Luísa Guterres passed away at the age of 52.

Full Stop

In the residence of the Portuguese Ambassador, a formal dinner in honour of the Prime Minister was well under way. It was October 1998 and Guterres was in Austria for an informal European Council meeting, a justifiable occasion for Pimentel to host the dinner.

At the table, placed near a balcony looking out over the historical centre of Vienna, places were set for sixteen people. Next to Guterres sat Seixas da Costa, the Secretary of State for European Affairs, and Pina Moura, the Minister of Economy.

As the dinner reached its end, the Prime Minister called them and Pimentel, their host for the night, to the television room, the same place where Pimentel had sat for hours on the telephone overseeing the Alpha Plan operations.

While the other guests were chatting over coffee, the Prime Minister informed his colleagues that he was unable to accept any international position. He ordered they cancel all plans to make him President of the European Commission.

"They were extremely disappointed because I said no," Guterres remembers.

However, by this time, the plan had gained a life of its own, and explanations would have to be given to the top of Europe's power structures that had already signed up to the Portuguese project. "Schröder even told me during a European Council meeting, 'We have here a consensus that it is you…,'" admits Guterres, who was then left with two children to care for. The youngest, Mariana, had just lost her mother at the age of 13. "I told him, 'I cannot do this and that's final. This is not a matter for discussion. These are personal and family matters.' At the time, I perceived that I should not leave Portugal. But, in fact, there was a consensus for me to get the position."

Schröder still maintains today that Guterres "certainly had all the qualities necessary to become the President of the European Commission."

7

THE PEBBLE IN THE SHOE

"Mr. Prime Minister, are you going to raise the issue of East Timor?"

"Are you afraid you will ruin the Summit?"

Wherever Guterres turned up those days, journalists would point their microphones at him always with the same question. Recently sworn in, the head of government either pretended not to hear or simply opted not to respond. But now, as Portugal approached the first Euro-Asian Summit, scheduled for March 1996, they kept insisting that, at some point, Guterres would have to break the taboo, and he promised to do so at the summit: "I shall not remain in silence."[1]

The summit would bring together in Bangkok the fifteen European Union member states and ten of the major economies in Asia, such as China, the Philippines and Indonesia. Wishing to engage with Asian markets, the Europeans were not keen to see their work disrupted, never mind ruined, due to a little island.

Located between Southwest Asia and Australia, Timor was a former part of the colonial empires of Holland and Portugal. The western half, which had been under Dutch control, became part of Indonesia following its independence in 1949. The eastern half, majority-Catholic, had remained Portuguese until 1975, when a local revolutionary movement inspired by communist ideology declared the independence of the Democratic Republic of East

Timor. The Portuguese government hurried to abandon the island and, in that same year, Indonesia seized control of the territory.

Portugal cut diplomatic ties with Indonesia and repeatedly protested at the United Nations, which had recognised the right of the Timorese people to self-determination.

However, the years went by, governments changed, and the East Timor dossier lay dormant despite the constant and gross human rights violations, widely covered by the international media. The international community only began paying close attention to the unfolding tragedy in 1991, when CNN aired the first footage of the Santa Cruz massacre, in which dozens of panicking young people fled Indonesian bullets, while others laid in pools of blood by the cemetery gates.

In Portuguese society, East Timor had become an open wound; a mixture of guilt and compassion—and mounting pressure on political authorities to take action rose by the day.

"I shall not remain silent." The words of Guterres echoed in Jakarta, and their reaction was quick. The Indonesians convened the EU ambassadors and threatened that, if Portugal were to raise the East Timor question, they would walk out of the summit. Guterres recalls, "I immediately began getting calls from my colleagues, European prime ministers, telling me, 'You watch it, don't ruin this.'"

Given Indonesian intransigence, the passivity of the international community, and Portugal's concerns, nobody could foresee a play capable of stirring these stagnant waters. Guterres had his hands tied and, when travelling to Thailand, he did not have any defined plan, only ideas.

Upon arrival, leaders were invited to a last-moment dinner to take place on the eve of the summit. This was perceived as an invitation to raise the East Timor issue on the margins of the official talks so that neither the Portuguese nor the Indonesians would lose face.

At the end of the meal, the Thai Prime Minister invited his guests to accompany him into an adjoining room to finalise the summit details. Guterres thought the host must have been improvising: none of this was planned and the room itself had a mixture of armchairs and armless chairs—protocol would never have allowed a meeting between heads of state and government to have different types of seats.

The host began by sharing some general information about the meeting before getting to the core point: "It's very important that, in the spirit of Bangkok, no controversial or bilateral subject is raised…"

Some of those present immediately concurred. Feeling targeted, Guterres asked to speak and attempted to reposition the debate: "Well, we are representatives of the most varied civilisations from around the world. I believe that, among us, we may raise any subject without any problem, in a diplomatic, constructive fashion…"

Nevertheless, practically nobody lined up behind his position—neither on the European side and definitely not on the Asian side. Guterres again moved to intervene, but the British Prime Minister, John Major, who would be ousted a year later by Blair's New Labour, closed the issue: "I'd make a proposal: should anybody raise a bilateral or controversial issue, they lose the chance to speak!"

They all began to get up. At that moment, the Portuguese leader, isolated and defeated, saw General Suharto, Indonesia's President. "He was there right in front of me… I went directly to him and said, 'Let us sit down here for a moment, sir. I need to talk to you'—and he did. I sat down by his side and said, 'Look, our relations have been deadlocked and I have a proposal to make to you: we agree to open a diplomatic representation and you release the Timorese activists you have arrested.' I based this on knowledge that Indonesians never say 'no' outright as a part of their culture. When it is 'no', they cover it up. And so, Suharto said something vague like he 'was not expecting that' and he 'had to consult the government.'"

With the improvised tête-à-tête over, Guterres told his team to immediately call a press conference. Shortly after, the Portuguese suite was packed with international journalists and, on the following day, the proposal and the daring offensive by the Portuguese Prime Minister made the newspaper headlines.

The summit began on the morning of 1 March, with the traditional family photograph of the leaders, who posed smiling in batik shirts typical of the region. With the guests in an oval layout, the Thai Prime Minister started to alternately hand the microphone to those sat on his right and then his left.

When it came to Suharto's turn to speak, the Thai host opted to skip the Indonesian General and pass to the following leader without any justification. Guterres did not need one: it was clear they wanted the Indonesian to speak after him.

In his turn, the Portuguese politician flourished some general and charming comments before getting to the point: "I would like to praise the spirit of Bangkok for this decision that was taken not to raise bilateral issues... one bilateral issue that we have with China and that is going very well, is Macau... another question we have that is not bilateral—it is a matter under the auspices of the United Nations—is about East Timor, but I wish to state here that I yesterday met with President Suharto, I made a proposal and I think this shall be the start of a new beginning, a new dialogue."

Guterres' initiative—and the silence of Suharto—required the Indonesian Minister of Foreign Affairs to engage in damage control. A renowned diplomat in the region, a one-time candidate for leadership of the United Nations, Ali Alatas had accompanied the East Timor issue since the beginning and had compared it to a "pebble in the shoe."[2]

About the events in Bangkok, Alatas later argued, "What was surprising was the fact that Prime Minister Guterres made it sound as if the proposal [...] was his or a Portuguese initiative and not [...] a proposal that Indonesia had accepted and Portugal had consistently rejected."[3]

It took some time, but the news from Bangkok finally reached Cipinang prison in Jakarta, where the Timorese resistance leader was being held. Fluent in Portuguese, Xanana Gusmão had led the guerrilla movement against Indonesia for almost two decades. He spent years hiding in his country's mountains until captured and sentenced to life imprisonment. "Nothing came out in the Indonesian media," Xanana recalls. "I found out from the international newspapers and felt extremely comforted."

Changes in Mood

This pressure for Portugal and the international community to intervene and resolve the East Timor crisis was mounting at the same time as the United States was working to oust Boutros-Ghali from the UN top job. In late 1996, there was finally movement on this. Washington had been supporting Kofi Annan from the start, but Paris only accepted his name after receiving assurances that after being nominated UN Secretary-General he would place a French candidate at the head of the Department of Peace Operations—and after confirming that the Ghanaian could get by in their language.

With this final resistance overcome, Annan took up the position in January 1997. In his first press conference, he raised the issue of East Timor, later writing that he saw the situation as "an opportunity for the UN to play a valuable role, as no major power had a strategic interest in the dispute—unlike, say, the case of the Middle East process where our influence was always limited by the US dominance of the issue."[4]

Negotiations began in New York in a climate of mutual suspicion and constant recrimination. At the same time, the Portuguese government was attempting to gather bilateral support among other countries, especially in the United States. Congress even sent a few positive signals, such as occasional resolutions stemming above all from initiatives launched by the Wisconsin Senator, Russ Feingold, and the Congressman from Rhode Island, Patrick Kennedy, both Democrats.

The White House remained silent and Prime Minister Guterres was the only one able to intervene at that level. In a conversation with Bill Clinton while walking in the Rose Garden in April 1997, East Timor had been the second topic raised by Guterres.

"António attempted to demystify everything that was being said about Timor," explains Pimentel, "because many people were afraid the country would end up with a regime answering to China, capable of destabilising the entire region. He replied that what would harm Indonesia was continuing to lie about the situation, about the violations of human rights that were already on all the international channels."

The White House visit forced the US President to take a position before the cameras:

"At the moment," a reporter said in the Diplomatic Reception Room, "the US recognises the incorporation of East Timor without maintaining that legitimate act of self-determination took place. Do you plan to review this position?"

"Well, my main concern now," the President replied, with Guterres by his side, "is to make sure that we have done everything we can possibly do to respect the political and human rights of the people in East Timor."

"But isn't self-determination the ultimate human right?" the press insisted.

"Well, that depends. That's a very complicated question. We fought a civil war over it,"[5] Clinton answered.

At this point, the Portuguese diplomacy was seeking every possible opportunity to weaken the Indonesian position, such as the visit of Nelson Mandela to Gusmão in June 1997. But only the change in leadership in Jakarta, in May 1998, enabled the beginning of a new chapter. As a consequence of the financial crisis in Southeast Asia, which had even forced Indonesia to ask for the intervention of the IMF, Suharto resigned from his post after thirty-two years in power.

However, while the general represented a symbol of absolutist power in his own right, a man with a deep voice who had been born in Java and spent his entire life in the country, someone whose personal experiences interwove with Indonesia's own national history, his designated successor, B.J. Habibie, the former vice president, was an aerospace engineer trained in Europe, emotional and mercurial in temperament, who did not expect to spend long in power.

The change in leadership had immediate effects on the East Timor issue as described by the Indonesian Minister of Foreign Affairs. Appointed to the position for his fourth term, Alatas discussed with Habibie the idea, formerly rejected out of hand by Suharto, of granting a statute of special autonomy to East Timor and, to his great surprise, "the President and the Cabinet approved it without much debate."[6]

Guterres agrees "the events advanced very quickly when Habibie turned up." East Timor and Indonesia finally opened up diplomatic offices and reached the beginning of an understanding. "We spoke with the Timorese resistance and we made an agreement with Indonesia. There were many doubts, but we thought it was worth it. The agreement was: we go for a broad autonomous regime for East Timor, agreeing to disagree; for Indonesia that is a solution, for us it is a transitory stage and the subject remains under discussion in the United Nations."

Despite the progress made, the Portuguese insisted on a written agreement that granted the Timorese people the right to decide after a certain period—maybe five or ten years—if they wished to continue to be linked to Jakarta or if they wanted full independence.

However, with the international pressure mounting on the Indonesian government, Habibie questioned Alatas on the real benefits of delaying this eventual plebiscite: "Why should we continue to carry the political and financial burden of governing and developing East Timor, continue to be responsible and be blamed by the world whenever something goes wrong and then, after five or ten years, only to be told by the East Timorese: 'Thank you, but we now want to be independent'?"

In January 1999, the Indonesian President surprised everybody. At the end of a ministerial meeting, he issued a statement stating that "a regional autonomy 'plus' will be accorded to East Timor. If this is not accepted by the mass in East Timor, we will suggest [...] to release East Timor from Indonesia."[7]

The referendum in East Timor, overseen by the United Nations, was set for 8 August 1999. Indonesia had backed down on every point apart from one: there would be no blue helmets in East Timor.

Convincing Bill Clinton

John Holmes was finally making his debut as an ambassador. Lisbon was his first posting at this rank but, instead of a welcoming committee, the British diplomat was received with a protest at his embassy: "I certainly remember the demonstration... people in Portugal felt very alarmed by what was happening in East Timor as

Indonesians were ruining the country and they were therefore quite reasonably trying to make sure that the international community could not ignore this. Actually, I think António Guterres played a very important part by being able to talk very frankly to people like Bill Clinton and Tony Blair to make sure the UN did not ignore it."

The wave of violence that broke out on the eve of the referendum had already forced its delay until 30 August. But, in spite of the overwhelming result—78.5 per cent voted for independence—there was no time to celebrate.

After the results were released, and with the Indonesian authorities turning a blind eye, pro-integration militias began attacking and killing. Timorese who had worked for the UN became key revenge targets, but the attackers also went after activists, teachers and Catholic leaders, such as the Nobel Peace Prize Laureate, Bishop Ximenes Belo.

By this stage, the UN Secretary-General was convinced that only an international force would be able to halt the violence in East Timor and avoid the errors of the Rwanda genocide.

Nevertheless, two obstacles blocked the dispatch of blue helmets. The first was the Indonesian President who, according to Annan, "was neither in control of his own armed forces' operation in the region in collusion with local militias, nor was he being told the truth about the killing and burning that they had unleashed."[8] Habibie, who even publicly recognised the results of the referendum, maintained it was a point of honour not to call in international troops to deal with a subject over which Jakarta held responsibility.

It seemed inevitable that the United States should step in and persuade Habibie. However, Clinton was very much resisting such an intervention, which was precisely the second problem. In Annan's opinion, "It became clear to me that the US President's major concerns were securing a Security Council authorisation for a mission against a key US ally and, at the same time, addressing congressional hostility to US participation in such an operation. The urgency of the situation on the ground did not seem to have impressed the President."[9]

Guterres was also trying to convince the US President of the urgency of action. He talked to Clinton by telephone twice in the wake of the referendum, while also insisting with British Prime Minister Blair to intercede. However, neither of these diplomatic efforts, nor the multiple interviews with international media outlets, appeared to move the White House.

Guterres even authorised his Minister of Foreign Affairs to put pressure on the US by obstructing NATO, deliberately delaying the authorisations enabling Alliance aircraft to fly over Portuguese airspace.

But the most assertive act of pressure that Guterres used was when he ignored the rumour about a threat made by Jaime Gama to Madeleine Albright. In an informal conversation, the Portuguese Minister of Foreign Affairs mentioned an eventual departure of Portugal from NATO should the United States not support its North Atlantic partner.

Then Guterres' impatience hit a new peak. On the morning of 8 September, the front page of *The New York Times* stated:

> The Administration, these officials say, has made the calculation that the United States must put its relationship with Indonesia, a mineral-rich nation of more than 200 million people, ahead of its concern over the political fate of East Timor, a tiny, impoverished territory of 800,000 people seeking its independence. [...] "Because we bombed in Kosovo doesn't mean we should bomb Dili," said Samuel R. Berger, President Clinton's national security adviser.[10]

Guterres immediately summoned the US Ambassador to Portugal and asked to speak with President Bill Clinton, who would shortly be touring Asia.

While waiting for the reply, the Prime Minister was following closely another day of demonstrations in Lisbon, which reached their high point in the late afternoon. A human chain stretching 10 kilometres managed to interconnect the UN office and the five embassies of countries with a permanent seat on the Security Council. The United States Embassy was one of the locations where most people were concentrated, chanting, "Bill, make war not love," a reference to Clinton's brush with impeachment the previous year over his affair with Monica Lewinsky. They also chanted to the United Nations: "UN in Timor, end the horror."[11]

Guterres decided to leave the office to join the chain, in a gesture that expressed both solidarity and impotence, until one of his aides came running out to tell him he had the White House on the phone.

"That was a dramatic conversation with Clinton," explains Guterres. "What I told him was, 'You have to be aware that you are not choosing between Indonesia and Timor, you are choosing between Indonesia and Portugal, which is your NATO partner. Regardless of my wishes, there is no chance of Portugal maintaining troops in Bosnia and in Kosovo, protecting Bosnians and Kosovans, and in an international situation not protecting the Timorese. That's impossible and does not depend on me. This is going to lead to a massacre. Don't think this is about lack of will, I cannot do anything else. I have my entire country out in the streets.' I know that afterwards Clinton spoke with Blair—because Blair told me—saying that 'António called me and, well, he might be right.'"

When he touched down in New Zealand, on 12 September 1999, to participate in the Asia-Pacific Economic Cooperation Summit, Bill Clinton finally announced a change in position:

> Let me address the deteriorating situation in East Timor. [...] It is now clear that the Indonesian military is aiding and abetting the militia violence. This is simply unacceptable. [...] The Indonesian Government and military must reverse this course to do everything possible to stop the violence and allow an international force to make possible the restoration of security.[12]

Immediately afterwards, the Pentagon cut military relations with Jakarta. The noose tightened still further when the Indonesian currency and stock market went into freefall due to fears over the suspension of vital assistance from the World Bank and the IMF.

Less than forty-eight hours after Clinton's declaration, Habibie gave way to international pressure and finally accepted UN peacekeeping in East Timor.

That sealed the greatest diplomatic victory in the career of Prime Minister Guterres, who would next proceed, just one month later, in October, to winning re-election for a second term as Portuguese Prime Minister. He then received the following letter from the US President:

Dear António:

Congratulations on your party's success in Portugal's recent national elections. I am delighted to have the opportunity to continue working with you.

[...]

I will never forget your untiring efforts to bring international attention to the situation in East Timor

[...]

I hope that we can work together to enhance our Transatlantic partnership to promote security, democracy, and prosperity for our citizens and people around the globe

[...]

Sincerely,

William J. Clinton[13]

8

THE PEOPLE SPEAK

4 February 1998. The usually silent galleries, visited only by a few curious onlookers, were packed and the atmosphere highly agitated.

The rules for parliamentary visitors are very clear: any citizen may attend plenary sessions, but applauding, whistling, cheering or booing are absolutely prohibited. However, the feelings prevailing among the 230 members of parliament had spread to the galleries to such an extent that the Parliament's President had been forced to interrupt proceedings to demand the silence of the passionate audience.

After all, what was under discussion was more than a political issue. Parliament was deciding on an ethical and religious question, a matter of justice and public health; an issue of personal conscience, but also of civilisation. Within moments, there would be a vote on draft legislation decriminalising abortion in Portugal. Even though the proposal was made by the Socialist Party, it was public knowledge that the legislation lacked the support of its leader.

This was not the first time that Guterres' Catholicism spoke louder than the progressive values proclaimed by the left. In the run-up to the parliamentary elections, a journalist asked the Socialist Party's Secretary-General for his opinion on homosexuality. Guterres answered:

Homosexuality is a complex problem. There are those who consider it a disease. Others consider it an option. I'm not going to go into this, we can say, question of technical nature [...] Now, it is a right that I recognise to whoever and in relation to which I believe that I have neither the capacity nor the right to interfere. This is not an aspect that particularly appeals to me, but it is above all something that I would never refer to in any type of political intervention.[1]

However, contrary to the debate on homosexuality, which attracted little public coverage, the topic of abortion motivated major civic movements.

The Portuguese law was among the most restrictive in Europe. The voluntary termination of pregnancy was acceptable in only three circumstances: danger to the mother's life, rape or malformation of the foetus. This excluded the woman's personal choice, but did not prevent many to still do it, even if illegally.

The Socialist Party proposal provided for the decriminalisation of abortion on the request of the woman during the first ten weeks of pregnancy "for the preservation of their moral integrity, social dignity or conscious maternity."[2] This differed from the proposal from the Communist Party (PCP)—rejected earlier in Parliament— that provided for a twelve-week framework for legal abortion.

"I was willing to advance with liberalisation, but with another justification," explains Guterres. "I told my comrades that we should approve PCP's draft law. However, there were some technical issues and the group decided to do something slightly different and so I told them, 'Please excuse me, but I think that is wrong. You want to corner me with something when I have already said that I wanted something else. Don't count on me.'" After this, he recognises how "the dialogue was not great" between the Prime Minister and his party. "I ended up getting somewhat irritated and taking the position that I took—and that I would not take today."

The conservative opposition was convinced popular opinion was on their side and kept calling for a national referendum rather than deciding the issue by parliamentary deliberation.

It was already after 9 pm when the law was subject to voting. The Parliament's President had not yet confirmed the results, but there was already applause coming from the Socialist bench and the galleries. By a majority of nine votes, the Portuguese Parliament had approved the legislation that would decriminalise abortion. The victorious parliamentarians launched themselves into a sea of smiles and long, warm and emotional embraces. For many, this was the culmination of a long battle that had lasted years. They would not forget that day, nor the important victory they thought they had won for women's rights in the country.

They were still celebrating when harsh reality came crashing down. It seemed difficult to believe, but in the wake of parliamentary approval, Prime Minister Guterres had granted the opposition leader, Marcelo Rebelo de Sousa, leader of the Social Democrats and a personal friend since the days of the Luz Group, his wish for a national referendum on abortion.

"We were profoundly taken aback and had no prior warning whatsoever," stated the parliamentarian who had sponsored the bill, Sérgio Sousa Pinto. "I remember seeing female Socialist parliamentarians crying in the corridors because that had been such a highly emotional moment and, therefore, people were not expecting such a turnaround. I remember that even some members of government were disturbed by this development."

Ten More Years

Good afternoon,

For the first time in history, the Portuguese are going to the ballot box to decide a law.

Everyone has the right to answer the question: "Do you agree with the decriminalisation of the voluntary interruption of pregnancy, undertaken by the woman's choice, in the first ten weeks in a legally authorised healthcare establishment?"

For the first time, it shall not be the representatives of the people deciding, but rather the people themselves.

This is the first referendum in this country's history.[3]

The special television broadcast began half an hour before the polling stations closed. Guterres and Sousa had managed to push the referendum through in the hope that the ballot box returned an opinion equal to their own and different to Parliament's.

Overruling the will of the nationally elected parliamentarians was a serious position, especially from a constitutional point of view. Pinto states, "We subjected to referendum a law already approved by the Assembly of the Republic! The Parliament has to be above the rule of referenda—that's why we have representative democracy and not a referendum pantomime!"

Due to the position of Guterres, the Socialist Party had not campaigned. Officially, the party line was that this was a matter for individual conscience with each voting according to their best understanding. However, this lack of engagement from the main force on the Portuguese left and government party naturally favoured the campaign against abortion, which was better regimented, more mobilised and with greater resources.

"This caused a problem in the party that is still talked about today," concedes Jorge Coelho. "In practice, I was the number two and I supported the 'yes' without any type of problem, especially on television. Now, the Socialist leader was backed into a corner given that the most active party voters were all in favour of 'yes'."

The pro-choice Socialist MP Sérgio Sousa Pinto recalls, "There was an environment of great disapproval against António Guterres in the party." In 1992, Guterres had opposed the idea of holding a referendum on the Treaty of Maastricht, under which Portugal had agreed to abolish the national currency in favour of the Euro without listening to the citizens; and now, this same politician was imposing a popular consultation process for abortion. There were those who put this all down to political tactics. They said that Guterres was not willing to throw away his chances for an absolute majority in the upcoming 1999 election by disturbing a predominantly Catholic electorate.

In a country without any tradition of referenda, this first experience was scheduled for 28 June 1998. It was summer, it was Sunday and the beaches were packed. And that same afternoon there were two World Cup football matches monopolising the audience. This all added up to a colossal abstention rate of 68 per cent.

To the rejoice of the conservative parties, the jubilation of the Catholic Church and to the natural satisfaction of Guterres, 'no' prevailed even if by the most minimum of margins. Despite the Socialist Party having been missing in action, 'no' made it over the line with only 50.9 per cent of the vote.

Today, Guterres accepts that on the topic of abortion, as well as on homosexuality, he thinks differently. "I think things are completely different. The world has evolved and these issues as well." It would be ten years before a second referendum in 2007 decriminalised abortion in Portugal—and the Portuguese still talk about it to this day.

Universal Basic Income

Despite television having been around since the 1950s and Portugal having already notched up twenty-five years as a democracy, before 16 September 1999 there had never been a televised debate between the head of government and the leader of the opposition.

Incumbent Guterres faced the brand-new Social Democrat leader, Durão Barroso. With less than a month to go until the elections, Guterres expected his party to win again, but this time with an absolute majority. Indeed, internal opinion polls pointed in this direction, even suggesting the Socialists might end up with as many as ten more parliamentarians than all the other parties combined.

More than just believing, Guterres felt he deserved an absolute majority. The GDP was increasing at a good pace with a continual slide in public expenditure deficit, and even unemployment was down to historically low levels. At least for the meantime, the apocalyptic forecasts of economists predicting financial catastrophe on the eve of the European Monetary Union had come to naught.

In the real economy, the number of households able to go on holiday and buy their own home was rising. The Expo 1998, held in Lisbon, had been a boon to tourism and construction. There was peace in the industrial sector partly due to the cross-sector agreement for increased salaries and a reduction in the working week to forty hours. About to complete their term, the first minority government to achieve this had not faced a single general strike.

The absolute majority seemed a fair reward, at least from Guterres' perspective. Should the electorate agree, his government

would secure greater political comfort and decision-making autonomy. This would leave behind four years of constant and laborious
negotiations with the opposition, now even more difficult under
Barroso. While the former leader of the Social Democratic Party,
Rebelo de Sousa, was a lifelong friend, the relationship between
Guterres and Barroso had always been cold and distant, and showed
right from the start during their televised debate.

"I've heard you use words such as coward, political fraud [...]
about me. I'm here to respect the opposition," said Guterres.
"Now, I also understand that there are rules and boundaries and I
think you have infringed on those rules and those boundaries, and
I hope that this is not repeated."

Guterres started out unusually aggressive, almost caustic. He
compared Barroso's proposals to "supermarket advertising" and his
electoral program to a "castle built on sand". He confronted his
opponent with question after question as if he was the leader of the
opposition. And Barroso felt the strikes: "Well, I didn't come here
to respond to an exam."

Guterres constantly interrupted his opponent, forcing the moderator to request some restraint on more than one occasion.

However, in the more experienced socialist narrative, some
components did not seem to make sense. Even while knowing the
electorate broadly ignored foreign policy, Guterres had just published a book in which he fundamentally reflected on international
affairs. To a certain extent, the book's title, *Thinking Portugal*, was
misleading as over half of the contents dealt with state-of-the-
world issues and not Portugal.

There was the speech on fair trade given at the Ibero-American
Summit that brought Fidel Castro to Portugal. Another approached
environment and sustainable development proffered to the UN
General Assembly. Yet another, a presentation to the Congress of
European Socialist Parties, proposed a European employment pact.

This was not work delegated to the party machinery.
"Mr. Guterres chose the texts and the key topics," stresses
Guilherme d'Oliveira Martins, his friend, and then Secretary of
State, who oversaw the compilation. "The book was under his clear
and unequivocal orientation. He did not want it to be a campaign

book, election-focused, for the short term. He wanted a publication that expressed his thinking."

The debate went on and Guterres sought to capitalise on one of his government's leading measures: launching a universal basic income at the beginning of his term, in 1996. The distribution of an allowance to those most in need had been implemented by almost every European Union state, and by the mid-1990s only two economies had failed to do so. They were the most backward in the organisation: Greece and Portugal.

"If we go to the United States and speak with your Chicago Boys," explains Guterres, "they will tell us that, instead of giving away general subsidies, there should be negative taxes, there should be direct support for the poorest families—this must be the only point on which the ultra-liberals agree with me. My vision is that people have the right not to die of hunger, that means the state has to guarantee the minimum. I have no doubt today in saying that, especially in societies that are combatting the industrial revolution that is on its way, with risks of generalised unemployment, there has to be a social network with a minimum level of coverage. Now, you may discuss whether or not this should be done via a minimum income."

In this part of the debate, Guterres argued that no government had battled poverty and its social ills with as much determination as his own. Alongside the minimum guaranteed income, measures also targeted juvenile delinquency and even child labour that still openly persisted.

The water glasses were almost empty, the shirts already creased. The clock on the lower right-hand side of the screen showed that the debate had lasted for over an hour and was therefore reaching its end. To finish, each participant had the right to ask a surprise question to their opponent.

Guterres went first with an economic issue. Then came Barroso.

"If you win, will the Socialist Party, or will it not, reintroduce the topic of abortion?"

"I have no such intention," shot back Guterres.

9

BETWEEN THE SWORD AND THE WALL

Luís Patrão had just moved out of São Bento to take up the position of Secretary of State of Internal Affairs. According to Guterres' former chief of staff, the new government that had to be formed after the October 1999 election was "politically less structured, shaped by party struggles and resulted from a series of trade-offs and balancing acts between groups that did not represent the interests of the Prime Minister, but their own centres of influence."

Their recent victory was bittersweet. The Socialist Party had failed to gain an absolute majority and remained hostage to the opposition for the approval of laws and national budgets. However, beyond the disillusion over failing to reach their key objective, the Socialists could hardly believe the makeup of the new Parliament.

PS had picked up 115 seats, exactly one half of the total 230, hence the same number as the opposition parties combined and just one short of a majority. "Election night for me was really negative," remembers Guterres, as "a 115–115 tie result takes away responsibility. I mean, the opposition could get all together and not approve anything and we also could not approve anything."

In his first speech before this Parliament, the socialist Prime Minister explained to the parliamentarians—and to the voters—the conditions under which he had agreed to govern for another term:

The Government shall not be blocked nor left paralysed should some successful strategy emerge designed to block the functioning of a relative majority system in this Chamber...[1]

[...]

I want to make it perfectly clear that if this Government is placed 'between the sword and the wall', it shall prefer the sword.[2]

Today, Guterres accepts that agreeing to govern under those conditions was "a total error in judgement. What I should have done was bring the whole thing down at the time of the first budget; I didn't do so in the name of stability."

Indeed, this need for stability was very much imposed by the rotating Presidency of the European Union, which Portugal was due to assume at the turn of the new millennium.

Extremist Populism

Guterres leaned back in the luxurious blue and gold armchair. Around him, there were the antiques, baroque works of art and fine tapestries that decorated the audience room in the Elysée Palace. It was, nevertheless, without diplomatic finesse, that French President Jacques Chirac announced his decision:

"António, I'm not going to appear in the same photograph as that gentleman."

"Well, you have already appeared with him so many times when he was Minister of Foreign Affairs..."

"But now he's Prime Minister and I really don't want that!"

Guterres attempted to outskirt the intransigence of his host and changed the subject. After all, the objective of this audience was to discuss the new economic agenda for Europe that the Portuguese Presidency would be presenting a few months later.

"Well, as regards the Lisbon Strategy that we shall approve at this summit..."

"António, have you heard me? You're not going to embarrass me by making me appear in the same photograph as Schüssel, are you?"

Wolfgang Schüssel was the new Chancellor of Austria.

In order to take office, the Christian Democrat had had to forge a coalition with the FPO, a far-right, anti-immigration party. In recent months, the FPO leader had shocked Europe after publicly praising the employment policy of the Third Reich and defended that the SS were worthy of honour and respect.

The decision to let a xenophobic party be part of a European government sounded alarms in other capitals, especially those already experiencing their own incidences of radicalisation, including Berlin and Paris. Then EU Foreign and Defence Commissioner, Javier Solana, wrote in the *Washington Post*, "Our post-war European democracies were built on the absolute rejection of fascism. When Haider praises the Third Reich or Nazi veterans, those words have to be taken seriously. We need to show prospective new members from the east that a community standing for democratic values cannot accept any forms of populist intolerance."[3]

The Portuguese Prime Minister thus found his EU Presidency overshadowed, even before starting, by this outbreak of extremism in Europe and the need to articulate positions with all partners on the Austrian problem.

During lunch at the residence of German Chancellor Gerhard Schröder, the Guterres delegation received a set of papers describing the steps that should be taken over Austria, starting with the imposition of sanctions.

On leaving the meeting, the Portuguese Prime Minister decided to sound out his peers. He asked one of his diplomatic advisers to get him in contact with every European head of government and transformed the car loaned by the German authorities into a temporary headquarters.

On the phone, Chirac immediately confirmed the intention of advancing with sanctions. From Spain, Aznar said the same and only Blair provided room for manoeuvre.

"António, it's in your hands. Deal with it as best you can. I'll support you."

The Lisbon Summit, when Guterres would finally get to present his strategy for solving the geo-economic stagnation facing Europe, was seriously under threat.

At the beginning of the millennium, the European Union needed to continue growing and affirm its role in the globalised world, competing with the American giant and the looming Chinese colossus, while simultaneously creating employment able to finance, over the medium and long term, the costly principles underlying the welfare state that configured political identity.

Furthermore, European people also expected their leaders to remain in the vanguard of the demands of civilisation, such as the defence of human rights. Hence, more than ever, governments were forced, whether by party convictions or popular pressure, to establish the European Union as a major global benchmark for international solidarity and the promotion of democratic values.

One path involved strengthening the competitiveness of the private sector, sacrificing some of the established regulations on minimum wages and workers' rights, in line with the greater flexibility of rival economies. An alternative hypothesis was to find leverages that would enable the EU to become the key centre for wealth creation worldwide.

Aware of these crossroads, the Portuguese Presidency of the EU set out a new paradigm for development by putting the pillars of innovation and knowledge at the centre of social and economic policies that would enable the Union to become the most advanced centre of global technological and scientific progress.

However, Guterres did not perceive the European project as a trade chamber. He sought to place the emphasis on social cohesion. This differentiated the Portuguese Presidency from the liberals, conservatives and nationalists. According to Luxembourg's then head of government, Jean-Claude Juncker, "He almost singlehandedly steered difficult discussions and was able to showcase how structural reforms could be the engine for growth. Given some of the strong personalities and differences of opinion around at that time, I can assure you that was no mean feat."

At the Lisbon Summit, Guterres managed, on the one hand, to convince all his partners to back a European strategy cautious enough not to raise the opposition of any country. On the other hand, he minimised the imposition of sanctions on Austria to a set of diplomatic measures, more symbolic than effective, accommodating the position of European partners seeking to clearly demonstrate their reproach without overly raising the hostility of the Austrian government.

At the end of the summit, Guterres was even able to get Chirac and Schüssel into the same photograph.

Messenger

On the first occasion that they met at the White House in 1997, Guterres had gifted him a panel of Portuguese tiles. The baroque set, typical of the aristocratic homes and palaces of the eighteenth century, portrayed two men in period clothing, greeting and inviting visitors to enter.

Bill Clinton had returned the gesture with the book *Monticello and the Legacy of Thomas Jefferson*, about the former US President, a founding father of the nation and a confessed admirer of Portuguese wine.

The following Christmas, Guterres had sent him a case of Portuguese red wine with best wishes for the holidays and for the greatest successes, personal and political, coupled with a piece of poetry:

> Dear Bill,
>
> Inspired by the Portuguese poet Sophia de Mello Breyner Andresen when she wrote:
>
> 'Evohe god, who gave us
> wine
> And in it men discovered
> The savour of the sun and rosin
> And a consciousness, multiple, divine'
> I thought that the best way to represent Portugal would be to offer you the sun and rosin turned into wine.
> [...]
>
> Sincerely yours,
>
> António Guterres[4]

Their contacts had intensified, especially during the East Timor crisis, and time had seen their working relationship transform into friendship. On the President's own indication, the letters drafted by the White House services began with 'Dear António', no longer with 'Dear Mister Prime Minister'. And when Zizas passed away, Clinton went beyond the traditional message of condolence.

"I should call him."

Furthermore, the President had attempted to get Guterres involved in a progressive forum that brought together leaders from both sides of the Atlantic. This forum had already met at its first conference in Italy, and the absence of the Portuguese Prime Minister had drawn Clinton's attention, who asked Blair, "I'm glad we let Cardoso come, but can you explain to me, in a European context, why we didn't invite Wim Kok or Guterres?"[5]

In June 2000, a second conference was taking place in Germany, and which formed part of Clinton's final tour of Europe. He also talked about this on the telephone to Blair: "I depart the United States on Monday… I have an EU thing in Portugal, then on to Russia, and then a brief stop in the Ukraine. I go to Portugal, Berlin, Russia, Ukraine, and then home."[6]

This was the first official visit to Portugal by a US President in fifteen years. Nevertheless, the core motive for Bill Clinton arriving in Lisbon was not bilateral. He was primarily coming to participate in the European Union-United States Summit hosted by the country then holding the organisation's rotating Presidency.

At 8 am, Guterres welcomed Clinton as he emerged from Air Force One. On that first day, the President spent more time with the Portuguese President than with the Prime Minister. In particular, he witnessed the parading of the Portuguese troops about to embark on the peacekeeping mission to East Timor.

The "EU thing" only took place on the following day—in an eighteenth-century palace that only opens its doors for state visits—that brought together Clinton, Guterres and Romano Prodi, the President of the European Commission.

In addition to the usual trade disputes, one of the most sensitive topics was the US intention to deploy an anti-missile system that China and Russia strongly opposed, but which also attracted little support from among the European allies. Some feared another arms race, others declared the project was in violation of the Anti-Ballistic Missile (ABM) Treaty signed with the Soviet Union in the 1970s.

Unsurprisingly, this topic opened the joint press conference in the palace gardens, with a first question for Guterres:

"In a few months, President Clinton will make a decision about a national missile defence system for the United States. For an American audience, can you explain any European concerns about deploying such a system and whether, in your just-completed trip to Moscow, President Putin expressed any flexibility about amending the ABM to allow such a system?"[7]

In fact, in his capacity as *pro tempore* President of the European Union, Guterres had a few days earlier met with the new President of Russia, a former KGB spy and head of the secret services, someone the West was then attempting to decipher.

"At the time," Guterres recalls, "Putin made a very strong impression—please note this was a Putin seen in a different light—for his mastery of the dossiers and for his capacity for negotiation. Even on European questions, especially commercial issues, he discussed without papers and in great detail; he was a guy who studied seriously."

From Moscow, the Portuguese leader had brought back not only a positive impression, but also a message for the US President. "Putin asked me to pass on a message to Clinton on the question of armament," recounts Guterres. "I even said to him, 'But why don't you talk to him directly?' He then insisted that I should be the one delivering it. Well, okay then. When Clinton came here, we had a few moments alone and I told him, 'Putin has a message for you about these treaties and preferred that I gave it to you.' Clinton then explained to me what their exact position about nuclear and conventional weapons was. Afterwards, I telephoned Putin, informed him I had talked to Clinton, as he had asked me to, and I told him everything that Clinton had told me. But then I got out of the game: 'Now, you can settle the rest yourselves.' So why did Putin think of me to intermediate that issue with Clinton? I still wonder today."

10

OUT OF THE QUAGMIRE

Accounts of an increasing lack of government leadership came spilling into the newsrooms directly from the indiscreet party corridors and porous ministry office walls.

Reports of unqualified socialists receiving nominations to senior state positions, and to the recently inaugurated institutes and foundations of dubious public utility, started to be widely discussed. Others told of chiefs of staff not answering the phone to their ministers.

Slowly but surely, this image of a government adrift began to take root in public opinion. A satirical television programme labelled the government as the "Big Bedlam", with ministers entering and leaving the "house" at almost the same pace as *Big Brother* contestants. The Prime Minister appeared in a constant state of frustration, vacillating with his hands on his head, looking for the character portraying Coelho, Guterres' old ally and most reliable problem-solver, and Melícias' advice. Guterres' constant absence from the country was also an inspiration for the programme's caricature.

Indeed, in the first six months of 2000, the Air Force Falcon that transported the ministerial committees spent more than 700 hours in the air, which was the equivalent to thirty entire days.[1] "The first stage of the second government was the Portuguese Presidency of the European Union," recalls Guterres, "and then a problem arose,

107

in that it was highly demanding, and so the internal issues were left somewhat behind."

Backstage, almost as an interim Prime Minister, chairing cabinet meetings, dealing with both parliamentary debates and behind-the-scenes disputes, as well as fighting the fires that kept flaring up, Coelho was attempting to square this circle: "How many times was António Guterres in Parliament and had to leave because there was a European Council meeting that night and he just had to go? Those were difficult times, but he adored foreign policy in general and European policy in particular."

However, Guterres invested little time in everything that he did not adore. "That which did not motivate him, he ignored," admits his friend Guilherme d'Oliveira Martins. "If something is off his radar, it does not interest him. He has no patience."

Yet, even during his second term when he found increasingly greater returns from international meetings than from internal quarrels, there was a domestic matter that was necessarily drawing the Prime Minister's attention: the annual state budget. Without a budget, he would not be able to govern because this document authorised both expenditure and tax collection. This authorisation had to be granted—or not—by Parliament, where the Socialist government still did not hold a majority.

We're Screwed with this Guy

António Guterres hates cheese.

His friends would not hesitate to consider him a sophisticated gourmand, a gastronomic savant. However, if there is one thing he cannot stand it is cheese, whatever its origin, smell or flavour.

It is also true that his time as Prime Minister would be indelibly marked by a politically indigestible cheese.

Without a parliamentary majority, the only way Guterres could get his budget through was by obtaining the favourable votes, or the abstention, of at least one—one was enough—opposition MP.

To approve the 2000 state budget, the Prime Minister had been able to reach an agreement with the small Christian Democrat Party, CDS-PP, in exchange for an increase on pensions. The then leader of this party, Paulo Portas, highlights: "On some things, Mr. Guterres agreed with the left, on others with the right, and this permanent zigzagging ended up creating some distrust across all party benches." Portas also remembers that "the key criticism made of him—and that we shared—was that he was a person with an obsession for consensus and this harmed the outcome of his decisions."

Now that the Portuguese Presidency of the European Union was over, along with the reputational damage that rejecting the budget and bringing down the government would carry, the opposition felt a lot more comfortable about saying "no" to the 2001 accounts.

This was the context in which one member of parliament, desperately attempting to prevent the closure of a cheese factory in his electoral district, came to appear on the radar of Guterres' team.

As time went by, this MP's affliction began to coincide with that of the Prime Minister, who was seeing the deadline for submitting the 2001 budget drawing ever closer without a whisper of support from any opposition party.

While there is no tradition in the Portuguese political system of negotiating ad hoc agreements between central government and members of parliament, securing benefits through individual negotiations on behalf of the regions they represent, the Socialists agreed to open a line of contact with the cheese parliamentarian.

However, for selling his precious support, countering the position of his own party that was voting against the budget, the MP now submitted a hefty list of demands: support for building a new dairy factory, roads and a fishing port, upgrading the hospital…

Coelho was once again in the eye of the storm: "I was Minister of Public Works, and what a lot he wanted to get from me! And it was not just things for his own council, but also for various mayor friends in other councils! I saw the list and said, 'We're screwed with this guy.'"

Against a chorus of criticism, both in Parliament and in public opinion, the budget passed: 115 votes in favour, 114 against—and one cheesy abstention. Once again, when confronted with the sword, Guterres chose to be pushed against a wall. "That was a total error in judgement," he now accepts.

The Collapsed Bridge

It was 3.30 am when the press conference began.

Six hours had passed since the tragedy. Behind a row of microphones, Coelho announced to the country that "guilt cannot die alone." There had to be "political consequences."[2]

Over the previous hours, the government's number two had spoken many times with the Prime Minister. Guterres had listened to all the arguments and had no doubt that the last thing that should happen was for him to be left without his "firefighter", as he knew Coelho was called.

Throughout the night of 5 March 2001, the head of government tried to maintain there was no responsibility to attribute. He would order an inquiry; that Coelho's resignation was not necessary, an exaggerated response; and that they would see what to do later.

However, Coelho was not to be moved and did not even wait for the following day. Before dawn broke, he confirmed that he had submitted his resignation to the Prime Minister.

When a bridge collapsed in northern Portugal with several vehicles crossing it, Guterres was left with no alternative—especially as Coelho had visited the same bridge just a few days earlier, verifying the poor conditions of the road. Surely there were deaths, but nobody knew just how many at that stage.

What was known was that at around 9 pm one of the pillars had suddenly given way and a section of the bridge had collapsed into the rapids of the river Douro below.

As the night advanced, it was discovered that a bus and three cars had plunged into the river. Only later would it be confirmed that, in a matter of seconds, almost sixty people had disappeared, the worst road accident in national history.

Guterres reached the site of the accident the following morning. On that cold, grey winter's day, the Prime Minister arrived to a wave of whistling and insults, jeers and shouts.

"Murderer!"

Surrounded by journalists, Guterres struggled to maintain his composure. At one stage, he avoided eye contact with reporters, preferring to gaze at the skies instead of looking at the faces in front of him.

1. Guterres with his first wife, Luísa, during a trip with friends to Southern Europe in 1978.

2. In the early days of Portuguese democracy, Guterres worked on expanding the Socialist Party across the country.

3. Guterres' speech to the III Congress of the Portuguese Socialist Party, held in Lisbon in 1979.

4. At the constituent summit of the CPLP (Community of the Portuguese-Speaking Countries), one of Guterres' many links with Africa.

5. With Jacques Chirac, Boris Yeltsin and the NATO Secretary-General Javier Solana at the signing of the Founding Act with Russia.

6. António Vitorino, the current Director General of the International Organization for Migration, was Guterres' Minister of Defence.

7. Guterres' close friendship with Hillary Clinton began in the early 1990s.

8. The conservative José María Aznar, who served as Prime Minister of Spain, became one of Guterres' best friends.

9. Toast at a state dinner with the Brazilian President Fernando Henrique Cardoso during Guterres' official visit in 1996.

10. Talking to Vítor Melícias, with whom Guterres has remained close friends for decades, and the Portuguese Foreign Minister Jaime Gama.

11. Meeting with the UN rising star Sérgio Vieira de Mello in the Prime Minister's official residence.

12. Guterres' decision to participate in NATO's interventions in Bosnia and Kosovo faced strong domestic resistance.

13. Tony Blair's campaign for the Third Way influenced Guterres' political vision.

14. With Mikhail Gorbachev, the last leader of the Soviet Union. Guterres advocated for a super alliance between the US and Russia.

15. At the 1998 Lisbon World Exposition with the UN Secretary-General Kofi Annan.

16. Guterres talks to Fidel Castro at the Ibero-American Summit in Oporto in 1998.

17. German Chancellor Gerhard Schröder persistently tried to persuade Guterres to lead the European Commission.

18. Guterres was received by the Chinese Prime Minister Zhu Rongji in Beijing.

19. The handover of Macau was an important milestone in Guterres' relationship with China.

20. Bill Clinton visited Lisbon in 2000, just as Portugal held the rotating presidency of the European Union.

21. Alongside the King of Morocco, Mohammed VI, during the first European Union-Africa Summit.

22. The first European Union-Africa Summit, in Cairo, was one of the main achievements of the Portuguese Presidency of the EU.

23. Nelson Mandela would play an important role in East Timor's road to independence.

24. With Xanana Gusmão in East Timor, the greatest diplomatic victory of Guterres' political career.

25. Guterres shakes hands with Boutros Boutros-Ghali at the XX Congress of the Socialist International, held at the UN headquarters.

26. As President of the Socialist International, Guterres mediated a meeting
between Yasser Arafat and Shimon Peres.

27. Guterres worked as an adviser for the Brazilian government led by Luiz Inácio
Lula da Silva before joining the UNHCR.

Rodolfo Lavrador, his then chief of staff who was accompanying him, remembers this as the first time he had ever experienced the "hostility of people in relation to António Guterres. Thus far, I had never encountered anything like that. So, I consider the fall of the bridge to be a political turning point."

After the abortion referendum, which had left wounds in the party, and after the cheese budget, which had left open sores in Parliament, Guterres now faced a popular tragedy that would leave scars in the country.

"In summary," argues Lavrador, "it's the political death of the government. That's the fall of the bridge and the departure of Jorge Coelho. From my perspective, this is the point of no return."

In fact, the popularity of the government was on the slide just as the economy was deteriorating. For the first time since PS had won the 1999 election, the public account deficit was rising, having doubled in just two years, and now even unemployment was on the rise too.

Heading into 2001, there had been an accumulated pile of warnings about the need to tighten the nation's belt. The Portuguese Central Bank was forthright that summer: "We have arrived at a situation when public consumption as a percentage of national income is the highest in the European Union. The costs of civil service staff, also as a percentage of GDP, are the highest in the entire Eurozone. And that is a situation that our level of development cannot tolerate."[3]

Guterres felt he needed to breathe new life into his government. He had to replace underperforming ministers, those focused on their own agendas or simply lacking the profile for the role. The situation forced him to do something he still abhors today: "Telling somebody that they have to go is horrible," he admits.

In fact, the ultimate consensus was that Guterres did everything feasible to avoid sacking anybody. There was even the creation of the Ministry of Equality—unprecedented, only temporary and never again replicated nationally—just to keep in government an exhausted Minister of Health who also happened to be a personal friend.

"For him, a cabinet reshuffle was a sacrifice from the other world," confirms Coelho, who remained a close adviser of the leader, even after having formally left the government.

Now Another Story Begins

Despite the difficulties in the government, the party and the country, Guterres did not let up on the international contacts.

On 29 June 2001, the very same day as the ministerial reshuffle, he hosted another meeting of the Socialist International to commemorate the 50th anniversary of the organisation. Yasser Arafat and Shimon Peres were among the 400 delegates.

The Israeli had been reappointed Minister of Foreign Affairs in the recently formed Ariel Sharon government and had not yet had any meetings with the Palestinian leader. This was partially due to the Middle East peace process going through one of its most delicate moments since the early 1990s.

The wave of violence known as the Second Intifada, which began in September 2000 and would last for five years, was piling up casualties on both sides. Shortly before Peres and Arafat touched down in Portugal, a terrorist attack on a disco in Tel Aviv had left over twenty people dead.

Even in diplomatic terms, these times seemed particularly barren for any new attempts at mediation. The second round of negotiations at Camp David, which Bill Clinton wanted to become a historic turning point, had failed. Even a proposal from Secretary-General Kofi Annan for Peres and Arafat to meet in New York under UN auspices was rejected.

When Guterres welcomed them in Lisbon, he reminded the two long-standing rivals that they had agreed to talk on the margins of the last Socialist International Congress in Paris (where Guterres had been nominated President). As such, the Prime Minister offered his good offices, as well as his own literal office in São Bento, so they could meet in private.

The recent positions taken by the Portuguese government on the conflict had contributed to both sides perceiving Guterres as a reliable interlocutor. The Israelis recalled his assertive critiques of antisemitism, and his visit to the Amsterdam Synagogue, marking the 500th anniversary of Portugal's royal edict expelling all Jews—many of whom fled to the Dutch Republic. The Palestinians recognised with appreciation that, under his leadership, Portugal had a diplomatic representation in Ramallah and authorised the inauguration of a Palestinian diplomatic mission in Lisbon.

Additionally, under Guterres, Portugal had granted a million dollars of financial assistance to Palestine, donated to support rehabilitation projects for historical buildings in Bethlehem and the building of a female residence at a West Bank university, which would be called the House of Portugal—and guaranteed support for "the establishing of a sovereign Palestinian state."[4]

The Peres-Arafat meeting lasted over three hours and ended after midnight,[5] but was inconclusive. However, it enabled Guterres to grasp a fundamental dynamic of the Israeli-Palestinian question: "Our role was that of hosts and we spent the entire night, until really quite late, waiting to see if they could overcome a series of problems. They did not reach any agreement but it was interesting for me to understand that there was a very intimate relationship, not only between the two leaders, but also between their staff. These people were in a great deal of contact and this gave me some hope. I mean, the meeting was difficult, but it was a meeting between people who already had relationships, and that surprised me. There was a lot of shared will there."

Three months later, in September, the Prime Minister's turning of diplomatic wheels led to the arrival in Lisbon of another distinguished guest—the first socialist Chilean President since Salvador Allende. Guterres had made a point of attending the swearing-in ceremony of Ricardo Lagos, who now came to meet his Portuguese peer at the start of a European tour. On the Chilean agenda were two core topics: promoting the signing of a trade deal with the European Union and learning about the Portuguese strategy against drugs.

They were lunching quietly at São Bento when they were interrupted by tragic and shocking news from New York.

"I'd hardly seen the footage of the Towers when I ran out of my office," the press adviser Miguel Laranjeiro recalls. "But when I got there, they already knew. Somebody had already been in contact."

The date, already known by all Chileans as the day General Pinochet overthrew Allende, would now be stamped on the world's memory: September 11, the date of the most mortal and symbolic attack on American soil since Pearl Harbour. This would be the day when Osama bin Laden shed American blood; it would become a day of Western rage against Arab countries.

"We still hadn't finished our conversation," wrote Lagos, "when the image of the Twin Towers falling, enveloped in flames, led us to a premonitory sentence: Today, the world has changed, another history now begins."[6]

The Fall of Man

The tragic events of 9/11 did not distract Guterres from his domestic priorities. Throughout his tenure as Prime Minister, drug addiction remained the most prominent national social scourge. This was an area of the exclusive jurisdiction of the Ministries of Justice and Internal Affairs, and a matter for the police and the courts. However, such an approach, whereby drugs are considered solely as a criminal issue, was to be definitively compromised.

With the topic of drugs at the top of popular concerns, the government met with a group of specialists to define an innovative strategy for liberalisation, while setting out only a single red line: the new strategy had to respect the UN conventions that stipulate sanctions for non-prescribed usage of psychotropic substances.[7]

The group recommended the decriminalisation of consumption, turning drugs into a public healthcare matter, not a justice one, and drug addicts into patients, not criminals. The government accepted, instituting in June 2001 the policy that still applies in Portugal today: whenever the police intercepts somebody with drugs, they are taken to a police station, the substance is seized and weighed and, should it exceed a certain amount, the case will go to court. However, if it is within the legal limits, the consumer is signposted to an entity set up under the Ministry of Health with the objective of identifying their needs and helping them to access treatment.

Despite initial resistance from the World Health Organization, time would confirm the effectiveness of this approach and turn it into an international case study, consensual on both the left and the right. Today, it is the United Nations—either the General Assembly or the

Economic and Social Council—that frequently invites Portuguese specialists to share their experiences and lessons learned.

During Guterres' second term in office, however, such long-term social progress generated little short-term enthusiasm in public opinion, and the disenchantment of the electorate seemed to be reflected in the polls ahead of the local elections that would take place at the end of the year.

Since entering politics, the Prime Minister had notched up three decades of campaigns, whether that be campaigning to get himself elected nationally or internally, or for the election of others in European, local and even presidential elections. He had travelled thousands of kilometres and contacted thousands more people.

Today, Guterres swears he went into those local elections with the same level of commitment as always: "I did that campaign seriously. I toured the country in support of candidates." However, those accompanying him on the road now admit that he was already giving them some signs.

Indeed, in mid-campaign, Guterres made a decision: "If we get a positive result, I will have to make an effort, but I shall continue. And for me, winning is getting more votes than [the Social Democrats]. Winning Lisbon. Winning Porto."

Meaning, if he won, Guterres was prepared to remain as Prime Minister—despite no local election victory being able to resolve the legislative and executive limitations that he had encountered over the preceding six years.

But, what if the result was not positive? In such a case, Guterres' opinion was that "everything gets paralysed, Parliament will not approve anything and we shall end up with new elections. I thought that, with me, the PS would win against the PSD, but would not be able to govern alone."

Local elections took place on 16 December 2001.

As the Portuguese cast their ballots and the votes were counted, the popular verdict on the political future of Guterres became increasingly clear.

From the party headquarters in Lisbon, the Prime Minister watched the first results as they came in. They reflected the disillusionment of the country and the defeat of PS soon became irreversible.

However, the sheer scale of the loss would only become clear when the party saw that some of its most emblematic strongholds had swung the other way. "On election day, Lisbon fell, Porto fell and we got fewer votes than PSD," recalls Guterres. "It was over."

One hundred and twenty-seven Socialist Party councils started to change hands one after another. Ten, then twenty, then thirty councils... At the end, PS lost control of forty-one municipalities.

Coelho spent the election night in PS headquarters, right in front of the Secretary-General's office. He was one of the first people Guterres spoke to: "We were listening to the results and he came into my office and told me what he was going to do. And I supported him immediately."

This sparked a debate in the PS citadel. The majority of the top leadership attempted to dissuade their leader from his intention. Never had such a thing happened in Portuguese political history. They tried to pressure him, convince him and propose alternatives. However, the leader was not to be moved and his decision was final.

The only thing missing was a public declaration. Called in for the Prime Minister's election night speech, journalists packed out the main hall in the former palace that served as the Socialist Party headquarters. Television cameras at the back, reporters to one side and photographers at the front, Guterres got straight to the subject:

> *If I let these elections pass, continuing to exercise the functions of Prime Minister, the country would fall into a political quagmire that would undermine the relationship of trust between the government and the governed. [...] I understand that my duty is to avoid this political quagmire. To this end, I shall ask the President of the Republic to receive me so that I may present him my resignation.*

PART II

ONE HELL AT A TIME

11

THE NETWORK

Sitting with his back to the restaurant door, Guterres tried to soothe the indignation around the table. He and his lunch companions had just returned from the inauguration of the next Portuguese Prime Minister. The aggressive comments Durão Barroso had directed his way were categorised by all as less than elegant. Nevertheless, after completing this final formality, he had little interest in the deals and schemes driving Portuguese politics or in the headlines accusing him of fleeing after having depleted the state's coffers. "I will never write a memoir," explains Guterres, "and I never take notes on what's going on around me. I don't even keep a diary, and I threw all my papers away. The great advantage is that each day we're thinking forwards, not backwards."

There, in a restaurant near Parliament in Lisbon, a bottle of white wine accompanied the meal and enlivened the conversation Guterres shared with his former chief of staff, Finance Minister, and the Secretary of State for the Budget, the latter being the youngest in the quartet and the least stoical about the criticism.

"They said we'd bankrupted the country," says Rui Coimbra, "and practically accused us of being dishonest. I didn't think that was acceptable and I wanted to go over the accounts right then and there, but Guterres really had detached himself from everything."

At the age of 53, and bidding farewell to all the trappings of being Prime Minister, Guterres once again took up the kind of social work that was reminiscent of his student days. Twice a week, he would arrive by himself at an African neighbourhood in Lisbon's suburbs, park in the street and make his way through identical four-storey-high apartment blocks, with ground-floor windows hidden behind bars and yellowing walls covered with graffiti, until he reached the doors of the parish church. Inside, in a room where catechism was sometimes taught, a group of high school graduates were waiting for him. They were young, in their early twenties, and still needed to pass the national mathematics exam to get into university.

"He seemed like a teacher," recalled the musician Isaías Trindade, one of Guterres' students. "You could tell he really understood maths and had experience. He made jokes, really dry ones, and put us all at ease. There was nothing formal about him, and he certainly didn't seem like a politician. If not everyone, then nearly everyone passed the exam."

It was not long before the journalists picked up on his teaching, even though Guterres had always refused to discuss his life outside public office. Many considered the articles that depicted him playing the role of the good Samaritan further proof of the rumours that suggested he would soon be running for the Presidency.

Guterres decided instead to return to his roots, turning full circle to when he had taken up a position at his old university, Lisbon's Instituto Superior Técnico in the 2003/04 academic year. However, this time he was not going to teach physics, but rather stage a series of seminars on global challenges. This was an opportunity for the former teacher to update the curriculum and bring international experts to the campus, such as Jan Pronk, a negotiator of the Kyoto Protocol, who had unexpectedly lost his bid to become the UN High Commissioner for Refugees.

Step by step, Guterres began to engage with some of the places he had left behind thirty years earlier, and now with another wife at his side. Catarina Vaz Pinto had joined Guterres' government as Secretary of State for Culture without even having spoken to the Prime Minister. Over time, they met in cabinet meetings and their relationship had evolved discreetly before becoming official in the summer of 2000, after Catarina had left the government. Their marriage had taken place in a chapel in Lisbon less than a year later and was celebrated by two priests: an uncle of the bride and Vítor Melícias. Guterres was still Prime Minister at the time, but had made a point of keeping the ceremony private.

Turning the page from six years of eventful governing, Guterres was starting to knit together his future, turning his back on party politics and on all political positions. All, that is, save one.

Bush Clones

Carlos Lopes, the new head of the United Nations Development Programme in Brazil, took office amid a shift in the local political scene. In October 2002, Lula da Silva, a man of ample charm and working-class roots, had finally been elected the Brazilian President on his fourth attempt.

During his campaign, Lula had promised to make social security and public welfare the flagship of his tenure. This agenda worried the financial markets, but pleased the United Nations, which saw it as the right approach for a country so rich in resources yet riven by inequalities.

From the beginning of his appointment in Brazil, one of the portfolios that occupied Lopes, an economist from Guinea-Bissau, was known as the "Bolsa Família"[1] or "Family Allowance" scheme. Through this programme, the federal government issues a small allowance to families in extreme need provided they meet certain criteria, such as enrolling their children into school and ensuring their vaccinations are up to date.

It was when searching for similar policies in other countries that Lopes once again came across the name of Guterres.

"I suggested the Brazilian government should take a look at the guaranteed minimum income in Portugal," Lopes recalled, "an idea they welcomed, especially as we were talking about a measure implemented by people from the left and, what's more, who also spoke Portuguese. After that, I got in touch with Guterres and we ended up twice appearing before the Brazilian Council of Ministers to present our ideas."

Guterres took full advantage of his new acquaintances among Lula's entourage to push forward a second initiative: to bring

Brazil's governing party under the umbrella of the Socialist International, of which he remained president even after leaving office. Besides, Lula was also the leader of the Workers' Party, the most powerful force on the Latin American left, a valuable addition to the club. Lula himself certainly seemed receptive to closer ties, hailing Guterres in 2003 as:

> *My Dear Friend António Guterres,*
>
> [...]
>
> *It is with great happiness that Brazil welcomes the Socialist International Congress to the city of São Paulo.*
>
> [...]
>
> *Here you'll meet important representatives of political forces fighting on the five continents for the social progress of their peoples.*
>
> [...]
>
> *To reach these objectives, we need to reconstruct the UN, adapting it to the new realities of the contemporary world, which are distant to those of its foundation.*[2]

On the very day he celebrated his 58th birthday, Lula opened the Socialist International Congress at which Guterres was scheduled to speak. In the modern Transamerica Expo Center, the Portuguese statesman argued in favour of establishing a "global coalition"[3] capable of responding "to the neoliberal ideology, to the neoconservative political agenda, and to the logic of unilateralism that sanctifies the market to such an extent that the person is sacrificed, along with attempts to dismantle or weaken the system of the United Nations."[4]

The Socialist International meeting in São Paulo took place in October, seven months after the invasion of Iraq, which meant that the Bush administration was the hot topic in most speeches. This was not the first time Guterres had publicly censored the Republican President. Right after the US invasion, he had participated in an anti-war march in Lisbon that coincided with protests worldwide. Simultaneously, he had made clear to the press the consequences of such an adventure, stressing in an interview that, "It's essential that the Muslim world does not see us as though we are all Bush clones."[5] "Iraq is being transformed into the world's most important training camp for terrorists,"[6] he would lament in another public appearance, a year later.

In this context, he thought the time was not right to accept the mission offered by Kofi Annan. The UN Secretary-General, who he had been in contact with since the crisis in East Timor, was trying to recruit Guterres to be his new special envoy to Iraq, filling the position left in the wake of the death of Sérgio Vieira de Mello, who had been killed when a truck bomb blew up the United Nations headquarters in Baghdad, in August 2003.

The invasion of Iraq, a US-led coalition with no clear mandate from the UN Security Council, reignited the long-standing debate over the need to reform the United Nations. Always in tune with global tendencies, and with an understanding that this was a golden opportunity, Guterres sought to update the Socialist International position on a possible UN reform, a task that began in São Paulo with the creation of a working group and that culminated in a thirty-seven-page report. At the time, this document did not attract a lot of attention. Today, however, it reveals some of the structural changes that the future UN Secretary-General wished to see implemented at the organisation.

More than just mulling over the problem, Guterres wanted to sit down at the same table with the decision-makers: "I had this strategic objective: to establish a network that would facilitate the Socialist International to be more in contact with the main powers, thereby creating possibilities for discussing the great multilateral questions. We were well represented in Europe, reasonably well represented in Latin America and Africa, but did not have this kind of relationship with the big powers, except in Europe."

One of Guterres' strategic targets was China. "There was no relationship with the Communist Party due to all the Cold War stuff," he explains. "The Chinese came to the big events, though not to the larger working groups, under the auspices of something called the Friendship Association, or whatever it was—a pretence. We thought this didn't make any sense at all and decided at the São Paulo Congress to open a strategic dialogue with them. We're not from the same family, but we speak to each other."

Along with the contacts established with emerging powers, Guterres began building connections with Washington, since "no transformation on a world scale happens today unless the United States takes part."[7] However, he was also certain that this could not happen with the Republican Party.

Among Democrats

One hundred thousand biodegradable balloons and over 400 kilos of paper confetti. Above the stage hung a 27-metre-wide and 5-metre-high screen for video projection, a scale never before seen in politics, not even in the United States.

Boston pulled out all the stops for the 2004 Democratic Convention. It was the first time the city had hosted the major event of its favourite party. In addition, it was one of their own, John Kerry, the Senator from Massachusetts, who would pick up the nomination for the first presidential election since 9/11.

Hemmed in by tight security, the Fleet Center arena hosted delegates from every US state and guests from around world, including Guterres.

In the early afternoon on the first day of the convention, he took part in a "Conversation on Democracy", staged by Madeleine Albright's National Democratic Institute (NDI), one of the many parallel events held in the city during that week in June.

Guterres was more interested in making contacts than attending every talk on the convention's agenda. For that reason, he missed the keynote speech by a relatively unknown aspiring Illinois Senator, Barack Obama.

Contacts with the Democratic Party had intensified in the aftermath of the Iraq War, since Guterres believed Europe had "to maintain a dialogue at all costs with those in America who believe that an international and multilateral order is desirable and possible."[8]

Following the first post-invasion parliamentary elections in Iraq, the Portuguese statesman had travelled to Baghdad at the invitation of the NDI. "It was a brief course about how elections are run," he recalls, "how to conduct a political campaign, given to some guys from secular Sunni parties. The NDI and myself were engaged in a variety of activities in the Middle East that had to do with the promotion of liberal and secular democracy among emerging parties in the region."

This bridge-building exercise with US Democrats also extended to other platforms. There was the newly formed "Building Global Alliances for the 21st Century", a progressive think tank run by Europeans and Americans, among them Guterres and two key figures from the Clinton administration: Secretary of State Madeleine Albright and chief of staff John Podesta.[9] "We were in touch regularly," says Guterres. "It was all done very discreetly because the term 'socialist' didn't work very well in America at that time."

On the eve of the annual G8 Summit—held that year on Sea Island, in the US state of Georgia—the Euro-American think tank proposed a new global strategy to combat the proliferation of nuclear arms and spoke out about two of the members of George W. Bush's "axis of evil,"[10] predicting that Iran would continue to camouflage its attempts to enrich uranium and recommending the White House open negotiations with the North Korea regime.[11]

A few months later, in November 2004, the nuclear topic re-emerged in a debate organised in Washington by Podesta's Center for American Progress:

Antonio, if I could turn to you.

[...]

If you could comment on whether UN reform is really feasible and why, in fact, to people who may be sceptical about the merits of multilateralism and rather see this as a weakness than as a strength.[12]

Responding to the panel's moderator, Guterres argued that international security depended on reducing the "flaws"[13] in the Treaty on the Non-Proliferation of Nuclear Weapons and reaching an understanding on the definition of terrorism at the UN level so that a shared and global strategy for fighting that threat might be implemented.

He also considered it imperative to define the circumstances that legitimise intervention in states, including militarily, in order to protect at-risk populations. In simple terms, there was a need to stipulate at the international level the moment at which the "sovereignty of the human being"[14] would overrule that of the state.

On this issue, he added he would like to see the principles set out in the report produced by an independent commission co-chaired by the former Australian Minister of Foreign Relations,

Gareth Evans, entitled "The Responsibility to Protect",[15] "incorporated in the United Nations doctrine."[16]

According to this report, humanitarian military intervention should only take place in the event of:

- large scale loss of life, actual or apprehended, with genocidal intent or not, which is the product either of deliberate state action, or state neglect or inability to act, or a failed state situation; or
- large scale "ethnic cleansing", actual or apprehended, whether carried out by killing, forced expulsion, acts of terror or rape.[17]

All of these realities would be one day faced by Guterres.

This kind of intervention would be equally legitimate whenever executed "as an anticipatory measure in response to clear evidence of likely large scale killing."[18] Otherwise, "the international community would be placed in the morally untenable position of being required to wait until genocide begins before being able to take action to stop it."[19]

In another passage, the report Guterres brought to the debate approached the question of authority. It was clear that "the Security Council should be the first port of call on any matter relating to military intervention for human protection purposes. But the question remains whether it should be the last."[20] How then should the organisation proceed if and when, in the middle of a humanitarian crisis, a P5 veto throws the Security Council into a state of paralysis?

Hypothesis 1: convene a Special Emergency Session of the United Nations General Assembly.[21] When this is not enough to save lives, an "overwhelming majority of member states"[22] taking a stand would pressure the Security Council into acting.

Hypothesis 2: intervene via a "regional or sub-regional organisation acting within its defining boundaries."[23] This would be accomplished through states that, given their geographic proximity, would be most impacted in various ways by the catastrophe, such as refugee influxes.

Club de Madrid

"Watch out for the question of Iraq. It will become very important."[24]

Boutros-Ghali really had hit the nail on the head. This had been his only piece of advice to the incoming Secretary-General at the end of 1996. For Annan, Iraq had become an intractable issue. He was forced to go on the defensive after the avalanche of criticism that escalated when a Republican senator called for his resignation in *The Wall Street Journal*.[25] A fresh start with the US administration was necessary, especially since, according to US Ambassador to the UN Richard Holbrooke, President Bush "had come out of the election believing that most UN staff preferred [John] Kerry and that the UN had taken steps that were perceived by the White House as being aimed at helping Kerry."[26] A clear sign of change came with the appointment of Annan's new chief of staff, the Briton Mark Malloch-Brown.

In addition to the Iraq crisis, there were claims of sexual abuse perpetrated by Blue Helmets in the Democratic Republic of the Congo. And the already difficult situation worsened in May 2004 when the High Commissioner for Refugees, the Dutch Ruud Lubbers, faced accusations of sexual harassment by a staff member. When the UN's internal report on the matter was leaked in early 2005, following weeks of controversy, media pressure rendered his resignation inevitable.

In New York, Malloch-Brown began working on a list of possible candidates for the newly vacant position. Above all else, the selection process depended on the good offices of Annan, who had once been the head of personnel for UNHCR.

In March, the Secretary-General travelled to Madrid to speak at the International Summit on Democracy, Security and Terrorism, organised by the Club de Madrid.[27] The forum brought together former heads of state and heads of democratic governments from around the world, and paid tribute to the 191 lives lost in that city a year earlier at the hand of al-Qaeda.

As a member of the Club, Guterres was present at the commemoration and it was there, in the midst of informal greetings and conversations on the sidelines, that his candidacy for High Commissioner for Refugees started to gain momentum.

"The Spanish Minister of Foreign Affairs said to me, 'You're the one that should run for High Commissioner. We have a candidate, but we're ready to support you,'" Guterres remembers. "Later, Kofi Annan came over to me and said, 'So, are you running there [in Portugal] for President, or not?' I said, 'No, I'm not running,' and he said, 'Ah, that's good,' or something like that."

After the episode in Madrid, Guterres did not take long to start working for the post. "It was the kind of job that attracted me. I made two or three contacts and ran without any guarantees that I would win, although today I'm convinced that Kofi Annan, when he came to talk to me, he already had an idea in mind."

In fact, as Malloch-Brown confirms, "The person who most defended the candidacy of Guterres was Kofi Annan himself." However, the British diplomat was against the idea: "I thought that he simply did not have the same historical tradition of working with refugees as the others. Furthermore, this made me think, 'Oh my God, no, we do not need another prime minister. They simply do not command things."

Around a month after the resignation of Lubbers, New York put forward eight candidates for the position. The list included the Tunisian Kamel Morjane—at the time the Agency's Assistant High Commissioner.

"We were very anxious because we needed a candidate able to survive the press scrutiny in terms of the type of behaviour for which Lubbers left... but he was never accused," Malloch-Brown outlines. "Kofi and I were convinced that we had to have a High Commissioner whose personal behaviour and integrity were untouchable."

However, not all the candidates reacted well to the selection criteria. The Australian Gareth Evans, a member of the High Level Panel constituted by Annan to study the reform of the United Nations, flared up during his interview and even accused Malloch-Brown of sabotaging his bid. The charismatic Bernard Kouchner, founder of Médecins Sans Frontières (Doctors Without Borders) and one of the most popular politicians in France, calmly placed all of his cards on the table.

"Bernard, is there anything in your past that might prove uncomfortable for you or for the UNHCR if you were nominated the High Commissioner?" asked Malloch-Brown.

"There is nothing uncomfortable from my perspective, but there may be a lot from yours," answered the French candidate.

In his report to the Secretary-General, Malloch-Brown detailed these episodes and added his own observations about which candidates should proceed to the second phase.

"And what answer did António Guterres give to that question?" inquired Annan.

"I'm even slightly embarrassed to put it like this, but the man breathes personal integrity—he's a member of Opus Dei, he was widowed and got married again just a while ago—I felt that his integrity was simply so obvious that I couldn't ask the question," explained Malloch-Brown, whom Guterres had also impressed with the volunteerism that motivated him to teach maths in the suburbs of Lisbon.

"Well then, that's our next High Commissioner," Annan concluded, according to Malloch-Brown.

However, the process was still to run its course, and five candidates proceeded to the following stage where they would be interviewed by the Secretary-General and his deputy. One of these candidates was Evans.

Had Evans also been encouraged by Annan to run? "No, it was my call," the Australian explained in his memoir. "I think I was seen as the best credentialed of those who formally applied and submitted themselves to the rather rigorous vetting and interview process. My understanding is that António Guterres was not initially a candidate but a late applicant promoted actively by Malloch-Brown, who had reservations about my suitability for the job. I was told, in effect, that while there was no question about my ability and experience, I was seen as likely to provide a little more colour and movement than the system would find it comfortable to live with. Brother Guterres, it seems, was a smooth man: I was a hairy one."[28]

In this phase, Guterres' campaign opted to strategically demonstrate his global support. This was a period when many networks came together to openly show their support: the Socialist International, the CPLP,[29] not to mention a number of European friends.

Efforts directed at Washington were simultaneously advancing. Moreover, old friends are handy in such situations, and one that came through was Blair. Similarly, Elizabeth Bagley, the former US Ambassador to Portugal, also answered the call: "I was asked to speak with Bill Clinton, who gave him his full support."

With the jury still out, Guterres continued his activities with the Socialist International. There was a looming meeting in the Middle East, a crucial opportunity to finalise the work ongoing since São Paulo for the reform of the United Nations, in particular that of the Security Council.

This subject was already on the agenda with the publication of reports[30] that Annan released as part of the discussions in the run-up to the 2005 World Summit. While these reports proposed adding more seats in the Security Council, Guterres continued to advocate a bolder restructuring of the system, including the creation of an Economic, Social and Environmental Security Council.[31]

In this new organisational architecture, there would be two bodies functioning in parallel at the peak of the hierarchy. The 1945 Security Council would take on the political and security issues, while its new counterpart would focus on sustainable development and would be responsible for coordinating the action of the economic and social agencies, as well as the Bretton Woods institutions governing world finance and the World Trade Organization.

In Guterres' vision of a new Security Council, decisions would be taken by a qualified majority—without vetoes. The weighting of the votes would depend on a country's population relative to the global population combined with its gross domestic product and its contributions to the United Nations budget. States with a seat on this new organ would be elected by the General Assembly and would preferably be represented by leading civil experts, instead of the traditional career diplomats or former foreign ministers.

The report also called for changes to the existing Security Council. It specifically singled out the right to veto as symbolic of the "UN's lack of efficiency and ability to tackle some of the most important conflicts in the world",[32] and recommended the organisation "should aim at a veto-free culture."[33] While a change of such magnitude might seem unrealistic, there should at least be an attempt to reduce "the use of vetoes based purely on national interests."[34] This might be achieved in two ways: pressing countries to present "a written, publicly accessible motivation for its veto with reference to the UN Charter",[35] or, alternatively, restricting the prerogative to situations perceived as threats to international security.[36]

Guterres had the report with him when he arrived in Tel Aviv on 23 May 2005 to chair the inaugural session of the Socialist International meeting dedicated to peace in the Middle East. The schedule was tight, and he was already in Ramallah that evening for a second round of working sessions. As he was leaving the meeting he had just had with the President of the Palestinian National Authority, Mahmoud Abbas, his mobile phone rang. It was the softly spoken voice of Annan: "It is you who I am going to propose to the General Assembly."

12

THE DIRT, THE MUD AND THE DUST

"Gutierrez?" A few months earlier, on hearing the name for the first time, Athar Sultan-Khan had no idea who that was. At the United Nations for over twenty-five years, this Pakistani, slender in build, with a high-pitched voice and thick hair, had been chief of staff to the previous High Commissioner for Refugees and would continue to hold the position until further notice. That was why he was standing in front of the Agency's glassy headquarters in Geneva. Guterres was about to arrive.

A diplomat in profession and in manners, Sultan-Khan greeted the Portuguese as he got out of his car and accompanied him into the building, making sure everything went smoothly for his new boss at each step.

The rest of the staff, having been warned about the imminence of the arrival, had gathered in the building's atrium, lining the railings between the upper floors and the ground floor, where the new High Commissioner was about to say a few words. In truth, many had hoped that the next leader of the organisation would be the man now standing on Guterres' right, Morjane, the Assistant High Commissioner since 2001. After the Lubbers scandal, people felt the need for a safe harbour and Guterres' political profile, as well as the gossip going around that presaged a faltering decision-maker, fostered a certain unease among the staff.

133

After his address, during which he invited Morjane to work by his side, Guterres was bent on learning his way around. He was now heading a humanitarian agency born out of the ashes of World War II to deal with European refugees and which had, at the time, only thirty-four staffers. The original idea had been that its mission would take three years to complete and the UNHCR would then cease to exist. However, post-war history had turned the protection of refugees into a permanent mission. Guterres was the organisation's tenth High Commissioner, which now had 6,000 workers on its payroll and worked to support the populations of 115 countries.

For these first few days, Sultan-Khan had scheduled meetings, put together a retreat for senior staff and even arranged for a BMW 740 as the official car. For a long period of time, he and the High Commissioner's driver had wanted to get rid of the dark blue Audi A8, which had already clocked up well over 100,000 miles and was pumping out levels of emissions frowned upon at Davos. He had hoped to work alongside Guterres just for a year to facilitate the transition and was dazed that Guterres did not bring anyone with him from Portugal, not even an aide or a secretary. "No, no, I'll work with whoever you have."

Raymond Hall, the UNHCR Director of Human Resources at the time, was also surprised by this approach: "Many people would have come in saying 'a new broom sweeps clean' while Guterres came in and broadly kept everybody in place. Some attributed this to his judgement that the organisation had already been through such a period of recent turbulence." He soon understood that Guterres preferred to come up with workarounds rather than outright personnel substitutions: "He sometimes feels that if a certain one of his senior staff is weak then he can cover for them; that it doesn't really matter as he can do it anyway. He's usually right but that's not good in terms of the overall structure of delegation."

Guterres rented a two-bedroom apartment in Geneva's city centre, overlooking the Rhône. He hurriedly picked up some furniture, brought over a couple of pieces from Lisbon and hung some contemporary art on the walls. This new address accessed what would become well-worn routes in the High Commissioner's daily life: either to the office or to the airport. Five days after taking up his position, his bags were already packed for a trip to Africa. But before leaving, he called Sultan-Khan.

"Was it you who ordered the car?"

"Yes, High Commissioner, it's a very practical car."

"Can you please cancel the order?"

The Pearl of Africa

Ron Redmond was relieved. For the UNHCR's spokesperson, Guterres' arrival in June 2005 meant the beginning of a new news cycle. Behind him were ten dark months dedicated to the sexual harassment accusations against Lubbers.

During those early days, Redmond took Guterres to the studio and offices of the communications team on the sixth floor to go over the general features of their strategy. He took this opportunity to get some insight to the High Commissioner: "I remember one of the first things he told me was that he did quite a bit of television as Prime Minister," the American recalls, "and would often recite the same line several times when actually doing the recording, but not live. Also, especially when he was going to do a live event, he would mentally think ahead about what he was going to say."

Redmond, a former journalist with United Press International, had been with the UNHCR since 1991. When he first arrived, relationships between journalists and the Agency were of low priority. By the time Guterres arrived, Redmond was working just a flight of stairs away from the High Commissioner's office and one of the most important annual tasks was preparing his boss for World Refugee Day.

Celebrated on 20 June, this commemoration provided a highly valuable opportunity to push the organisation's agenda. The occasion was usually marked with a field visit by the High Commissioner, but not necessarily to places as remote as Northern Uganda.

The bumpy road, rocky and full of holes, made for slow progress. Each of the humanitarian trucks carried about twenty Sudanese refugees and their scarce belongings, which constantly bobbled and shook on the uneven pavement. The convoy advanced as best it could through the dense green and endless forest. In one of the trucks, underneath its canopy with sun-faded blue UNHCR insignia, Guterres talked with the Sudanese. They had spent years fleeing warzones, first from the civil war in their own country that pitted the Muslim North against the majority Christian and Animist South. After that, they fled the horror of the raids by the Lord's Resistance Army and their medieval-style pillaging, as well as the kidnapping of children on the border with Uganda.

Some of the refugees Guterres was talking with had received small plots of land in Uganda to grow potatoes, corn and other vegetables—not only for their own sustenance but also, whenever possible, to sell. The more self-sufficient they became, the less the effort required by the government and the lower their dependence on foreign aid: a model the UNHCR would have liked to replicate in other countries.

Guterres' presence was intended not only to thank the host country for such generosity, but also to warn the world about the endemic lack of money for African operations. What most disturbed him was the lack of food at some refugee camps. In Moya, one of the areas he visited in Northern Uganda, food rations had recently been reduced and was no longer possible to guarantee the recommended daily intake of 2,100 calories, the minimum for a healthy life.

Known as "The Pearl of Africa" for its astonishing fauna and flora, Uganda had become used to sheltering its neighbours, whether Congolese, Rwandan, Burundian, Somalis coming through Kenya, or the Sudanese. Many of these refugees were not even processed by the UNHCR verification centres. They entered, circulated and settled on the shores of the Great Lakes, perhaps even returning to their own countries, but always staying outside the system.

The majority of the 230,000 refugees officially taken in by Uganda were Sudanese.[1] After the January 2005 peace agreement between Khartoum and the southern insurgents these refugees could now return home and perhaps even participate in the urgent task of reconstruction. It was precisely one of these repatriation projects that Guterres was accompanying and, after two hours—that Redmond thought were taking forever—they crossed the border and reached their destination.

"When we arrived at this village in South Sudan that they were returning to," explains Redmond, "[Guterres] went straight into the home of one of these refugee families and spent time there in order to see the entire process. That was quite impressive to me and to the other UNHCR staff who saw he was willing to get involved, to get out in the dirt and the mud and the dust in a very uncomfortable situation. This was no shock to him."

They were housed in a government facility in the tiny agricultural village of Kajo-Keji. At around 8 pm, from the courtyard Guterres spoke with international stations via satellite telephone. It was normal to take advantage of the spotlight cast by World Refugee Day to provide the global media with an updated perspective on the prevailing situation. Even more so when, at the time Guterres had become High Commissioner, there was good news to tell the world: the number of refugees worldwide had fallen to 9.2 million, the lowest since 1980—notwithstanding the fact that, in counting asylum seekers, the repatriated, stateless persons and the internally displaced, situations that also merited the attention of the agency, that number had actually soared to 19.2 million.[2]

Statistics, however, are versatile narrators and Guterres knew of other numbers that told a very different story, including that which detailed how he had inherited a serious financial crisis at the heart of the UNHCR.

The Implementation Gap

Guterres arrived at work each day at around 9 am. On normal days, his morning was spent responding to emails and taking part in meetings, whether with ambassadors, NGOs or his own staff.

Occasionally, in the middle of these tasks, he would take the atrium elevator down to the ground floor for a coffee, crossing the various departments that comprised the organisation:

Sixth floor: Foreign Relations.

Fifth floor: Division of International Protection.

The UNHCR headquarters comprises two wings that form a "U", with Guterres' office on the top floor, parallel to Avenue de France. Except for the yellow doors and window casings, the interior colour scheme was dominated by cold and sober hues, with grey flooring and the main support pillars painted blue.

Fourth floor: Human Resources.

Third floor: Bureau for Asia and the Pacific.

Second floor: Operations.

Guterres was never without a jacket and tie. Whoever ran into him in the elevator would usually greet him with a few cordial and brief words, to which he did not always respond.

First floor: IT

Ground floor: Cafeteria and Travel Agency.

During his first months in office, the second half of 2005, the meetings were, above all, an opportunity for the High Commissioner to examine the various teams he was working with and, simultaneously, for the organisation to size up its new boss.

Was he a hesitant leader too fixated on consensus, as initially rumoured, or an expeditious decision-maker after all? Erika Feller, the UNHCR's Assistant High Commissioner for Protection between 2005 and 2013, states, "I have worked with many people who spent a lot of time informing themselves and being very nervous about acting on the results of this information. That was not Mr. Guterres. I think he was a very good decision-maker. Sometimes, however, he had to bring in perhaps too many layers of people into the consultation process."

Was he a delegating High Commissioner, focused only on the most important dossiers, or a micromanager? Nick van Praag, the Director of External Relations between 2006 and 2009, puts it this way: "He's just very keen to keep control of the whole narrative and he likes working directly with people. He wants to be on top of all the details."

For staff who were reluctant to work in the field, the most important thing was understanding if there were significant changes on the horizon. In truth, there were contradictory signs. Guterres said at the beginning of his tenure that he was not about "to shoot in all directions." However, he also noted in another internal speech that much of what had been produced, and was still being produced, the guidelines and new policies, have "not yet become integral to the way we work [...]. We have an 'implementation gap'. To address it, we must set priorities, take care to match our objectives and resources, and ensure this consolidation draws the headquarters closer to the field."[3]

What he did not specify on that occasion was that the most disconcerting gap was budgetary. Sultan-Khan was with Guterres when the financial director explained what was at stake: "He said to him that we have a gap of 20 per cent in the budget and we may not even have the money to pay for the following month's salaries."

Unlike most United Nations agencies, the UNHCR's budget depends almost entirely on voluntary contributions. Every year, the organisation starts over again from zero and sometimes the available funding reaches the red line far too early.

The donors are the UN member states, starting with the United States, at that time responsible for 32 per cent of the UNHCR's annual budget of a billion dollars. In a distant second place came Japan, followed by the European Commission and by a dozen European nations, plus Canada and Australia.[4] Guterres depended on donations for practically everything and was not always able to put money where it was most needed, as most state contributions had to be channelled towards regions, countries or projects within the donor country's sphere of interest.

The expectation of being adequately represented in the UNHCR's management structure also represented another collateral for state donations. It was already an unwritten rule that the organisation's second in command, the Deputy High Commissioner, had to come from the US, but the other funding nations also shared with Guterres their requests, suggestions and complaints.

As stakeholders, states are also sensitive to the solvency of organisations and the quality of service they provide. Taking too long to resolve problems may lead to donor fatigue, just as spending too much money within the organisation can cause sinking levels of confidence. On this matter, Guterres understood how the unbalanced budget was sending out the wrong message: "The UNHCR found itself in a completely unsustainable situation. The level of financing was more or less stagnant, and as the fixed costs, in terms of personnel and administration, went up, operational expenditure was going down. There was actually a moment when they would cross. We had to work hard to turn this around."

We Reject Local Integration

On Thursday mornings, the directors of the different bureaus ascended to the seventh floor. They sat in low-backed, yellow chairs around a long, light brown, rectangular table, usually supplied with three thermos flasks of water. The weekly meeting took place in a room named after Sérgio Vieira de Mello, the late UN envoy to Iraq and a former UNHCR staff member. Mello had wanted to solve complex problems in difficult environments, which were precisely the kind of situations under discussion at such meetings. When he was in Geneva, Guterres presided over these meetings, which used to take several hours and involved calls to officers directly in the field. Guterres used to sit at the head of the table with his back to the four clocks on the wall: for Geneva, New York, Tokyo, and Greenwich Mean Time. Time was of the essence and his teams knew that.

"He had little patience for esoteric discussions," recalls Dominik Bartsch, who was appointed Representative of the UNHCR to Jordan in 2020. "You're there for a reason; you're there to support refugees. It's to keep the eye on the ball, okay? I think that may have also been a message to senior managers who he wanted to challenge by saying, 'Look, you cannot get away with knowing less than I do.'"

At the start of each meeting, there was time to hear the department heads. As the work progressed, however, attention might be funnelled in a particular direction and, in late 2005, that meant Egypt, a country well known in the corridors of the United Nations for its ability to punch above its weight. "It was his number-one problem at the time," recalls Radhouane Nouicer, the Deputy Director of the North Africa office.

It all began in September with a small-scale Sudanese protest in front of a UNHCR office in Mustafa Mahmoud Park, Cairo, a popular area for its restaurants, stores and movie theatres. This was not just any field office. It was decided here who was, and who was not, a refugee: a life-changing designation as the Egyptian government only recognised those sanctioned and stamped "approved" by the UNHCR. In addition, it was one of the most over-worked offices in the world, which did not always correspond with the financing available.

Simply by crossing borders does not turn a foreigner into a refugee. Protection under international law requires proof, which can be challenging when more often than not applicants are not in possession of any sort of documentation and do not understand the local language. Victims of trauma, unaccompanied children, the mentally ill, all are required to prove, in one way or another, they are in danger in their own country. In the first phase of this process, the UNHCR gives asylum seekers a yellow card which protects them against deportation. A verdict is reached after a series of procedures. The approved refugees receive a blue card, while all others whose requests have been rejected are left to their own devices, usually falling into the informal economy.

In the case of Cairo, the discontent prevailing among the Sudanese was well known. There were multiple complaints of sluggishness, allegations of arbitrariness in the decision-making process and even the way staff handled refugees. These frustrations had deepened when the UNHCR suspended all pending cases after the ceasefire between the government in Khartoum and the Sudan People's Liberation Army, the precursor to the peace agreement. This agreement had now opened the door to undesired repatriation, unquestionably contributing to the protest in Mustafa Mahmoud Park.

The majority of refugees in Egypt came from the south of Sudan. The two neighbours were formerly a single country and, as a result of the peace treaty of January 2005, people could circulate, work, live and buy property—the so-called four freedoms—on both sides of the border. However, the realities many Sudanese in Cairo faced did not coincide with the benevolent provisions of the pact.

Contrary to the Sudanese whom Guterres had met in Uganda earlier in the year, the protesters at Mustafa Mahmoud Park had no intention of returning to their country. Nor did they want to remain in Egypt. Most shared the ambition of making it to the West.

Organised by a group of Sudanese, the protest coincided with the beginning of Ramadan and aimed to grab the attention of both the authorities and the international media. After a month, around 2,500 Sudanese were living in the small park. The full picture became most apparent at dusk, when the men arrived from their daily activities around the city, and on weekends, when still more people arrived out of solidarity. The conditions were precarious. During the day, there was little shade under the few trees around the park and, with winter approaching, nights in the open would become increasingly harsh.

Slogans such as "We are the victims of mismanagement" and "We reject local integration" were attached to the park's low railings. Such messages soon turned into demands that were listed in Arab and in English.

These demands led the UNHCR to question its initial view of the situation, and to conclude that many demonstrators, perhaps the majority, were not refugees and, therefore, not their responsibility.[5] As time passed, the growing number of protesters and the rising impatience led the Agency to open negotiations and finally, on 17 December, to sign a written agreement with five Sudanese representatives. The UNHCR committed itself to re-evaluate all cases and to distribute immediately "a one-off financial assistance for housing" for all registered cases,[6] on the condition the protestors demobilised within five days. However, the protesters winced at the offer. They wanted additional guarantees that the agreement would be fully honoured and they intended to remain in the park until that happened.

New York was monitoring the situation, but believed "this had to be resolved at the UNHCR level." Secretary-General Annan's chief of staff, Malloch-Brown, explains: "I think that we did not have any direct political influence in Egypt and their ambassador to the UN was a particularly inflexible defender of the regime and, therefore, we left António Guterres to deal with this."

With no solution in sight, Guterres decided to send Nouicer as an emissary: "I met with the people in the park on three occasions and you cannot imagine their level of stubbornness," Nouicer remembers. "They believed the only solution to their problem was to get a plane to come and take them out of Egypt."

To the surprise and concern of all, on the afternoon of 29 December, 4,000 police officers flooded into the area around the park. On the following morning, the day marking the third month of occupation, the protesters were informed they were to be transferred on buses, by force if necessary, to camps where they would receive water, food and shelter.

In the following hours, as water cannons were fired on the crowds, successive attempts at negotiation were made, to no avail. At a given moment, the police began chanting nationalistic slogans and marching up and down as if warming up for battle.

By 5.30 am, the park was empty and reduced to silence, even though many objects were still lying around. Left behind were hundreds of mattresses and suitcases, toys, photographs, pieces of clothing and several identity cards, both blue and yellow. The initial death toll was twenty-seven, of whom half were women and children.[7]

"It was a particularly difficult and painful moment," explains Guterres, "because we don't have a police force, and depend on the local police, and we also couldn't criticise them because they were there to protect us. It's complicated because the Sudanese benefitted from the four freedoms regime in Egypt. They were under a form of protection which was better than the status of refugee. But that didn't always function as it should and I was always in doubt whether or not our team was doing the right thing or if it was also partly responsible for what happened."

After this incident, the UNHCR in Egypt relocated to a new office and reformulated its service, but it was not enough to deflect the rising criticism. In a letter addressed to the UN High Commissioner for Human Rights, twelve Egyptian NGOs called for an investigation that included the "conduct of the UNHCR."[8] But the letter pointed above all to the long history of "excessive use of force and other human rights violations committed by the security forces,"[9] providing, as an example, the recent "severe beating of peaceful demonstrators protesting President Mubarak's decision to rerun for the Presidency."[10]

Guterres' first reaction was to issue a statement declaring that "there is no justification for such violence and loss of life,"[11] words that were not well received by the Egyptian authorities. Responding in a *note verbale* to the UNHCR, Egypt's Permanent Mission to Geneva expressed "its astonishment,"[12] reminding that "the UNHCR Regional Office in Cairo called on the government of Egypt on 22 December 2005 to take appropriate measures to resolve this situation as a matter of urgency."[13]

In response, the UNHCR concurred that it had indeed solicited the intervention of the government, but "through peaceful means, without violence."[14] The message ended by reiterating "its appreciation of the Egyptian government's long and positive tradition of asylum,"[15] and making themselves available "to alleviate the impact of these events on the affected populations, and to support the Egyptian authorities in their future actions towards the protection of refugees."[16]

Seoul Train

It was March 2006, and Ron Redmond, the High Commissioner's spokesperson, was once again on a plane. It was going to be another long trip and Guterres' proposal was impossible to turn down. "I'm 6 feet 5 inches tall," says Redmond, "and he told me, 'I'm giving you special dispensation from flying economy class. I will fly economy class, you fly business class, but you have to carry my clothes.' He's very protective of his clothes; he likes to look good. He's always carrying his extra suits in a clothes bag and he has got his shoes all shined up. So, he said: 'You have to take my clothes into business class and make sure they're hung up properly in a closet and not wrinkled.'"

Departure: Geneva. Destination: Beijing. Flight time: ten hours and twenty minutes, announced the senior cabin crew member before take-off.

Guterres was the first High Commissioner for Refugees to catch this flight in nine years, although he had recently been to China, in his previous position as the leader of the Socialist International before joining the United Nations, and had met with President Hu Jintao.

Although China's paltry contribution of $250,000 to the UNHCR budget rivalled that of Liechtenstein, the relationship stretched back several decades, with its ups and downs, and always with an irritating stone in the shoe.

"When I was there," states Raymond Hall, who had worked in the UNHCR office in Beijing in the late 1980s, "China had very recently signed the International Refugee Convention, which was tied up with the major refugee influx coming from North Vietnam in the late 1970s. China sort of looked to the UNHCR then for assistance, but also as a vehicle for good publicity. Our relationship in those days with China was very close and it was very senior level—I met with people like Zhao Ziyang who was Prime Minister. Today, of course, having evolved so much, the UNHCR's access to the Chinese Government will be at a Director of Foreign Affairs level at best."

On the eve of the trip, Redmond had brought Guterres into the studio to watch a 2004 US documentary. *Seoul Train* denounced China's deportation of thousands of North Korean defectors who, when sent back to Pyongyang, faced torture, forced labour and even execution. Redmond thought the documentary, critical of the UNHCR, might shed some light on the array of reactions their visit to China was bound to provoke.

"It was an extremely difficult issue to deal with publicly," says Redmond. "We didn't want to blast the Chinese because there were certain actions that allow us to help North Korean refugees who were able to reach us. We had safe houses, that kind of thing. Also, we did not want to damage the situation of other refugees. For example, there are Central Asian refugees or even African refugees in China that the UNHCR was caring for. At the same time, we were being attacked by international NGOs and Christian organisations in the US for not doing enough. Some went as far as asking us to shut down our operations in China."

During the visit, which lasted three and a half days, Guterres came across an old acquaintance. China is vast, but the world is small, and Tang Jiaxuan, the Minister of Foreign Affairs with whom Portugal had negotiated the transfer of Macau, was now a member of the State Council, China's supreme centre of executive power.

This time around, however, the bilateral agenda was incomparably more delicate. The visit, notes the then UNHCR Director of the Asia-Pacific bureau, Janet Lim, "took place at a time when our relationship with China was difficult and tense and ordinarily we would not have been received at the level we were." Lim accompanied the High Commissioner to the official dinner with Jiaxuan and other Chinese officials, an evening which inevitably ran aground on the North Korean problem.

"China did not want to destabilise North Korea," says Guterres, "and wanted to avoid a massive influx of North Koreans. Every once in a while, they would send North Koreans back, saying they were not refugees but economic migrants. We would say that although the majority were migrants, there were political cases, and this created the need for very complicated negotiations. The Chinese always said, 'We're dealing with this according to national and international law.' And I would say, 'Fine, the problem is when national law is not in sync with international law.' But all of this needed quite a lot of discussion because with the Chinese, as everyone knows, there's a fundamental question: not losing face. Nothing is ever achieved by debating these things in public."

In the middle of dinner, with a high-stakes sparring match well under way, Guterres received a profoundly troubling report. News from Seoul was broadcasting the Chinese deportation of a North Korean who had played a central role in one of those very political cases.

Guterres recalls how he ended the dinner with Jiaxuan, who immediately scheduled another meeting for the next morning: "You know, the first thing is that I simply don't agree; secondly, it's when I'm here that you guys pull something like this?"

According to Lim, the High Commissioner, visibly disturbed, "spent sleepless hours strategising just how he might confront the Chinese over the incident without jeopardising the goodwill the visit had built up. During the meeting, he did not hide his emotions and his hurt and was quite honest, even while maintaining his politeness and decorum. It did appear that the incident had not been known to the higher authorities in Beijing."

Before returning to Geneva, there was still time for a press conference that began with a lengthy statement by the High Commissioner.

In the midst of a well-wrapped diplomatic speech, full of tributes to frankness, to openness, to dedication, to dialogue, to work, and to the inestimable cooperation of Beijing, Guterres referred *en passant* to his "clear objections in relation to news that there had been a recent deportation, in my opinion in breach of the 1951 Convention."[17] In sum, he accused China—on Chinese territory—of violating international law.

However, the press were so intent on accusing Guterres of inaction over North Korea that his allegation was lost in the commotion. The accusation was never raised in the press and not even the Chinese diplomats present at the briefing bothered to protest.

"It was a very important and very difficult visit," Guterres concludes, "even though the Chinese have always treated me very well. As for them, I was—and continue to be—a friend, because of Macau and because of all the gestures made by the Socialist International."

13

THE NURSE AND THE SURGEON

Raymond Hall did not return with good news from India. The former Director of Human Resources, now in charge of reforming the UNHCR, was seeking an ideal location for a variety of administrative and operational services that would be moving out of Geneva. "I would have been very inclined to support a proposal for Chennai. The problem was that the Indian government wasn't willing to consider it. The UNHCR has this particular albatross, that it has to carry around its neck, of governments saying, 'Well, thank you, we're not so delighted that you want to open an office here because it might actually attract refugees, even though it's just a back-office function.'"

Previous High Commissioners had experimented with changing the way resources were managed and working more closely with field operations, but had never gone as far as Guterres envisioned. The plan was daring, even for the UN framework. "He was one of the first," recalls Josette Sheeran, Executive Director of the World Food Programme between 2007 and 2012, "to really realise that the era of the mainframe computer—one organisation and one place flinging outputs around the world and bringing them back to home base—really needed to change. I think the step was then replicated by many agencies and the secretariat itself."

Initially, twenty possible sites were considered for the new UNHCR centre. Following a thorough selection process, led by

PricewaterhouseCoopers, four locations were shortlisted: Chennai and Kuala Lumpur were rapidly discarded due to lack of political will in India and Malaysia; which left Bucharest and Budapest.

As recent arrivals to the European Union, Romania and Hungary displayed similar advantages, starting with their proximity to Geneva. Budapest, however, offered more compensations: up to $80 million of savings over a decade. The decision was made when the government came up with an offer that was impossible to refuse. The Hungarian socialists, after winning the elections—beating the Viktor Orbán-led opposition—were willing to provide high-quality, well-equipped and furnished premises in the capital's downtown, cost free for the next ten years.[1]

As expected, the move generated controversy among staff in Geneva, especially from those who feared redundancy. They even appealed to the UN courts to try to ensure their jobs would not be at stake. Perhaps due to his socialist background and experience in working with trade unions when he was in government, Guterres took part in discussions with the UNHCR staff council and gave instructions to mitigate the impacts caused by the move to Budapest.

In the end, suitable solutions were found for nearly all of the staff involved. "There were only two left out," Guterres remembers, "and we solved their problem as well, and there was no collective firing, but it was a very difficult situation at the beginning."

Nevertheless, there were human resources problems the move to Budapest was unable to solve. For example, Pricewaterhouse-Coopers' diagnosis identified huge failures in performance evaluations. It seemed strange that "no single case of unsatisfactory performance was recorded in 2005"[2] and that there were apparently "no ongoing sanctions or corrective actions for underperformance."[3] "One of the problems he was not able to solve," notes Feller, "was how to actually dismiss people, due to the nature of the contract, the length of the contract and the rules about the field rotation policies."

By demonstrating its capacity as an organisation dedicated to cutting costs and to improving services, Budapest was the perfect calling card for mending relationships with creditors. This aspect was, by far, what Guterres most valued: "We multiplied our activity by three or four times, all the while lowering our expenditures for personnel, and this meant that we had a huge surge in donor confidence."

A Lawless Land

"How am I going to get out of this one?" As he landed in Tehran, Guterres sensed he was already on very thin ice. Iran was high on George W. Bush's wanted list and was once again under sanctions due to its nuclear programme. Further complicating the situation, the recently elected president, Mahmoud Ahmadinejad, had rapidly confirmed his reputation as a hardliner. The High Commissioner's main interlocutor within the government on the subject of refugees was the experienced Minister of the Interior, Mostafa Pourmohammadi, who was about as popular in Washington as Ahmadinejad.

Above all else, Guterres needed to come out of Tehran retaining the support of two apparently irreconcilable adversaries: on the one hand, the United States, UNHCR's most important donor; and on the other hand, Iran, the world's second-largest recipient of refugees. The trip's central theme was vital to both powers; allowing himself to get too close to either one would offend the other.

In 2006, for the twenty-fourth year in a row, the world's largest single population of refugees came from Afghanistan. Such a massive and prolonged exodus reflected the history of one of the poorest places in the world. Ever since 1979, after the overthrow of the Shah, belligerence was a constant and governance seemed impossible.

Over the decades, each new assault on power had given Afghans new reasons to leave. There were around 900,000 Afghan refugees in Iran alone. Some had been born and raised there without ever having set foot in their own country, and only a small minority lived in refugee camps. The situation called for periodic visits by the High Commissioner, especially since "Iran was never an easy country because they didn't want us to be involved," underlines Lim. "They just want to deal with everything themselves."

Despite this, Guterres respected Iran's maturity—a rare attribute in the region: "We were involved in complex negotiations, but people should be aware that Iran is a real state, that Iran functions. For better or worse, it functions."

In the wake of the American military invasion and the election of President Hamid Karzai at the end of 2001, nearly 800,000 refugees had returned to Afghanistan from Iran, many by their own means, others under the auspices of an agreement established between Kabul, Tehran and the UNHCR. Whether as the result of a downturn in the economic well-being of Iran, or an uptick in political pressure, authorities here and there had sought to hurry Afghans out of the country.

At this precipitous juncture, the High Commissioner needed to guarantee that the repatriation process would continue to unfold gradually and, above all else, on a voluntary basis. However, upon arrival in Tehran, on his first official visit to the bastion of Shia Islam, Guterres hardly exuded confidence: "I was worried because Ahmadinejad had been elected and I thought to myself, 'These guys are going to kick all the Afghans out.'" During the first twenty minutes of the meeting with Pourmohammadi, at the Ministry of the Interior, Guterres' initial concerns were confirmed: "It was a diatribe against the West, against the United Nations, against the Americans. It had nothing to do with me, but I had to listen to all of it." Nevertheless, at the end of his blunt and truculent sermon, Pourmohammadi surprised the Portuguese High Commissioner by confronting him with an argument that would profoundly mark his mandate at the UNHCR:

"I know why you came here. You came because you're worried. You think we're going to mistreat and expel the Afghans. But have no worry because God commands us to protect our brothers and sisters."

Iran, however, represented only one dimension to the Afghan refugee problem, and not even the largest part. That role was played by Pakistan, where the sprawling power of the military hindered the work of the UN and demanded a different approach from the High Commissioner. Under the command of General Musharraf, the country with the world's largest refugee population had long since announced what kind of strategy they would be adopting.

Larry King: "The refugees, how are you handling the problem? How many are coming over the border?"

Pervez Musharraf: "This is causing a great concern to us [...] we already have about 2.5 million refugees here in Pakistan. And you can compare this when you think of Australia not accepting even 200 refugees [...] our point-of-view has always been that we must establish camps across the border in Afghanistan and all assistance to the refugees must be given there, so that people go back to Afghanistan instead of making them comfortable here in Pakistan."[4]

But the head of the UNHCR saw Afghan refugees as a problem and a responsibility to be shared by all three governments— Ahmadinejad's Iran, Musharraf's Pakistan and Karzai's Afghanistan. Hence, Guterres' trip involved two additional stopovers: one in Pakistan and another one in Afghanistan. In Kabul, he met Karzai at the presidential palace and the conversation made clear the fragility of his negotiating position: "There was enormous pressure to reduce the number of refugees in Iran and Pakistan," remembers Guterres. "Knowing that the conditions weren't great for reabsorption, our strategy was to keep telling the government of Afghanistan that, 'You have to make an effort to show that you want this, even if later you find out that you can't do it. What you can't do… is to say you don't want it. You have to show that you have policies in place for the reintegration and return of the refugees. We know that you won't be able to do this in large numbers, but you have to show your willingness so that I can try to convince the Pakistanis and the Iranians to put up with them for a little longer. So I can tell them that this will take time, but that you are working on it.'" The problem was that "Karzai… didn't seem to care much about what I was saying."

In addition to the government's lack of interest, the latest news on the ground raised further concerns. The number of returning refugees was decreasing and attacks were going up. Just a few weeks before Guterres' arrival, in May 2006, an NGO's medical team had been ambushed and killed in southern Afghanistan, in Kandahar Province—a known bastion of the Taliban—where there was a UNHCR office.

With the political meetings wrapped up in Kabul, Guterres travelled about 90 miles east, almost to the Afghan border, where he met with a few hundred families, recent arrivals from Pakistan, living in an extremely isolated location. Close by, on the other side of the border, was a region well known to the intelligence services—with around five million inhabitants in an area the size of Massachusetts—which the Pakistanis referred to as "the lawless land" and which Guterres, in private conversations, described as the most worrisome zone on the planet.

Inhabited by tribes that still preserved the independence granted during British colonialism, Pakistan state law did not apply in these parts.[5] Misrule, banditry and illiteracy offered the ideal conditions for movements such as the Taliban and organisations like al-Qaeda, to train soldiers, plan attacks or exchange information, while evading capture or targeting by American drones.

The Afghans Guterres met near the border had until recently lived in these tribal areas, in one of the thirty refugee camps that Islamabad had ordered to close under the justification of national security. The UNHCR was sympathetic of such reason, given the pall of insecurity disrupted the flow of essential humanitarian supplies. However, the Agency had often been in disagreement with the restrictive target dates set for closing the camps and the excessive speed with which these closures took place. In many of these diplomatic altercations, the High Commissioner attempted to persuade the Pakistani authorities by employing their own security argument, but with a slight twist.

"I had a meeting with Musharraf," Guterres recalls, "which I will never forget, and I told him, 'You have an army, you have secret services, here in your own territory all is under control. Now, imagine what it's like over there—there's no army, no secret services, there's nothing. You send them over there and whatever happens to them is up to God. You'll create a security problem for Pakistan that you'll never be done with.' He looked back at me and it seems that he believed what I was saying because the campaign that had already begun was brought to a halt."

Having witnessed the poverty with which Afghanistan welcomed back its own people, one of the UNHCR representatives under Guterres in the country would later classify the operation—which had been launched during the Lubbers period—as "the biggest mistake the UNHCR ever made,"[6] in the sense that "we thought if we gave humanitarian assistance then macro development would kick in."[7] Speaking to Agence France-Presse, Peter Nicolaus pulled no punches, arguing that what the Agency overlooked was that "it's the income that counts, the livelihood" and "in very simple terms" they needed not just to facilitate Afghans' return, but to ensure that this was in the long-term interests of the returnees, "to find jobs for people coming back."[8] In a rare moment of self-criticism, he even shared an example from the field: "You can build five roads to a village and the farmers will benefit because they can go to the next town to sell their vegetables. But the returnee doesn't benefit at all. He has nothing to sell at the market."[9]

In any case, during those first years at the UNHCR, the Afghan-Pakistan-Iran triangle became an important showcase for the partly political, partly humanitarian style of the Portuguese statesman. His capacity as a diplomat undoubtedly began to be put to the test and he would now have to apply it to yet another dangerous mission in the region.

If This Fails, Everything Fails

After a period spent in Lisbon, John Holmes had been Ambassador to Paris for five years. Now, in 2007, it was time to take up a new post, which was precisely the reason why Prime Minister Blair was calling. He should get himself to New York as soon as possible as the process of assigning senior positions at the United Nations was already underway. Objective: to regain the leadership of the Department of Political Affairs.[10]

Holmes followed his instructions, but when he met with the Secretary-General elect, South Korean Ban Ki-moon, he realised he had arrived too late: "He did not say so directly, but [Ban] had already promised the position to the Americans in exchange for their support for his candidacy."[11] The alternative proposal, the position of Under-Secretary-General for Humanitarian Affairs, was hardly playing to the diplomat's strengths. "I explained that I knew nothing about humanitarian affairs. Moreover, I was not sure that, being British, I had the right nationality for the job. We were seen by many as military interveners, particularly after Iraq—not the best recommendation, even if the UK was a generous aid contributor. Ban was unimpressed by these arguments."[12]

In April 2007, after four months in the position, John Holmes crossed the Atlantic to participate in a humanitarian conference on... Iraq. Contrary to what the UNHCR had predicted, the US invasion had not unleashed a huge flow of refugees, at least not in the first years. Indeed, following the fall of Saddam Hussein, 300,000 Iraqis had returned to the country—many were Kurds returning from Iran. However, in recent months the panorama had shifted, especially in the wake of the bombing of the al-Askari Shiite shrine in Samarra,[13] in north-west Iraq, and everything that followed: reprisals, numerous attacks on Sunni targets and hundreds of deaths.

The rise in tensions was also reflected in the growing number of refugees. There were now two million of them, mostly concentrated in Syria and Jordan.

Bringing up the subject in a call with Annan, who at the time was easing his way out of office, Guterres put forward his strategy: "This is getting out of control. We have to do something; we have to set up a conference. Either you do this in New York or I'll do it in Geneva. See what you want to do."

The High Commissioner had already been engaging with this particular issue prior to taking up his UN position, when he was with the Socialist International. As well as visiting Baghdad at the behest of the National Democratic Institute, he had also sponsored an initiative in Rome that brought together several Iraqi politicians to talk about the future of their country.[14] One participant, Hoshyar Zebari, was now the Foreign Minister, while another participant, Jalal Talabani, also Kurdish, had ascended all the way to the top, serving as the President of Iraq from 2006.

In any case, the event in Geneva incurred some serious risks. According to Sultan-Khan, "This conference was the first major undertaking by António Guterres as High Commissioner and it could have gone totally wrong. He even told me once: 'Look, if this fails, everything fails,' as it would immediately have affected his mandate and he had only been in office for less than two years."

To heighten the stakes further, the leading players at the confer-ence had hardly ever agreed to appear on the same stage together. Bringing together such impulsive temperaments, each with their own contrasting agendas, and at a time when 150,000 American troops were on the ground in Iraq, could have easily led the discus-sions to descend into inflamed rhetoric and revanchism.

Guterres diligently set about working on the preparations. In addition to giving a speech to the Arab League,[15] he persuaded Zebari to attend the conference, and he met beforehand with Condoleezza Rice in Washington. One of Guterres' goals, his spokesperson Ron Redmond recalls, was "to raise the profile in a way that didn't upset the Americans because the UNHCR [had not been] saying a lot about the devastation that the US involvement had caused in Iraq and that was a politically sensitive situation, since ultimately we had responsibility for those refugees, and the NGOs were becoming increasingly vocal about why the UN was remaining silent."

In the early morning of 17 April, the traffic of diplomatic-plated vehicles and taxis around the European headquarters of the United Nations, the Palais des Nations, in Geneva, was intense. One of those cars drove John Holmes to the doors of the complex which, on this occasion, was hosting the US Under-Secretary of State, the Syrian Vice Minister of Foreign Affairs, and the Iranian delegation, headed by the Ambassador and including an adviser to the Minister of the Interior, all under one roof. Adding to this list were Zebari, several senior representatives of the Jordanian Crown, and the regional Red Cross leadership.

"It was excellent to get all those agencies and governments around the table in a way that few other people could have done," relates Holmes, who found himself just a few metres away from the High Commissioner as he officially opened the conference. "Guterres has that combination of commitment to humanitarian issues, but also a strong awareness of the links to sort of understand the broader con-text and to understand how to make things happen."

Excellencies, Distinguished delegates, Ladies and Gentlemen, [...]]Iraq is probably the best-known conflict on the globe. But, despite the global spotlight, Iraq may also be its least well-known humanitarian crisis.

[…] In the most significant displacement in the Middle East since the dramatic events of 1948, one in eight Iraqis have been driven from their homes. […] It is the biggest urban caseload ever dealt with. […] More important than terminology—whether a state calls a person a refugee or not—is the tangible protection afforded that person.[16]

When, after the end of the conference, he once again went before the cameras, the High Commissioner arrived with Foreign Minister Zebari at his side to announce the single most important accomplishment of the congress: the Iraqi government had committed to launch a $25 million aid programme for refugees, thereby lightening the load for neighbouring Syria and Jordan.

"That was the first time the [post-Saddam] Iraqi government had contributed to any refugee operation," points out Nouicer, the UNHCR operational coordinator. "This was also the start of very generous contributions, and, from that time onwards, we never had any financial difficulties in providing assistance and support to Iraqi refugees in the region."

Despite this, it was a long time before the Iraq programme saw the light of day. In fact, months dragged by and the $25 million was still being delayed. In his contacts with donors, Guterres complained—not about Zebari, whose support he continued to praise, but rather about Prime Minister Nouri al-Maliki's sectarian attitude.

Maliki seemed to perceive the Iraqi exodus—mostly Sunnis—in light of the repression and exile that he had experienced as a Shiite under the previous regime. "He did not believe these people were truly refugees," claims Nouicer. "He just thought they were Saddam Hussein supporters who had left the country out of fear of prosecution by the new government."

On his return to the region, in February 2008, Guterres finally met with King Abdullah II of Jordan, and Syrian President Bashar al-Assad, two of UNHCR's most valuable partners in the Iraqi crisis.

Before leading the UNHCR, Guterres had never visited Syria, nor had he ever engaged in a face-to-face conversation with Assad, who was sixteen years younger and nearly a foot taller. During their meeting in Damascus, the High Commissioner was particularly interested on a comment made by the young Syrian: "A great worry of his was, 'You should not allow religious sectarianism among refugees. You should be careful of Islamic NGOs, and some of the Christian ones, that come here and engage in proselytising. Protect the secular character.'"

Maintaining a positive attitude regarding refugees, Assad raised no objections to the list of requests the High Commissioner had brought with him. However, Guterres recalls, "It was already very clear" that neither the word nor the powers of the President were absolute. "On a number of occasions he agreed to things that we were not able to bring to fruition later because his subordinates did not follow through. Or rather, he wasn't in complete control of the governmental apparatus and I think that still today he does not control it. There are various centres of power there. He's a kind of central figure and nothing will get done without him. He's a fundamental reference, but he doesn't run everything."

At that time, Syria had already overtaken Iran as home to the world's second-largest refugee population. According to estimates, the total was already as high as 1.5 million, and packed buses and taxis brought in new arrivals every day.

The refugees lived mostly in rooms or apartments in urban areas and, at the time of Guterres' visit, only 10 per cent had registered with the UNHCR.[17] The Agency was expanding its operations and, through agreements with ministries, acted at times as a development bank, financing the construction of schools and the acquisition of ambulances and, at other times, as a health insurance agency, covering medical treatments and supporting Red Cross clinics, which supported the most vulnerable in Damascus, Aleppo, Homs and Idlib.

UNHCR's positive relations with the Syrian government were such that one agreement even allowed staff from the US Department of Homeland Security to work in Agency offices in Damascus. Washington did not even have an accredited ambassador there, and maintained a lengthy, long-established list of grievances and sanctions deriving from Syrian ties with Moscow, Tehran, Hezbollah, and even Pyongyang. Nevertheless, the Iraqi refugee issue contained common interests both sides wanted to safeguard—that is, without losing face. "The United States had an extensive programme to resettle Iraqis," recounts Guterres, "but to resettle a person in the United States an interview was first necessary and the person had to be verified, etc. Many of those people were in Syria, but the United States and Syria did not have [full diplomatic] relations. The agreement reached was that Homeland Security would conduct interviews at UNHCR premises. They couldn't happen in the American Embassy—because the Syrian government wouldn't permit that—but they let them go ahead in the UNHCR premises."

There were other UN agencies and resources on the ground, and one of Holmes' tasks as Chief of the Office for the Coordination of Humanitarian Affairs was to keep everyone in contact and, whenever possible, working harmoniously. "We ran into difficulties with the UNHCR. We thought they were keeping us too much at a distance. The programme was heavily financed by the Americans and the Americans had particular views about how that should be done... We weren't sure UNHCR always got that one right."

In fact, by 2008, relations between the UNHCR and the United Nations headquarters in New York had trodden quite a complicated path for some years.

Peace-building

The United Nations presents itself as a single body, cooperative and synergetic, but the different agencies do not always behave as such. The UNHCR had long viewed New York as some kind of remote headquarters, bureaucratic and disconnected from the field. As for New York, by the time Guterres took office, they also had their long-established opinion about the UNHCR: an agency that was overly defensive of its own jurisdiction and which was not shy of reminding partners that its mandate came directly from the General Assembly.

"They [the UNHCR] didn't have a very strong representation in New York," says Holmes, "and they somehow seem, not to me necessarily, but to others, a bit distant, a bit separate. There were these issues which arose in certain circumstances where we wanted to coordinate all humanitarian work in a country and the UNHCR would say, 'Well, we will work with you but, when it comes to refugees, that's our responsibility. It has nothing to do with you. You stay away from that.'"

Of his time as Under-Secretary, Holmes also recalls how "the UNHCR and António Guterres were always the most sensible and the most committed to humanitarian principles—they were sort of more in line with the NGO's slightly more purist view—which wasn't necessarily the case of all the UN agencies." Nevertheless, "he was the one whose views I respected most and to whom I would turn if we were having a difficult problem."

He was highly impressed with the conduct of the High Commissioner—even more so than during the Geneva conference on Iraq—during his intervention in South Ossetia, in the summer of 2008. The risks in going to the Caucasus during a time of escalated tensions between the separatists—supported by Russia—and Georgia, at the time vigorously flirting with NATO, were clear.[18] Redmond, who had been with the UN for twenty-seven years, was surprised at the results of Guterres' meeting in Moscow with the Russian Foreign Minister Sergey Lavrov: "He was the first UN official to actually go down into South Ossetia. During that mission, we also visited a big emergency centre that was run by the government. I don't know how many international visitors were ever given access... It was quite impressive, a huge building, one floor with hundreds of workers and all sat at computer terminals with big-screen televisions across the front of the room featuring different emergencies—weather disturbances, earthquakes, any kind of civil defence problem anywhere in the former Soviet Union."

On one of his first trips to New York as High Commissioner, Guterres delivered a speech on the role of the UNHCR inside the UN's broader structure, addressed to the Department of Peacekeeping Operations. The Under-Secretary-General responsible for the department, Jean-Marie Guéhenno from France, thought Guterres' testimony would motivate his staff by evoking the human side of their work, which was not always visible due to the excessive focus on the Security Council. After all, the man in charge of refugees had previously been Prime Minister, he had run a government before leading the UNHCR. In describing the scope of the former and the nature of the second, Guterres resorted to a metaphor about the way hospitals work: "Look, we are just the nurse. What we can do is give the aspirin and help staunch the blood. But the surgeon, who will really heal the patient, that will make sure the underlying problem is dealt with, that's you guys."

In addition to New York, the High Commissioner's itinerary in the United States would often take him to Washington, where he engaged with US members of Congress. He had good relationships with the Democrats, especially with Senator Patrick Leahy of Vermont. He also began to grow closer to the Republicans, in particular with Lindsey Graham, Senator for South Carolina, who Guterres today calls "a great friend."

When in Washington, he might also attend a university conference, present an award or meet certain of his civil society partners. There were commitments of a more informal nature than others and, at one particular dinner, he sat next to Samantha Power, a White House staff member. Guterres was already a familiar name to President Obama's human rights adviser, and not only because he was the High Commissioner for Refugees. Power had written a biography on Sérgio Vieira de Mello, and Guterres' name had come up in the chapter on East Timor. Guterres would later write the preface to the Portuguese edition of that book. Nevertheless, this was the first time they had met face-to-face.

"I have never before heard anybody bring up Jürgen Habermas at a Georgetown dinner party," states Power, "especially in the context of talking about refugees and democracy, which I believe was the topic of the evening. He was clearly cut from a different cloth than the average UN official. He kind of shines the light of his intellect on the world's problems; he's not interested in theory for theory's sake."

Both the Portuguese and the American had only just landed in their positions. Guterres was hardly planning to become the Secretary-General of the United Nations, nor did Power imagine she would be sitting in the Security Council at the very moment of his election.

14

SPRING TIDE

Guterres looked at Geneva simply as a place to work. "It's the most boring place on Earth, there's nothing else to do but work," he would occasionally confide to his closest staff. His UNHCR working day rarely finished before 8 pm, when the High Commissioner would customarily retire to his apartment. On the way, he might ask the driver to stop over at Payot, one of the few bookstores nearby, to purchase another history book and dedicate the evening to a long-standing hobby. "For the last fifty years, I read a bit of history each night, from all periods and about everything. I went through a phase when I was fascinated with the French medieval-ists—Duby, Le Goff, Braudel and even Chaunu. I moved on to the English and my favourite is A. J. P. Taylor. And later I discovered that it's in American universities that the best history is being written today. Many of these books are by authors who seem foreign, because the names are South Korean, Japanese, Chinese."

Guterres lived alone in Geneva and took advantage of most of his free weekends to spend time with his family in Portugal. Once in a while, there was enough time to meet with Melícias and other old friends who concurred that the post of High Commissioner seemed to have been invented for Guterres. It not only responded to his long-standing restless and Christian urge to care for the most vulnerable, but it also allowed him to travel the world building

163

bridges between adversaries who, despite their close proximity, remained trapped in their antagonistic positions. Patching estranged relationships through dialogue was inherent to Guterres' nature; much more so than the conflicts and ruptures which form such a part of the brutal game of national politics.

His five-year term at the UNHCR would last until 2010, and by 2009 the habitual diplomatic consultations for a second term were afoot. Guterres was gearing for an expected second mandate under considerably different circumstances from the ones when he first came to the job. There was a new President of the United States, an African-American and a Democrat, to whom Guterres had written on the occasion of his inauguration, and who had even chosen Guterres' close friend, Hillary Clinton, as the new Secretary of State.

Although officially apolitical, the UNHCR was keenly sensitive to the trends in political opinion in general, and to the thoughts of Washington in particular. After all, US foreign policy frequently had an impact on UNHCR's actions. In fact, during the first month of his presidency, Obama confirmed major changes in Iraq and Afghanistan, from where came nearly half of the refugees currently under the Agency's protection:

> Good morning Marines. Good morning Camp Lejeune. Good morning Jacksonville. [...]

> America can no longer afford to see Iraq in isolation from other priorities: we face the challenge of refocusing on Afghanistan and Pakistan. [...] The first part of this strategy is therefore the responsible removal of our combat brigades from Iraq. [...] Let me say this as plainly as I can: by August 31, 2010, our combat mission in Iraq will end.[1]

At the same time that the Democratic administration was reorganising troop deployments in the Middle East, they were also adding new issues to the global agenda, such as closing down the prison in Guantanamo Bay, support for which they convened Guterres' team. "The US approached us about any assistance we might be able to offer regarding Guantanamo prisoners," Erika Feller reports. "Such matters were always discussed with the High Commissioner prior to settling on the UNHCR response. I believe limited assistance, essentially of an advocacy type with selected governments, was undertaken in some cases."

In addition to the new US President, there was also a new UN Secretary-General. Lacking the charisma and media-savvy approach—not to mention the articulate English—of Annan, the South Korean Ban Ki-moon took some time to assert himself in the West. Guterres had never met Ban personally and, in contrast to the Annan years, his relationship with the new head of the United Nations was notably more distant. Courtesy had replaced friend-ship, and duty took the place of admiration. Time would soon tell that this was no trivial issue.

Another looming change came from the new economic cycle. Guterres' second term at the helm of the UNHCR (2010–15) coincided with the most serious international economic crisis since the Great Depression. Some of the main humanitarian donors were experiencing recessions and rising levels of unemployment, all favourable forces towards a rise in xenophobia. For those trumpet-ing forms of nationalism—a rapidly spreading phenomenon—the solution was, as always, more than evident: closing ranks against illegal immigrants, whether those already in the country or those trying to get in.

History was once again threatening to repeat itself, as it had done so in the many well-documented stories that lined Guterres' bookshelves. Of the French historians he had read with great atten-tion, Georges Duby asserts the existence of the absolute foreigner in the Middle Ages, "the one who did not belong to the Christian community—the pagan, the Jew, the Muslim."[2] He even reminds us—recalling what people of the period might themselves have said—what fate held in store for them, "these infidels, either con-vert them or, if not, destroy them."[3]

Another of Guterres' French historian references, Fernand Braudel, examined this "game of the strong,"[4] as he called the per-sistent clashes between peoples. In his writings, he argues how, before a culture reaches maturity, "adjacent civilisations exploit it in a thousand ways."[5]

Many of the books in Guterres' library analyse the topic of hubris, as is the case with a work by A. P.J. Taylor that relates how, in 1930s Germany, "unemployment, the result of the economic crisis, sapped the spirit of the skilled workers, who were the only reliable republicans";[6] and how, in the run-up to World War II, the German middle class had become "half-hearted, indifferent to events, feeling they stood for a cause which was already lost, ready to respond, though with shame, to a 'national' appeal."[7]

Whether resulting from the twists of history or the individual turns of the present, Guterres knew the landscape had already shifted by the time the United Nations General Assembly renewed his mandate as High Commissioner for Refugees for another five years, until 2015.

African in Spirit

"Look, if you are refugees, cross the border and I'll help you. But if you stay on the other side..."

Speaking about this absurdity was inevitable among UNHCR colleagues. In the end, this was an old dilemma, now becoming increasingly pressing: how to deal with those who were internally displaced from their "former habitual residence,"[8] due to persecution "for reasons of race, religion, nationality, membership of a particular social group or political opinion,"[9] but who could not be formally considered refugees? They were just as much in need of shelter and support, thus meeting all the requirements under the Refugee Convention... with one exception: they were still within their country's borders.

If they haven't taken that last step—that which, on any administrative map, would place them over the border—the international community refers to them by another name: internally displaced persons (IDPs).

Without the official refugee status, some might say they do not fall under the responsibility of the UNHCR even though, given the flexibility with which the human spirit sometimes supersedes the law, the Agency has been assisting multitudes of IDPs since the 1970s.

The issue was attenuated in 2011, following a timely division of functions among UN agencies.[10] "We certainly welcomed the fact the UNHCR wanted to take more responsibility for IDPs because if they didn't, no one else was going to do it," recalls John Holmes, then the Under-Secretary in New York responsible for humanitarian affairs, "but I think the issue was controversial both inside the UNHCR and inside some countries that said this was going to dilute our attention to refugees."

Even though the subject divided opinion, everyone in Geneva had known for quite some time which side Guterres favoured. "In the very first meeting which I attended after he became High Commissioner," describes the then African bureau chief, the Ugandan George Okoth-Obbo, "he said to us that he saw the UNHCR's engagement with IDPs as a life and death matter."

It was undoubtedly a humanitarian imperative but also a means for the UNHCR to assert its relevance: "Human displacement was becoming much messier," adds Raymond Hall, the man largely responsible for the sweeping Budapest reform Guterres had ordered in his first term, "and Guterres very quickly saw that, in order to remain relevant both with governments and within the UN system, and get the funding to address the needs of its core beneficiaries, who were the refugees, the UNHCR had to demonstrate it was important in terms of the work it was doing with internally displaced peoples, returnees and so on."

Broadly off the public agenda, the number of internally displaced persons by conflict or violence had climbed to 27.1 million people by 2009, more than double the number of refugees under the jurisdiction of the UNHCR.[11] Around 40 per cent of the displaced were in Africa, where in October 2009 Guterres was part of the first real high-level political effort to discuss the subject. The High Commissioner travelled to Kampala, Uganda, to attend the signing of an unprecedented convention on the protection of the displaced, an initiative of the African Union supported by the UNHCR from the outset.

The High Commissioner invited Okoth-Obbo to accompany him on this trip, since the Ugandan had participated in drafting the convention. The meeting was held at Speke Resort, on the banks of Lake Victoria, one of the few four-star hotels in Kampala with one of the equally few conference centres large enough to accommodate the thirty-six countries attending the Convention for the Protection and Assistance of Internally Displaced Persons in Africa.

From the stage, Guterres could easily take in the whole measure of the hall, and it really did seem like a session of the UN General Assembly circumscribed to African countries. In the absence of the Secretary-General, that role fell to Guterres, who read a declaration to the whole continent on behalf of Ban Ki-moon. In those moments, before an audience of heads of state, ministers and ambassadors, his voice was that of the Secretary-General, his words were those of the Secretary-General. In that moment, Guterres was the Secretary-General.

The convention was already well underway when Guterres spoke again, this time as the High Commissioner. Given the sensitivity of the issue, the efforts were not a mere formality, and the proceedings even had to be suspended at one point to respond to the objections of the Zimbabwe President, Robert Mugabe. Nevertheless, at the end of the conference, the Kampala Convention was approved, setting an official definition for IDPs as those who, due to not only violence, but also "natural or human-made disasters, [...] have been forced or obliged to flee or to leave their homes or places of habitual residence",[12] while still remaining in their own country.

He drew loud applause when he introduced himself as "European by birth, yet African in spirit," recalls Okoth-Obbo. In fact, Guterres had maintained a special relationship with Africa, dating back to his earliest days at the Socialist International. Whenever one of the UNHCR African service directors met with the High Commissioner in Geneva, his advisers could practically sense the purse strings loosening. "How much will this meeting cost us?" they would wonder. However, this affinity was not simply abstract; it was also visible out in the field. With twenty years of UNHCR experience over Guterres, Okoth-Obbo travelled the region with his boss and notes, "He evinced exceptional knowledge of African culture, which was often disarming, and helped create a good ambience for engagement and dialogue. He also conveyed what I might call the right attitude, including being anti-colonial, anti-imperialist, anti-hegemonic and pro-Pan Africanist. In a number of meetings with leaders, some would actually refer to him throughout as Prime Minister and not as High Commissioner."

This was certainly not the case with the President of the Democratic Republic of the Congo, the African country with the most internally displaced persons, apart from Sudan. Most were located in the turbulent region of Kivu, where the Congolese army, supported by the largest contingent of Blue Helmets deployed worldwide,[13] fought several local militias. One statistic pointed to 5.4 million deaths by 2007, making this the bloodiest conflict since World War II.[14]

Covering an area larger than Mexico, the Congo, once the King of Belgium's private property, abounded as much with raw materials needed for the production of arms, automobiles and smartphones as it did in violations of human rights. Slavery, torture, civilian massacres and the generalised use of child soldiers were widespread. Furthermore, violence against women was practically the norm in this brutal, protracted civil conflict.

Dubbed by the United Nations as "the rape capital of the world,"[15] the Congo was a place where women knew that danger was always imminent. The accounts of victims were abundant and travelled fast. They knew what might befall them during the next raid. Each lived in the constant torment their turn was just around the corner, to be kidnapped, tied to a tree and repeatedly raped by her kidnappers for weeks at a time. That gang rape could happen in her own village, in front of her neighbours, and even her own family, in various, increasingly horrific manners. That contracting HIV was a likelihood, as was pregnancy without the possibility of abortion. After forced sex, she could be disfigured or murdered. If she survived, she would likely be banished and abandoned by her husband, which added guilt to the trauma. Still worse, as if there could be anything worse, to witness their own daughters, sometimes still toddlers, or their own mothers, aged 60 or more, go through the same agony of being taken as sex slaves and then returned months later permanently scarred both mentally and physically by their ordeal.

For humanitarian workers, Congo represented one of the most hostile places their career could lead them to. UNHCR offices there were not immune to the fires of conflict, forcing the Agency to suspend work in various areas for months at a time. In mid-2010, it seemed the minimum required conditions were once again in place to restart operations. So Guterres was once again back in the country.

The most notable feature of this visit to North Kivu was perhaps the fact the High Commissioner was not alone. He was accompanied by the World Food Programme (WFP) Executive Director, the American Josette Sheeran. Two voices speak louder than one, and many at the UNHCR perceived the WFP as their sister agency, unlike the International Organization for Migration (IOM) or the Office of the High Commissioner for Human Rights, with whom they shared some grudges.

It was a period of relative calm and nearly 900,000 Congolese had returned home over the previous months. Nevertheless, Guterres and Sheeran visited camps in Nyanzale, still packed with displaced persons, sheltering thousands of people, where security remained precarious, as a group of Congolese women explained to them. "The women were telling us," Sheeran recalls, "that they had to sleep out in the woods at night because marauders would come and rape them inside the boundaries of the UN working there. I was so upset I could barely talk. I was ready to just go and yell at the whole UN, but Guterres would always try to calm me down... his ability to stay present when we're hearing simply the worst things, to be able to give them the dignity of being heard and then to work together to try to find solutions that could make life easier for them was extraordinary."

Despite the clusters in Africa, it was actually in other regions of the world that the number of internally displaced persons was rising. This had become a chronic issue in Colombia, Iraq and Somalia, even though the deteriorating crisis in Yemen stood out at the time. Here was yet another country where refugees and displaced persons lived cheek by jowl inside the same national boundaries.

The refugees were mostly in South Yemen. They were above all Somalis who had survived the perilous crossing of the Gulf of Aden. The internally displaced were concentrated in the mountainous north that had experienced the Houthi insurgency against what they claimed was a corrupt regime that discriminated against them. These were Zaydi rebels, a minority branch of Shiites, who lived on both sides of the border between Yemen and Sunni Saudi Arabia. It was common knowledge there were foreign powers engaged in a behind-the-scenes tug of war, furnishing weapons and money, helping with propaganda or simply serving as inspiration. What was equally certain was that no ceasefire had lasted and the intensity of the combat had left an estimated 250,000 displaced,[16] with the majority having to fend for themselves. However, in reality, due to the restrictions on access to humanitarian aid, there was no clear certainty how many there were or even where they were.

Guterres visited the country in January 2011, and once again, he did not go alone. On this occasion, he was accompanied by the new European Commissioner for Humanitarian Aid and Civil Protection, the Bulgarian Kristalina Georgieva, an economist formerly at the World Bank who had held various high-ranking positions, including as its director based in Moscow. Although the European Union had long figured as one of UNHCR's largest donors, this was the first time the two institutions had officially made a joint visit to the field.

During the three-day visit, Guterres and Georgieva met with the different factions in conflict. In the South, they met with the Yemini Prime Minister and visited the refugee camp in Kharaz. In the North, they made their way to Sa'dah city, the heart of the rebellion, as reflected in the buildings reduced to mounds of rubble on which children played while military patrols marched by.

There, an opportunity arose to meet one of the Houthi leaders face-to-face. While not unprecedented, it was rare for the High Commissioner to be out in the field negotiating directly with armed groups.

Accustomed to the ever-present dangers, the local UNHCR staff strongly advised against such adventuring. But Guterres wanted to go and the Yemeni government authorised the trip, and so he met with the Houthis outside the security perimeter: "We met in a long room; they were sitting around and we were on one side. Their chief put his Kalashnikov on the floor, took a foot out of his sandal and rested it on the rifle and that is how we talked. Georgieva was with me and the truth is we reached an agreement about humanitarian access which they followed through."

However, conditions in the field were about to deteriorate even further. A few days after Guterres and Georgieva's visit, the revolutionary winds already gusting through North Africa began to blow in Yemen.

#Bouazizi

It seemed a day like any other in the small city of Sidi Bouzid, in the middle of Tunisia, far from the capital and the Mediterranean beaches packed with European tourists during the summer. The national economy was growing at a good pace, even if Sidi Bouzid remained a city of few opportunities, where even the most qualified, many of them young and with university educations, found it hard to avoid lengthy spells of unemployment.

The international community might not have known their names, but they did know their history. The loudly debated reports emanating from the United Nations Development Programme (UNDP) about the Arab world would, year after year, set out the dangerous and persistent disparities in the region.

2002: "Out of seven world regions, the Arab countries registered the lowest freedom score in the late 1990s."[17]

2003: "Access to digital media is also among the lowest in the world. There are just 18 computers per 1000 people in the region, compared to the global average of 78.3 per 1000 persons."[18]

2004: "With a few exceptions, some of which are cosmetic, free presidential elections involving more than one candidate do not occur in Arab countries."[19]

2005: "In most Arab States, reformers and human rights advocates have become open targets of official repression."[20]

2009: "Human insecurity is palpable and present in the alienation of the region's rising cohort of unemployed youth and in the predicaments of its subordinated women, and dispossessed refugees."[21]

In spite of such warnings, Arab dictators and dynasts remained sure that time was on their side. As always, they assumed, the cycles of governance would outlast those of the daily news, especially as the West found few friends among the ranks of their opposition and few motives for changing allegiances. After all, they valued the Arabic political stability, autocratic but secular, and they certainly treasured the petroleum and natural gas flowing uninterruptedly from the region.

The day of 17 December 2010 seemed like any other in Sidi Bouzid, and in the life of Mohamed Bouazizi. This young man of 26 years, with light brown eyes and short dark hair, was his family's primary breadwinner after his father had passed away. At one point, Bouazizi had begun searching for a more secure occupation—such as military service—rather than his usual work as a street vendor working out of a wooden cart. However, the doors he knocked on were all locked.

That morning, as normal, he loaded his cart with fruit and vegetables and was on his way to the souk, pushing his cart along, when he was stopped by the local police. This was a common occurrence, attempting to pocket a few dinars in exchange for turning a blind eye to the lack of a licence or some other bureaucratic infraction that probably did not exist.

At first, Bouazizi seemed to have escaped. After a heated discussion, the policewoman who had stopped him turned and walked away. But not for long. Quickly changing her mind, she insisted on a fine of 10 dinars—equal to Bouazizi's daily earnings. Then, when he refused to comply, she slapped him across the face, insulted the memory of his father and confiscated his electronic scales and all his produce.

Humiliated in public, Bouazizi took himself off to the city hall to protest and to get his belongings back. In vain.

Increasingly furious, he then tried the regional government headquarters. To no avail.

Exasperated with the indifference he encountered on all fronts, he bought a can of gasoline and returned to the governor's building. He doused himself in fuel, struck a match and set himself on fire.

Burning and writhing in the middle of the street, his skin melting under the flames, he screamed, "How do you expect me to make a living?"

In Geneva, Guterres had just attended the commemorations of the UNHCR's 60th anniversary when the first reports of the incident began filtering in. Al Jazeera reported that "footage posted on the Facebook social network site and YouTube showed several hundred protesters outside the regional government headquarters"[22] in Sidi Bouzid. Even though the state network had completely ignored the subject, "there were many messages of support for Bouazizi and the protest posted on Twitter."[23]

In reality, a protest was breaking out every morning somewhere in Tunisia and, for better or worse, the national authorities were dealing with them. Until the day, much to general amazement, the protests reached the capital. Then they spread across the country before engulfing the whole region. In the midst of this, Bouazizi succumbed to his burns, missing the political fires he had sparked.

By the time Guterres landed in Tunisia, in March 2011, the rioting had already spread to the other side of the border: "The crisis in Libya was erupting and we had a massive exodus into Tunisia of something like 20,000 people each day."

In Libya, the military—along with African mercenaries—loyal to the dictator Colonel Muammar Gaddafi responded to the uprising with an iron fist, firing not only on crowds, but also at the ambulances that came to evacuate the wounded.

In international politics, everyone had heard the whisperings of Gaddafi's eccentricities: his obsession with looking young, the luxurious Bedouin tent in which he lived, the Ukrainian nurse always tending him, the sinister all-female guard who protected him. In power for forty-one years, he had repaired his relationship with the United States in the 2000s by renouncing his nuclear programme and cooperating in the pursuit of Islamist radicals in North Africa, many of them al-Qaeda sympathisers. He was also simultaneously raking in millions of euros from Europe for the vitally important job of helping keep the Italian coast free of African migrants, both by making their departure from Libyan ports difficult and by taking back those who had managed to set sail, but who had been intercepted by the Italian coastguard.

Gaddafi, who never completely trusted the West, took every opportunity to remind everyone of the strategic importance of his leadership, especially when hosting important visitors. "I went to Libya several times," recalls Erika Feller, "and there was once an unexpected meeting offered to the heads of delegations during an African-European migration discussion held in Tripoli. Gaddafi rounded us all up and took us to an undisclosed location where we all sat, and then he came and spoke to us. Over a two-hour speech his message was very clear: 'If you depose me, you will unleash an absolute flood of illegal migrants on Europe, and you will reap what you sow.'"

In March 2011, the same month Guterres visited Tunisia, the work of the Security Council had already done much to justify the colonel's insecurity by clearly identifying him as a marked man. Referencing "the responsibility to protect"[24] the Libyan population and justifying it with irrefutable evidence of his regime's failure to carry out this duty, the United Nations had opened the door to military intervention under NATO's command.

Votes in favour: The United States, France and the United Kingdom.

Abstentions: Russia and China.

Votes against: None.

The forecasted rapid fleeing of people was already underway, but no one had predicted a refugee crisis. Rich in petroleum, Libya carried itself like a Persian Gulf state, and their citizens lived relatively comfortably, basking in the shade of oil income and gladly ceding menial labour to immigrants.

"Can you tell us, please, what happened to you?" In eastern Tunisia, about 7 kilometres from the border with Libya, Guterres questioned a group of men who were seeking a safe haven. With the authorisation of the Ministry of Defence, which had selected this strategic location, a transit camp had been erected in the middle of the desert with more than 100 tons of humanitarian aid: tents, blankets, plastic awnings for shade, sleeping bags, cans for transporting water, and cooking equipment. The cargo was flown in by aeroplane and then distributed with the help of the Red Cross. In the meantime, a medical centre had been set up, as well as a mosque, since, in situations like these, hope for the soul was every bit as vital as comfort for the body.

"Why did you leave?" It was not an idle question. The UNHCR did not have a single international staffer in Libya, so information was hard to come by and what got through was vague. Guterres, so close to the warzone, was trying to make his own assessment of the situation. He enquired how they had arrived, how long it had taken, what dangers they encountered along the way, and if it was true there were still people hiding in Libya who were trying to leave but not doing so for fear of being mistaken for mercenaries.

But soon, following the High Commissioner's visit, other questions came up in the media and on social media. Even if the camp was being run by the UNHCR, and even if Guterres was accompanied by the Director-General of the IOM, and even if there were some refugees in amongst that sea of people, wasn't it above all a problem of migration? And, if so, why was the High Commissioner for Refugees taking the lead?

Guterres says he takes "particular pride in the rapidity" with which the Libyans were evacuated from the camp. "What we said was, 'This doesn't make sense. We have two operations here; let's put everything together,' and we arrived at an agreement with the IOM. We set up a joint operation centre and there was a massive airlift to get people back to their countries of origin, with funding from those countries and from UNHCR and IOM funding campaigns. Those who, in the meantime, were recognised as refugees stayed in the camp, and later this was steadily taken care of with the Tunisian authorities. The overwhelming majority—we're talking about hundreds of thousands of people—were not refugees."

After seven months, the IOM had accounted for 706,000 people who had left Libya and declared it "one of the largest migration crises in modern history."[25] The majority escaped overland to Tunisia and Egypt. However, there was another exit route: by sea.

15

AT EUROPE'S DOOR

Spokesperson Ron Redmond was ready to retire and, after so many years at the agency, he was reluctant to leave the choice of his successor to just anyone. He had someone in mind, an American like him, who seemed interested in the job, and good sense dictated he should arrange to get her into the same room with Guterres. He called Melissa Fleming, spokeswoman for the International Atomic Energy Agency (IAEA) and asked her to come to Geneva.

"I met with Guterres and there was a really good rapport from the beginning," Fleming recalls, "but I didn't really know too much about him, so I asked my boss—Mohamed ElBaradei, who was then leaving the IAEA—and he said, 'You should take the job. I sit in this UN meeting with heads of organisations and he is the only one who has any vision.'"

When she arrived at the UNHCR and began working with Guterres, Fleming immediately realised how the High Commissioner "was really constantly also very in touch with what was in the news." So much so that if something relevant cropped up, even outside working hours, she could expect a call from her boss.

"Melissa, did you just see Al Jazeera?"

"No, I'm cooking for my kids and I don't have the TV on. I've got the BBC on the radio, but…"

For Sultan-Khan, this was something he was obviously already accustomed to. "Athar, look, sorry, are you watching Euronews? Did you see the footage? All the trucks are there, but UNHCR trucks are not there. Find out what happened to the UNHCR trucks... You call everybody!"

Fleming's first task every morning was to scrutinise the media and, during the 2011 uprisings in North Africa, she and her team began to notice a growing number of references to the UNHCR. This particularly held for European outlets highlighting the agency's warnings of Africans embarking in boats and heading for the Italian coast. The distance from Tripoli to southern Italy was only 180 miles, even less from certain Tunisian ports. Paradise was but a step away and Gaddafi was now encouraging—if not actually forcing—these departures, launching migrants off to Europe as payback for the NATO bombings. Fleming was frequently quoted in the media, whether when updating the world on the rising number of crossings or sharing stories of survival.

Actually, these routes across the central Mediterranean, or even the shipwrecks, were not new. Back when Guterres was still Prime Minister, the UNHCR had already begun lamenting the deaths in that sea and censuring Europe for repelling those desperately knocking on its doors. In his role as High Commissioner, Guterres had returned to the issue on certain occasions, and a scheduled speech at the European Court of Human Rights, in Strasbourg, had invited him in January to speak out once again on the subject.

However, at the opening ceremony for the 2011 judicial year, EU member states seemed more concerned with the ongoing fall-out from the 2008–09 financial crash than with the plight of refugees and other migrants from the Middle East and North Africa. Just as Guterres was in Strasbourg condemning how "persons seeking entry into Europe for the purpose of claiming protection are increasingly detained on immigration grounds, irrespective of their specific situation,"[1] Germany was debating the virtues of reprinting marks and abandoning the euro. As he was alerting the venerable court about how "persons fleeing violence are also often told by European asylum authorities that they could have found safety in another part of their own countries,"[2] France was trying to come to terms with polls that had the extreme-right making it into the second round of the presidential elections. And, while arguing before the most honourable judges that there was "a certain irony in the fact that, while European instances meticulously examine whether the intensity of an armed conflict or the individual level of risk is sufficient to justify granting protection, in Africa and Asia, states are taking in hundreds of thousands of persons fleeing from precisely the same situations,"[3] European banks were undergoing stress tests and the stock market was considering which govern-ment, besides Greece and Ireland, would be the next to need an IMF bailout.

Meanwhile, off the small Italian island of Lampedusa, the bodies continued to wash ashore. This rocky piece of land, comprising just 8 square miles, surrounded by translucent turquoise waters and inhabited by 4,500 locals, was located closer to Africa than it was to Italy and, for this reason, it was the first target zone on the European shores. Making landfall there was the goal of everyone crossing the Mediterranean, and 40,000 Africans fulfilled that dream in the first months of the Arab Spring, from January to July 2011.[4]

Guterres intended to visit the island and, during preparations to do so, they decided to bring in reinforcements: an A-list actor who had also been a UNHCR Goodwill Ambassador for the last decade. "Angelina Jolie is somebody who draws a different kind of attention than he does," Fleming explains. "We thought it would be an excellent combination. We also had a journalist from the BBC with us who did so much coverage of the day."

A clear sky, warm air carried by an onshore breeze, the arrival of summer was only days away. With his shirt cuffs rolled up, Guterres walked shoulder to shoulder with Jolie, who was holding a notebook and pen. A UNHCR staffer gesticulated explanations, while a few steps ahead photographers were jostling for the best shot. Security guards and the rest of the entourage followed close behind, mimicking the measured pace of the main protagonists.

They were approaching the overcrowded reception centre, attracting the attention of everyone they passed. People crowded the windows, hung over railings and filled the stairways to get a glimpse of the show. Some tried to get closer to Jolie, if only to shake the hand of a movie star. Once at the centre, Guterres and Jolie sat down and talked with a group of Africans, nearly all young men in their twenties, whose initial shyness Guterres tried to overcome by putting out his usual feelers: "How did you come across the boat? Did you have to pay? How much? 150 euros?"

Although refugees were the minority among the arrivals,[5] and the UNHCR did not actually operate in Lampedusa (which belongs to one of the world's richest countries, Italy, a G7 economy), there was the High Commissioner informing himself, and broadcasting—through the megaphone of Jolie's world fame—how this situation was becoming intolerable for everyone. Intolerable for the Africans, because the process of transferring them was so slow and there were, at certain times, hundreds sleeping out in the open on Lampedusa docks; intolerable for the Italian government, as the rest of Europe refused to share even a fraction of the burden; and finally, intolerable for the inhabitants of this seaside resort who, as high season started, were seeing a lot of empty hotels.

If this was too many people for one small island, for Europe as a whole the numbers were but "a drop in the ocean,"[6] Guterres argued to the press. "Less than 2 per cent"[7] of those who had fled Libya had tried to cross the Mediterranean. If the borders of Tunisia and Egypt were open, how strange it was that Europe's were closed. What he said to the journalists he repeated on the telephone to the President of the European Commission—his old rival in Portuguese politics, Durão Barroso.

As if to drive this point home, his last act on this springtime visit took place on the island's southernmost tip, the land that first comes into view for those arriving from Africa. There, on Europe's doorstep, in front of a gate sculpted out of clay and iron—a towering structure 5 metres high and 3 metres wide, commissioned by various NGOs to an Italian artist, in honour of those who had set out for the island but never arrived—a ceremony took place. The microphone passed from Guterres' hands to Jolie's, then to Lampedusa's priest and its mayor. The speakers pleaded for solidarity and favourable political winds, all of which would soon be falling on especially deaf ears.

Today, Guterres recognises that the Arab Spring was "a great leap forward, the moment in which the situation became much more complicated, because new events followed on from each other so quickly. We had Libya, Syria, Yemen and, at the same time, huge new departures from Somalia because of the drought, and everything also interconnected with Islamic radicalisation in other places. There were starting to be refugees in Nigeria, because of Boko Haram, then Mali... there was a series of crises related to this radicalisation."

In fact, the tide had definitely turned when yet another alarm sounded in New York. In October 2011, the Security Council vetoed a proposed resolution which referenced the Syrian government's "responsibility to protect"[8] its population and condemned "the continued, grave and systematic human rights violations and the use of force against civilians by the Syrian authorities."[9] The same text appealed to states to exercise "restraint over the direct or indirect supply, sale or transfer to Syria of arms and related material of all types, as well as technical training, financial resources or services, advice, or other services or assistance."[10]

Votes in favour: The United States, France and the United Kingdom.

Votes against: Russia and China.

16

FAITH AND PROTECTION

Monday, 31 October 2011. 6 am, Kandahar, Afghanistan.

The van, packed with explosives, was facing the target: a two-storey house protected by a tall and sturdy wall.

Alone inside the van, the driver scanned the line of cars parked in front of the wall. He needed a gap large enough to drive the van through, as only a direct, frontal impact would bring down the towering barrier.

As soon as he found the opening, he sharply turned his steering wheel and accelerated towards glory. In a few seconds he smashed against the wall. A deafening boom and a huge plume of dust rose into the air—just the sign the other assailants were waiting for.

Three armed men rushed the breach on foot, ran rapidly across the courtyard and entered the building. Their guns raised, shooting to kill. Aiming at UNHCR staff.

For High Commissioners, the darkest hour must be the death of team members in the field. Senior humanitarian officials commonly say that the first experience of mourning produces the deepest sorrow, the sharpest pain. But that was not exactly how Guterres experienced it. He had been in office for two years when one of the most violent attacks committed against the United Nations happened in Algiers, in 2007. "We were in another building, on the same street," Guterres explains, "and two of our drivers were caught up in the explosion. These were truly horrible and worrisome moments, but the attack was not against the UNHCR. If it had been, it would have been much more complicated."

In any case, the terrorism strike in Algiers had brought the Agency's morale to a new low. It was an injustice, wicked and self-defeating; a direct blow to the gut. In addition to the discouragement, many UNHCR officials felt suddenly vulnerable. The death of colleagues had brought back memories of dangerous situations they had been through in the field and would very probably face again. These ideas had pricked their conscience, forcing them to reflect on those left widowed in Algiers, and how their children might well have been their own.

As always in these circumstances, Guterres had instructed that the families of victims should receive the maximum compensation possible. He had also received them at the headquarters, in the conference room next to his office. Many issues had been dealt with in that room, with its two burgundy sofas facing each other and its low table between them: presidents, heads of government, ministers and ambassadors were received and consulted there. On the small wooden shelves and on the windowsill, there were medals of honour, sculptures, handicrafts and other trinkets gifted to the High Commissioner and to the Agency by visiting dignitaries.

The families had made themselves comfortable and Guterres had taken his usual position in the armchair next to the sofas, from where his regardful gaze embraced those present, including his chief of staff, whose sombre expression over the preceding few days had been unusual for the Pakistani.

"As the UNHCR Representative in North Africa," explains Sultan-Khan, "I was based in Algeria for a long time and the drivers were my lifeline. They did everything: they drove, they worked as interpreters, even giving me political insights I could never pick up in any local newspaper. They were the ones who got killed, so meeting their wives was a very emotional moment for me. When I was younger, you showed your UN papers and people respected you. You wore the UN flag, nobody touched you. However, the global security situation changed after 9/11—now they target you."

In fact, the United Nations insignia—a projection of the world map, held up by a crown of olive branches—provided an increasingly diminishing guarantee of safe passage in conflict zones. The War on Terror had pushed divisions to a new extreme, leaving little—or no—space in the middle. From the insurgents' perspective, unarmed humanitarian workers claiming neutrality, without any explicit allegiance, were not their friends, so they could only be their enemies—just like the Blue Helmets.

The rising hostility was increasingly apparent. In 2008, the numbers had reached levels never seen before: 165 attacks that resulted in the deaths of 127 humanitarian workers, half of whom were United Nations staff.[1]

Some of the incidents that Guterres dealt with personally had positive outcomes, such as the release of the UNHCR coordinator in Quetta, Pakistan, after months of captivity—a case worked in coordination with the FBI since it involved a US citizen. Other episodes, however, had a tragic end, such as the suicide of an Agency official, a victim of rape in Sudan, after her return to Geneva.

The norm dictated that the most afflicted places on the planet were the ones most in need of the UNHCR. So much so that nearly half the Agency staff worked in so-called "D" and "E" posts—the most dangerous.[2] In some of these theatres of war, in areas with out-of-control epidemics, staff were not even allowed to bring family along. They were expected to last at least two years in post and, to reward such resilience, salaries were topped with a special subsidy for which the Agency bureaucracy—usually so nimble at creative linguistic choices—did not find a better designation than "danger pay".

Every year, the United Nations evaluates the level of risk of each post, designating a "letter" after taking into account security, the degree of isolation, climate and available healthcare, among other such factors. As of January 2011,[3] Moscow and Beijing, for example, fell among the "A" destinations, providing the most comfort, if such is the term. Damascus and Aleppo were in group "B", in conjunction with the Saudi capital, Riyadh. Tehran, in turn, fell into "C" even though other Iranian cities were already categorised as "D".

HONEST BROKER

Then there were countries like Afghanistan, with no apparent differences between working inside or outside the capital, deep in the countryside or on the border, because all operations were ranked "E". Kandahar had long since figured definitively as the benchmark for "E" zones.

On receiving news of the 31 October attack, which had already been claimed by the Taliban, Guterres caught the next plane to Afghanistan. The Secretary-General, the UN General Assembly and the Security Council had all condemned the strike, but it was the head of UNHCR who had to decide the next steps. It was a long-haul flight and Guterres spent it dealing with questions and dilemmas that, in situations like these, always tested the High Commissioner's judgement. What additional security measures could be taken? Would it not be better to evacuate all personnel from Kandahar? What would be the fate of refugees left there without UNHCR's presence?

In general, "his inclination was that it has to be pretty bad before an organisation, which is funded and set up to assist people on the frontline, pulls out," states Erika Feller. "There was a lot of discussion internally as to whether there was sufficient concern about the safety of the staff versus the continuity of the operations."

Guterres holds the view that "the greatest protection comes out of direct contact with the populations," and that, in these terms, "the UNHCR had more capital than other UN agencies." Nevertheless, on arrival in Kandahar, he was leaning towards suspending the operation, at least for the time being: "It had been an attack on one of our guesthouses, and only out of luck no one had been inside, apart from the three guards who were killed."

His visit to the site of the attack—a white house with its windows all blown out, bullet-pocked walls and floors carpeted in shrapnel, some even blood-stained—made vivid the carnage that might have happened. He began on the ground floor, moved to the second floor and then out onto the roof. The higher he went, the more certain he was about evacuating the rest of the staff as the only means of guaranteeing their safety, especially since this was no isolated incident. The recent torrent of attacks against UN targets had been so incessant that, following the attack on the

186

UNHCR, the UN Staff Union[4] requested Ban Ki-moon to rethink the deployment of personnel to Afghanistan.

That same morning, Guterres called a staff meeting in another Kandahar facility. There were about twenty officials, many of them Afghans still disoriented by the recent events. The High Commissioner expressed his regret for what had happened and was quick to assure that nobody else would lose their life there. He was hoping that his words would be reassuring and that those present would sigh with relief on learning they had the option to move to a more secure location. However, the reaction was not at all what Guterres had expected: "It was an incredible moment, one of the most amazing things I've ever experienced because I wanted to end the discussion there and these staffers didn't let me. They all told me, 'No, we're not going anywhere, we're going to continue working here.'"

Guterres points to Kandahar, perhaps more than any other act of terrorism, as a standout incident that left enduring marks on his tenure. "After that particular event," recalls Janet Lim, who Guterres had promoted to Assistant High Commissioner for Operations in 2009, "he started speaking a lot about the security environment and there were quite a lot of domestic changes within the security management structure of the office. In fact, we set up a system so that, when there were cuts, the security budget would not be affected. There was also some review of the kind of insurance coverage local staff had because it used to be a bit different from that of international staff."

It was after his return to Geneva that, piece by piece, an alternative, seemingly reliable, version of the events began to emerge. A Taliban spokesperson corrected their initial declaration and explained the target had not been the UNHCR, but rather an American NGO—International Relief and Development Inc. (renamed Blumont) which operated out of a building adjacent to the agency. Apparently, due to the vehicles parked outside, the driver had exploded his van in the wrong section of the wall and the rest of the assailants, inflamed by the mission, carried through with the plan without noticing the mistake.

Musta'men

> I know why you came here. You came because you're worried.
> You think we're going to mistreat and expel the Afghans. But have
> no worry because God commands us to protect our brothers and
> sisters.

Mostafa Pourmohammadi's comments during that first visit to
Tehran occasionally reverberated in Guterres' head. "Have no
worry because God commands us to protect our brothers and sisters." Fundamentally this meant that sheltering refugees was tan-
tamount to an obligation for all Muslims as "the word of God".
Should this be the case, it meant "God" himself might turn out to
be a unique ally in the region.

However, this was not the religion that Guterres had first heard
about from his next-door neighbour as a child. This was the message of a different religion, one with which he was not familiar; the
message of a distant, mysterious belief. Invoking it out of context
or inappropriately would be to insult Islam, to sin in another faith.
Guterres set about learning everything he could about "the will of
Allah".

"I found the Koran to be very merciful and tolerant," Guterres
reflects. "There are some exceptions, like the fact women are only
allowed to receive half of their inheritance. But there is an explanation: it's because, if the husband dies, someone has to take care of
her. It's important to try to understand these things, which seem
so shocking to us, in their historical context. In fact, when Christ
comes across the woman who has committed adultery, she was
about to be stoned to death—those were the habits of the day. In
spite of everything, I think the Gospels (not the Old Testament,
where our own Saint Paul comes up as a bit misogynistic) have
something extraordinary which the Koran doesn't: their timeless-
ness. That's why I continue to be a Catholic, or I'd be something
else or nothing by now. The Koran is not as perfect, but it is much
more humanist than people think. Most of the doctrine is extremely
geared towards peace and the concept of jihad is much more connected with inner reform than it is with warfare."

However, men tend to differ in their interpretations of divine
instructions. What some denounce as moral weakness, others see

as purifying the soul. What for some demands mercy, is for others a call to vengeance. What some read as an appeal to peace, others take as their marching orders.

Bearing this in mind, shortly after his conversation with the Iranian minister, Guterres had solicited an academic study of the right to asylum under Islamic law. The idea was to produce an unbiased synthesis of everything that, in Islam, "God commands" regarding refugees. He tried to reach an agreement with the Arab League, but it was through a partnership with the Organisation of the Islamic Conference that the task landed on the desk of Professor Abou El-Wafa, Dean of the Law Faculty at Cairo University.

Published in Arabic and English in 2009, *The Right to Asylum between Shari'ah and International Refugee Law* includes a preface by Guterres in which the United Nations High Commissioner writes that, "More than any other historical source, the Holy Qur'an, along with the Sunnah and Hadith of the Prophet of Islam, are a foundation of contemporary refugee law."[5] In support of this view, he notes how the custom of protecting the *musta'men*, the asylum-seeker under Islamic law, predates by many centuries the consecration in international law of the principle of *non-refoulement*, which prohibits the return of refugees to places where their lives would be put at risk.

In his study, El-Wafa, copiously citing classical Arab poetry and the Koran, maintains that "the right to refuge or protection is a genuine and non-derogable Islamic practice[6] [...] granted to who-ever solicits it, regardless of religion, race, colour or fortune."[7] This is further grounded in widely known principles in Islam, according to which "before the world's calamities, all sons of Adam [human beings] are equal."[8] This is also referenced in numerous verses in the Koran, such as "Those who give [them] asylum and aid—these are [all] the believers in great truth: for them is the forgiveness of sins and most generous provision" (Surah al-Anfal 74).

Or even: "And should any of the disbelievers seek your protection, then grant him shelter so that he may hear the word of Allah, and then escort him to where he will be secure" (Surah 9:6).

According to this study, the definition of "refugee" in Islam is broader than that inscribed in the Geneva Convention. Firstly,

189

since it establishes that "asylum may be granted to any person, who wishes to reside in Muslim land, because he embraced Islam or because he wants to live as a non-Muslim under protection in a Muslim land."[9] Therefore, the Islamic refugee doctrine should not be viewed as a right limited to foreigners subject to persecution in their own countries. Likewise, under Islam, asylum is not an exclusive state prerogative, it can also be granted by individuals. Finally, once obtained, asylum is theoretically valid across all Muslim land.

This study had quickly become a working tool for the High Commissioner. The majority of refugees under UNHCR's protection were of Muslim origin, which was one of Guterres' primary reasons for devoting so much time and energy to visits and meetings with the leaders of the Muslim world. He sensed that invoking the sayings of the Prophet Muhammad (may the peace and blessings of Allah be upon you) would go further than repeating the worn-out pieties of the United Nations. "He used that book as his calling card all over the Middle East," explains spokesperson Melissa Fleming. "When we travelled to the region, he'd give a copy to kings, heads of state and emirs, and then appear on these major talk shows quoting sections of the Qur'an."

For example, Guterres offered a copy of the study to the Saudi Prince Naif bin Abdulaziz on the occasion of its launch, at Naif University, in Riyadh. In 2009, Saudi Arabia was only sheltering 548 refugees[10] and, despite the wars unfolding on its doorstep, this G20 country seemed reluctant to take in more. Nevertheless, Guterres, armed with his book, stressed once again "the protection of refugees, and of their property and families, not to mention the civil character of asylum and voluntary repatriation, are all subjects addressed in the Holy Qur'an."[11] His message was clear: more than just an international legal obligation, receiving and caring for refugees was a moral duty for Muslims.

In order to deepen ties with the Islamic world, Guterres went one step further. Every year, the High Commissioner showed up in an Arab country—usually a source or a destination of a large flow of refugees—in the middle of Ramadan. During the "Ramadan Solidarity Initiative", as he called the visit, he behaved, as much as a Western Catholic could, like a Muslim.

"When he was in a Muslim country during the Holy fasting month of Ramadan," says Nasser Judeh, Jordan's Foreign Affairs Minister at the time, "he would not eat in public out of respect for the people who were fasting. On several occasions he actually observed the fast fully, like any other Muslim. As a non-Muslim, he could easily get a daytime meal in his hotel or with friends and colleagues. But he did not. This was highly appreciated by all those who knew him and worked with him."

The Mediterranean Style

The empathy Guterres inspired outside the office and in the field contrasted with his lack of popularity at headquarters. Cold, distant and unapproachable were among the most cited adjectives at the Geneva office during the inevitable water cooler chats about the boss.

"There were many in the UNHCR," admits Feller, "who would have liked to have closer contact with him. There were those who said he was not the most... that he didn't give enough social time to staff, that his vision was more outside."

At one stage, Guterres would arrive unannounced in the agency's departments, sometimes just to say hello, on other occasions with questions about various items on the agenda. What might have seemed for him an act of camaraderie made many colleagues feel uncomfortable. The normal and expected procedure would be for the Office of the High Commissioner to announce a visit ahead of time so that people could prepare themselves, get their desks in order and, above all, be certain they were in the right place at the right time.

However, what really raised plenty of hackles among directors and made them feel overruled was the way Guterres disregarded organisational structure without even realising it. "There is a huge hierarchy in the UNHCR," says Fleming, "and most people are very respectful of this. He was not. He went to the people he knew he was going to get an immediate answer from. So, he was constantly calling people in the field, heads of operation or even officers a layer down."

Much less of a problem was the High Commissioner's habit of heading down to the ground-floor cafeteria for a glass of orange juice, which he began to favour over coffee, and to eat two energy bars, which for him served for lunch. Gone were the days when Sultan-Khan, Guterres' chief of staff, would take him out into the city for lunch once a week. These meals were put on hold when they both agreed the High Commissioner, incapable of resisting a chocolate dessert, had begun putting on weight.

During these ritual cafeteria breaks, it was usual for the small team on the seventh floor to accompany the boss. Within his own office, at least, Guterres managed to overcome his reputation for distance. They would gather around one of the standing tables. In addition to Sultan-Khan, there was the High Commissioner's secretary Micheline, his adviser Sophie, and speechwriter Katharina. They discussed their weekend plans, banter about something in the news before moving on to other trivialities, anything to help them disconnect from work for fifteen or twenty minutes. At the end, Guterres and Sultan-Khan would argue over who would pick up the tab, which always made everyone smile.

This kind of conviviality was common on the seventh floor. For example, they would talk about how their boss, a committed socialist, religiously read the liberal *The Economist*, which recently featured his colleague and presidential candidate Françoise Hollande, or, in the magazine's view, "the rather dangerous Monsieur Hollande."[12]

Guterres' troublesome relationship with technology was also a source of amusement and it was said that, "The world had changed when the High Commissioner got an iPhone." Nevertheless, there still remained a lot of work ahead to truly bring the boss into the digital era, even though he had already learned how to check and delete emails in the palm of his hand, something he now did constantly. Before he had a smartphone, he got so flustered when away from the office that they sent him documents through his wife's email.

Still, whenever talking to other staff, Micheline Saunders-Gallemand, Sophie Muller and Katharina Thote had the impression there was one High Commissioner on the seventh floor, and another less favourable version on the other six floors, an unfriendly political strategist who was obviously jockeying to become Secretary-General. The stories they shared between themselves reflected a certain human warmth: the time he refused to return from Burkina Faso without Sophie when the plane was overbooked; when he was one of the first to visit Katharina in the maternity ward and told her right there and then that she should have more children; how he always shared detailed travel tips with his staff… these seemed like fables to the ears of those who did not have this close relationship with the High Commissioner.

His bad temper, however, was well known. This was particularly evident in the way he tacked the informal Portuguese "pá" onto the end of his English sentences in order to express his frequent irritation: "This thing doesn't work, pá!" Sultan-Khan, the High Commissioner's first line of defence, downplayed these exclamations, maintaining they were just part of his "Mediterranean style". And whenever Guterres raised his voice at someone, his chief of staff would remind people what was really going on: "Remember, he's not yelling at you, he's just yelling at the situation."

Working in close vicinity to their boss, Sophie and Katharina witnessed his audible frustrations. Nevertheless, Athar Sultan-Khan always stepped in with comforting words: "Now that's all, ladies, he's behaving better." So much so that he no longer threw pens on the floor as he used to. Well, at least not as much. In truth, Sultan-Khan recalls that his impatience never faded with the years: "When he asked for something, it was to be done immediately because he would soon ask again and, on the third occasion, he would say, 'Look, I can do it myself.' What really made him angry was when I told him, 'I'm sorry, Mr. Guterres, the UN rules…' He would get very annoyed at that."

The lives of Athar, Sophie, Katharina and Micheline were all coupled to their boss' agenda. They knew that, no matter how many unforeseeable events occurred, unexpected crises, last-minute trips or urgently called meetings, there were also commitments every year that the High Commissioner simply could not miss.

At the beginning of October, there was always the annual meeting of the UNHCR Executive Committee, in Geneva. This body, now made up of representatives from eighty-eight states, functioned to a certain extent as the Agency's General Assembly, approving the budget and issuing instructions to the High Commissioner—although this latter rarely occurred in practice. The UN Secretary-General would sometimes attend the week-long meeting and the occasion always required the High Commissioner to prepare a meticulously crafted speech address-ing—no more and no less—the state of the world.

Two months later, in mid-December, the High Commissioner's Dialogue on Protection Challenges took place, an event launched by Guterres in 2007. This was a kind of reinvention of the General-Estates Guterres had organised in the 1990s as the leader of the Portuguese Socialists. He now adapted its structure to that of the UNHCR in order to bring state and United Nations' officials together with actors from outside the system, mostly academics and NGOs, to discuss topics informally and without any pre-pro-grammed conclusions. The High Commissioner would inaugurate the proceedings and close them by summarising the leading find-ings from the panels, round tables and side events.

In previous years, the subjects discussed included international migration, humanitarian work in urban contexts, and seemingly end-less refugee situations, as was the case, as Guterres remarked at the time, of the Rohingya Muslims who were already fleeing Myanmar to Bangladesh and continued to live in deplorable conditions.

The time to choose a theme for the 2012 Dialogue was upon them, and that was the reason the High Commissioner convened one particularly significant meeting of his UNHCR directors. Not all were in Geneva. Had this been the case, there would have been ten men and ten women in the Sérgio Vieira de Mello Room.

As the proceedings kicked off, the Director of International Protection, Volker Türk, in charge of organising the Dialogue, took to the podium. Guterres admired the Austrian's intelligence. With pale complexion and smooth head, his blue eyes stood out behind wire-rimmed glasses as he approached his 50th birthday. Guterres consulted him frequently and saw him as one of his right arms at the agency. As Türk, who is not a religious man, recalls, "I had a couple of ideas and I remember I suggested 'faith'. If you go into any humanitarian operation you see that faith communities are the first to provide assistance."

However, the proposal triggered some pushback. "Faith" was perceived as too dangerous a journey for a secular organisation like the UNHCR. The agency might be exploited, putting itself at risk—at the slightest false step—of being accused of favouring one or another religion, disrespecting one or another belief. Not to mention that not everyone supported ecumenical dialogue, and to place the United Nations under the same roof as all the world's squabbling religions might cause unwanted results. The risks were obvious and the benefits merely hypothetical.

In reality, this strategy was not without precedent at the UN. The year before, UNICEF had launched an initiative designed to strengthen ties with religious communities.[13] According to Türk, Guterres "was immediately convinced and then just said, 'Yes, great idea, let's do it.'"

And so it was decided. "Faith and Protection" would be the theme for 2012. Now, along with everything else, the High Commissioner's opening speech needed to be written.

The Stranger

During a short visit to New York in December 2016, UNHCR staffer Katharina Thote wrote a long memo to her successor. She had been Guterres' speechwriter for four years while he was High Commissioner and, in regards to his public speaking, the German knew better than anybody what Guterres was capable of.

> Mr. Guterres delivers speeches at about 120 words a minute when speaking English, but speaks more slowly (around 100–110 a minute) in French or Spanish.

> Accent: He cannot pronounce the aspirated "h" (enhance, heart, etc.) and usually says "s" instead of "th" at the end of a word (face instead of faith, youssss instead of youth).

> Unlike in French, he has a very strong Portuguese accent when he speaks Spanish—pronouncing every "s" as "sh", which he doesn't do in any other language—so it's good to keep the Spanish bits short.

195

She had applied for the position, without great expectation, in 2011. She had been with the UNHCR since graduating from university, but did not have any experience as a speechwriter, and English was not even her native language. Moreover, she was clearly not on Guterres' radar. Her contact with the High Commissioner had been limited to a meeting here and there in which she participated as a note-taker from the back row.

> He does not like teleprompters (though he will use them to record video messages).

> He is so anti-acronyms that, at one point, I had to explain the meaning of ASAP.

> Salutations: He is very anti-protocol when it comes to himself (does not want anyone to call him Excellency for example) and will not spend a lot of time on this on his own speeches (like naming every present head of state individually, etc.).

Everything that Thote assumed would be a disadvantage turned to her advantage. Guterres hardly knew her, which is why he gave her the benefit of the doubt. And Thote, honest about her inexperience, embraced the job with humility. There was no literary presumption that so often contaminates professional speechwriting. She wrote in a simple, stripped-down, linear style—indeed, the only style that Guterres would really tolerate.

> NEVER distribute a speech before he has finished delivering it. He hates it when people read along while he speaks.

> He usually does not want to expand in detail on papers or reports that are being presented at whichever occasion he is speaking at; he prefers to leave the "bureaucracy" to others.

> He can be quite sarcastic off-line, but doesn't like irony in his speeches, or funny remarks, he might make them off the cuff but he is not a crowd-warmer.

Grateful for the opportunity, she never felt slighted by how the High Commissioner preferred improvising while reading her speeches. She even thought it was funny how he joked about the subject. "Katharina, I need you to write another one of the speeches I'm not going to read." What did frustrate her was the institutional need to rewrite the same message over and over again and always with a different twist.

> He loves history, likes to make references to history (Middle Eastern and European in particular), as well as references to values and the world's major religions. He also likes numbers a lot so, if there is a good way to illustrate a point with numbers, he will be very interested to use statistics.

> He might make references to his past on strategic occasions (like framing the 1990s and early 2000s as the time when he was Prime Minister), to subtly remind the politicians in front of him that he understands their concerns back home very well and isn't just preaching to them from a multilateral pulpit.

In any case, she followed his instructions to the letter. So much so that Guterres would often be surprised at the final result: "Man, this sounds like me speaking." Before Thote came along, dealing with speechwriters had proven a real headache. Guterres was never satisfied and always ended up reworking the texts himself. "Oh please, not another butterfly and water lilies speech."

> He used to like playing with a big paper clip when we were working on speeches or in internal meetings. It helped him think, and we had a big flower pot full of broken paper clips by the time he left. He says he is now losing the habit but, just in case he ever asks for a paper clip, it's the jumbo size.

In those last days of November 2011, two weeks before the Dialogue on "Faith and Protection", the speech was still a blank page. Thote had prepared a list of key messages, but she wanted to get some feedback from Guterres before starting to write. Her boss made a point of participating in the process, so much so that they would meet once, twice, three times if necessary, for the text to reach its final form.

On these occasions, Thote remembers, "Sometimes he would get up and walk around his office and start writing a paragraph or a message in his head, sort of saying it out loud, and then he'd say, 'No, no, not this,' and cut it out before starting again, while I would take notes and make suggestions on how he could express it differently."

Brainstorming nearly always took place in the High Commissioner's office with its spare wall free of prizes, diplomas, magazine
covers, articles in frames or photographs taken with politicians,
sporting or other famous figures. The only pictures visible were
those of his family, including one of his first wife, Zizas.

While they chewed over the theme of "Faith and Protection",
one of the ideas that came up, Thote recalls, was to broaden the
scope of Professor El-Wafa's study: "I think the whole idea of the
speech came from that book. He thought, 'Well, let's look, at all
major religions and value systems, for something that says, "Take
care of people who are fleeing".'"

There was no need to waste time consulting the Internet or
much less send anyone to the library. Guterres picked up the telephone, rang the office of a Sri Lankan UNHCR colleague and asked
him what the Buddhist texts said on the subject. He repeated this
with a Hindu official and then proceeded systematically until he
had gathered enough input from as many religions as possible.

Thote could now begin to write. The first draft finished, she
once again met with the High Commissioner. Waiting in silence
for Guterres to read the text, she reacted with wide-eyed wonder
at his comments: "Usually, he would make me take out all the 'I's'
in the speeches, but on that occasion he was like, 'Oh, let's make
this a little more biographical.'"

Over the following days, drafts were traded back and forth. The
High Commissioner was constantly travelling, so Thote would
always have the latest version printed out. She knew her boss might
call at any hour and ask her to add or cut content. By the eighth
draft, the speech was finally ready.

On 12 December, Guterres woke up with the flu. The medicine
was slow to take effect and the freezing Geneva weather was not
helping. Thus, he asked Volker Türk and Erika Feller to host the
private meetings with religious leaders—collectively representing
over three-quarters of the world's populations—that were scheduled for the morning before the formal opening of the Dialogue.

Afterwards, the doors of Hall XVII of the Palais des Nations
opened to host around 400 guests. The oval auditorium, lined
with vertical wooden panels and lit by a white ceiling, was

designed to ensure everyone sat at the same level, including the High Commissioner for Refugees. Feeling somewhat better, Guterres put his glasses on, connected his microphone and delivered the opening speech:

> Excellencies, Ladies and Gentlemen, Friends, it is my pleasure to welcome you to Geneva for this year's Dialogue on Protection Challenges. [...]
>
> Faith lives in the heart and mind of every individual and represents the deeply personal way in which each one of us relates with the transcendental dimension of our lives. I would therefore like to start with my own personal testimony about the connection between faith and humanitarian work.[14]

Sitting in the row behind Guterres, Thote followed every word of the speech because her boss had a habit of scribbling changes, even as the curtain was going up. The definition of faith had come straight from his dictation. Then came the passage from "The Parable of the Talents", related to the work done as a student volunteer in Lisbon's poorest neighbourhoods, as well as the mathematics lessons given after serving as Prime Minister... all topics her boss had never discussed when they were drafting the speech.

> When I came here, I soon discovered [...] the values of caring for those in need were equally shared by all major religions. [...] The Exodus of the people of Israel from slavery in Egypt is a central story to the Jewish faith. In Christianity, the Holy Family's flight from Bethlehem is studied by all children in catechism. And for Muslims, the Islamic calendar begins with the year the Prophet travelled to Medina to seek protection. [...] In the Hindu Upanishads, the mantra "atithi devo bhava" or "the guest is God" expresses the fundamental importance of hospitality. [...] There are many different traditions of Buddhism, but the concept of "Karuna" is a fundamental tenet in all of them. It embodies the qualities of tolerance, non-discrimination.[15]

From where she sat, Thote had the same view as her boss. To her left, she could see the General Secretary of the World Council of Churches, the representative of the World Assembly of Muslim Youth, and the President of the Lutheran World Federation, who wore the clerical collar.

A little further back was the Archpriest of the Russian Orthodox Church, with the traditional pendant cross visible against his breast, and an American rabbi, the author of various books, who had travelled from Los Angeles. The President of the Hebrew Immigrant Aid Society had also made the journey from the United States.

In the middle of the auditorium, there was the CEO of the World Evangelical Alliance, the Sheikh of the Muslim Council of Liberia, and the Archbishop of the Episcopal Church of Sudan.

Finally, to her right, she could identify the Archimandrite of the Orthodox Church of Greece wearing a black cassock and cap, and the Director of Migration Policy from the US Conference of Catholic Bishops.

They all listened in silence with their eyes glued to Guterres.

> For the vast majority of uprooted people, there are few things as powerful as their faith in helping them cope with fear, loss, separation, and destitution. [...] Faith-based organisations have an important role to play in promoting reconciliation and peaceful coexistence—in the country of origin after a conflict, during refugees' stay in exile, and upon the return of the displaced, facilitating the reintegration into their home communities. [...]

> I thank you very much for your attention and look forward to engaged and inspiring discussions.[16]

According to the General Secretary of the World Council of Churches, which brings together around 350 religious denominations, the speech said "a lot about his openness to everybody who is willing to work for the same victims. I think it was an important message and he said it in a much clearer way than we had heard from UN leaders at the time." The Lutheran pastor Olav Tveit added that, "In line with people such as Dag Hammarskjöld [UN Secretary-General, 1953–61], António Guterres voiced a very strong ethos and a perspective that goes beyond the interests of one state, one party or one religion."

Tveit also pointed out how the dialogue continued outside the UNHCR. This was most notable in the implementation of one of Guterres' recommendations at the end of the event: to create a code of conduct for faith leaders facing refugee and displacement situations.[17] Religious representatives and academics met again in the following months to develop this code that became known as "Welcoming the Stranger: Affirmations for Faith Leaders",[18] now available in six languages.

Sultan-Khan was also present at the speech, listening to each and every word. The Pakistani diplomat, who initially thought would only spend a few months as Guterres' chief of staff, had now clocked up seven years of service. Hence, everything indicated he would be accompanying the High Commissioner through to the end of his second mandate in mid-2015.

There was still time, and Sultan-Khan was well aware how the end of this second term broadly coincided with presidential elections in Portugal and that the Socialist Party was once again calling for Guterres to return.

He also knew that the High Commissioner was preparing to take up a supervisory position at Portugal's largest private foundation dedicated to promoting culture and education. His relationship with the foundation was long-standing and he was simply awaiting Ban Ki-moon's authorisation, which was slow in coming. It was a part-time position with no salary, but which might lead him to take up the position of its president, should he so desire, after leaving the UNHCR.

But either option, whether returning to Portuguese politics or semi-retiring as a distinguished benefactor of the arts, seemed a step backwards. Sultan-Khan had greater ambitions in mind and he finally decided to share his thoughts with his boss: "Mr. Guterres, when I heard you the other day, I heard the voice of the Secretary-General."

17

THE GREAT MARCH

The Security Council was seized by paralysis. New York was lagging behind in getting humanitarian aid to Syria, and the UNHCR director responsible for the Middle East seemed in no hurry to address the situation. So, Guterres set himself to work on the problem.

Damascus didn't authorise entrance through Turkey? Okay then, you make an air bridge to Latakia Airport, in the north-west of Syria, and then transport the cargo over land to the border. The Red Cross cannot free some trucks? You have got to insist on it. Give them some alternative dates and drive the point home that the UNHCR would have difficulty mobilising vehicles on its own. Saturday is the safest day, isn't it? In that case, the teams need to be ready to move during the weekend.

After torturous months navigating obstacles and calculating dangers, Guterres gave the operation the green light in January 2013. This was going to be a high-risk move. The High Commissioner oversaw everything in real time from his Geneva base. Those accompanying him said that they had never seen their boss so nervous. "He acknowledged afterwards that he took such a risk for the convoy that if something had happened, he would have had to resign immediately," relates the then Assistant to the High Commissioner, Sophie Muller. "He himself became a senior logistical officer for 72 hours."

Out in the field, white Toyota jeeps, displaying UNHCR and United Nations flags, escorted eight trucks loaded with 15,000 blankets and 3,000 tents; all duly identified also with the red crescent. They were heading to northernmost Syria, where thus far nearly no one had reached the masses of displaced people trying to survive the winter. That this was still an untested itinerary in the middle of an active warzone fed into everyone's worst fears.

Latakia Airport, the operational starting point, was 200 kilometres from Aleppo, Syria's largest city. From there to the final destination, Azaz, there would be still another 50 kilometres to travel. Glued to the telephone, Guterres was in constant contact with events on the ground while simultaneously phoning the UNHCR representative in Syria and coordinating with authorities along the route.

Dark clouds filled the overcast sky when the convoy finally reached its destination, Kerama refugee camp. Men and women, the old and the young, swarmed around the vehicles. Were all the provisions unloaded? Was everyone safe? They were and, to celebrate, the whole team took some photos in front of the UNHCR jeeps.

"It was amazing but that's how cross-line[1] assistance started in Syria," says Guterres. "Before that, there'd only been some small stuff from the Red Cross." As in other situations, he had negotiated directly with Assad, was in contact with the Foreign Minister Walid Muallem, with Deputy Foreign Minister Faisal Mekdad, and even the Syrian Ambassador in Geneva, Faisal Khabbaz Hamoui.

On one occasion, he took the latter three to dinner on the outskirts of Geneva—far from the city centre and UNHCR headquarters. They all served a regime that had been denounced by the United Nations for war crimes and crimes against humanity. Nevertheless, without them, the UNHCR would hardly have been able to provide for the victims of these same atrocities. "As long as Assad is the sovereign leader of Syria, I have to deal with Assad," Guterres confided to those closest to him. "I'm not going to jump, like the Americans, like the British, like the French, and only start dealing with the opposition groups."

Nevertheless, with just the government's approval, they were not going to get very far. By mid-2013, it was estimated that 60 to

70 per cent of the territory was under rebel control.[2] "Initially, we had a good level of rapport with the opposition because they needed us to deliver assistance," notes the UNHCR regional coordinator in Syria, Amin Awad. "So we talked to different groups, except for the radical ones that didn't want to talk to anybody. However, we went to over 200 armed groups inside the country. The turning point was the foreign fighters—over 40,000 entered Syria."

The different rebel groups that had taken up arms since the Arab Spring reached Syria in March 2011 and shared the objective of defeating Assad, but seemed to differ on practically everything else. This fractured opposition, radicalised and internationalised, raised enormous barriers to humanitarian initiatives. Firstly, they waged war on a number of fronts—and the longer the time passed, the larger the multitudes of refugees fleeing warzones, and deeper was the suffering.

The numbers from Syria shocked even the most experienced experts in lasting conflicts: 6.5 million people internally displaced in just over two years.[3] Secondly, Syria was transformed into a maze of battles with populations corralled in between, in both cities and the countryside, and beyond the reach of the UN. These constraints worried the head of the UNHCR and caused him great indignation. "Guterres was always pushing for 'access, access, access'!" explains Awad. "But distances were a big problem for us, especially when you look at northern and eastern Syria. It takes nine hours to drive the 360 kilometres from Damascus to Aleppo because the highways are controlled by different groups, so you have to go around side roads or even cross back and forth over borders."

The situation continued to escalate and Guterres had his hands full, just like other UN leaders. "We are doing our best, but let's be honest: we are not doing enough," he admitted to journalists.[4] He had never faced a situation that was so out of control and with that kind of intensity and magnitude. The torrents of displaced people seemed unstoppable and with increasingly frequent human rights violations carried out by the government or by the opposition.[5]

It was one thing to lay siege to populations, letting them rot with hunger, cold and disease, just as the Romans did to Jerusalem, the Vikings to Paris, and the Serbs to Sarajevo; to blow up schools and hospitals, raze crops, bomb bakeries first thing in the morning when people queued to buy bread; to summarily execute hundreds of kneeling, blindfolded men, their hands tied behind their backs. It was one thing to arbitrarily take people prisoner, beat them, humiliate them, electrocute them, and hang them by their arms for hours before throwing them into overcrowded cells that were filthy, full of insects, with no water or toilet; to rape women and men with impunity, while under interrogation, or while their homes were raided. It was one thing to kidnap international journalists, such as the American reporter James Foley; to destroy World Heritage Sites...

However, the "red line,"[6] the act that was a "totally unacceptable"[7] practice, a "game changer",[8] to quote the words of the President of the United States, would be the use of chemical weapons by Assad's regime.

On 21 August 2013, suspicions over the use of prohibited chemical weapons in Syria were confirmed. Amateur footage of what happened that morning in Eastern Ghouta, in the suburbs of Damascus, left no doubt. In a speech delivered in the White House, Barack Obama described the images everyone was watching on the television and the Internet: "Men, women, children lying in rows, killed by poison gas. Others foaming at the mouth, gasping for breath. A father clutching his dead children, imploring them to get up and walk. On that terrible night, the world saw in gruesome detail the terrible nature of chemical weapons."[9]

The eloquence of his words masked the feeble decision he would deliver to the world. With Congress, public opinion and the armed forces still nursing their wounds after the invasion of Iraq, the President would not be intervening militarily in Syria. Hence, a war that had been based on lies was now blocking another one grounded in facts.

Instead, Obama decided to pursue what then seemed a timely diplomatic initiative put forward by Russian President Vladimir Putin, Assad's most important ally, which involved destroying Syria's chemical arsenal. This was an option that "would come to have far more serious consequences than we imagined, for Syria and for the entire world," argues François Hollande, then President of France.

Hollande had become the first socialist to occupy the Elysée Palace in nearly two decades. At the start of his mandate, which would fundamentally mark Guterres' career, he achieved levels of popularity that exceeded 60 per cent.[10] The new President would gain international support for sending troops into Mali and the Central African Republic, two former French colonies—just like Syria. Hollande recognises that, "The Security Council would never have authorised an intervention to punish Bashar al-Assad." Even so, Hollande is critical of Obama's strategy: "When a great country like the United States considers that there is a red line, and this line is crossed without military consequences, the other powers conclude that they have a kind of authorisation to go even further—and we can all see how Putin later used this 'non-intervention' to push into Ukraine."

Following the chemical attack in Eastern Ghouta, it became even more evident that Syria had become—as was already said privately within UNHCR corridors—"the mother of all proxy wars". It was an entanglement of conflicts: between Sunnis and Shiites; Kurds and Alawites; Salafi-jihadis and moderates. These simultaneous conflicts swept nearly the entire country and fed century-old heresies, while intersecting the interests of nuclear powers, such as the United States and Russia, and great regional powers, especially Iran and Saudi Arabia. These were conflicts that involved Syria's sensitive neighbours—Israel, Iraq, Lebanon and Turkey—and pitted states against armed non-state groups. All had some kind of role to play: selling weapons, contributing soldiers and supplies, transferring money, sharing information, forging alliances, imposing sanctions, shifting responsibilities and spreading lies.

The further events strayed from their normal course and the more contaminated diplomacy became, the more Guterres had to strive to keep channels open. "When things get too complicated, two things are important: to have ideas and have nerves of steel," he regularly told his UNHCR teams. "We are not here to be politically manipulated by anyone. We need to be the ones everyone respects and trusts. So, be transparent and loyal with the governments you work with and be loyal to your partners." Any support was as essential as it was scarce. And as chaotic as the situation became inside Syria, the UNHCR's main responsibility remained the protection of refugees; those Syrians that had fled across national borders looking for safety.

Bang, Bang, Bang

By the time they finally arrived here, out in the middle of the desert, many families expected to stay a month or so, maybe even less. Sleeping in cramped, dusty tents would be a merely temporary discomfort. In no time at all, they told themselves, they would be back home.

They were exhausted. Many had walked 40 kilometres or more just to reach the border, travelling by night so they might elude the indiscriminate gunfire of war.

By the time Guterres paid them a visit in June 2013, the families were still there, exhausted and with few or no belongings. A year had now passed and the temporary holding camp had become a refugee settlement with many of the tents replaced by trailers. Hope had given way to despondency.

Guterres had made the journey to commemorate World Refugee Day. Indeed, few places deserved visiting more in 2013. Located in the north of Jordan, just 11 kilometres from Syria, Za'atari had grown into the second largest refugee camp in the world.

The site now housed 120,000 Syrians.[11] For many of the refugees, their real homes were so close that, from Za'atari, they could still hear the rumble of explosions and gunfire. So close, in fact, some even risked returning to the warzone. They said that not even camels would spend a night in the camp, that it was better to die a quick death than to perish slowly, day by day.

Nevertheless, the majority considered it too dangerous to return and too expensive to live elsewhere in Jordan. Although the camp was overflowing and, according to the UNHCR, "lawless in many ways,"[12] at least there they were not paying rent.

Divided into districts and laid out according to a grid, with streets running parallel and perpendicular as though this were a capital city, Za'atari sheltered a range of groups. Organised crime networks lived alongside Syrian opposition groups, as well as professors, university students and small business owners, whose careers, plans and professional commitments had suddenly been interrupted. Rather than a new life in the wealthy West, many only wanted their old lives back, with or without Assad at the helm.

Even though they were able to keep in touch—via WhatsApp and Facebook—with family members and friends who were still in Syria, it was particularly difficult to endure the long hours of forced idleness and frustration. The temperatures, freezing cold in winter, intensely hot in summer, did not encourage outside activity. Some refugees found a certain emotional and intellectual relief in art projects: painting, sculpture or model building, objects they later tried to sell.

The best place to buy and sell in Za'atari was on the Champs-Élysées. This was the camp's main street, named after the famous avenue in Paris. There one found stands selling cell phones, tobacco, tennis outfits, fruit and vegetables, carpets and other household products, even pet birds. Those planning a wedding— and at least one took place every weekend—could find ceremonial clothes and musicians for hire. Those with newborn babies—and dozens were born each week—could buy what they needed.

Guterres' visit was thoroughly scheduled. So much so that, before entering a tent to talk with Syrian refugees, someone from the local UNHCR team would check the schedule and remind him how much time he had: "We have twenty minutes here."

The High Commissioner went in, took off his shoes and sat down with his legs crossed on the tent floor, between the parents of a young family. There was nothing there except for the red and beige carpet unrolled in the centre. More than the conversation itself, the behaviour of a child attracted his attention. "There's this four-year-old child who spends those twenty minutes shooting a plastic pistol—bang, bang, bang—at everyone around him," recalls Guterres. "The father and mother tried to calm him down a number of times, even I tried, but he just continued shooting. I was watching this and thinking, 'What is this kid going to grow up to be in life? We don't have any psychiatrists to treat him. We don't have the resources for that…' And then I thought, 'He's hardly the only one with problems…'"

At the time Guterres visited Za'atari, the number of Syrian child refugees verged on a million.[13] The majority were aged under eleven and the war had taught them new words, such as "sniper" and "martyr", and had prompted them to draw rockets, ambulances and bloodstains in their sketchbooks. Guterres saw some of these illustrations while flipping through the self-portraits made by children in the grip of war. He also met boys and girls who had been struck dumb by their experiences, who suffered night terrors, and he knew they were easy targets for recruitment by armed groups, child labour, underage marriage, and sexual and domestic violence.

School, perhaps the best defence against war, was available only to a minority. According to the UNHCR Coordinator for Syria at the time, this was a lost generation: "The Syrians praise education compared to other Middle Eastern countries. They used to have a 95 per cent literacy rate and now there is a generation that completely missed out on school. A child who was 6 when the war started, is today about 12 or 13… their entire primary education never even began."

Despite Za'atari being a favourite topic for the media, 80 per cent of Syrian refugees hosted by Jordan had lived in urban areas.[14] The kingdom kept it borders open but such generosity began to generate resistance. "In the early months of the crisis," says Nasser Judeh, then Foreign Minister of Jordan, "the numbers were not too alarming, but in 2012 they started to rise significantly, reaching several thousand crossing into Jordan every day. We are one of the poorest countries in the world in terms of water resources, and we purchase 97 per cent of our energy needs from abroad. We always say that a refugee coming into Jordan is not carrying a bucket of water with him or her."

As the flow of refugees increased so did the country's needs, and all against a backdrop of an economic slowdown exacerbated by the proximity of war, which further dampened trade, foreign investment and tourism. In an effort to alleviate these difficulties, the UNHCR distributed a guaranteed minimum income, a grant for refugees facing situations of extreme vulnerability.

Just to the north, a small, arid territory was suffering the same dilemmas as Jordan. In a year, Lebanon's refugee numbers had surged from 157,000 to 850,000, roughly one-fifth of the country's population and taking it to a level that—by the laws of nature—should only be reached in 2050.[15] At a conference, Guterres explained that would be the equivalent "to 66 million refugees arriving suddenly in the United States, 17 million in Germany and over 280 million in China."[16]

The influx of Sunni refugees worried some religious sectors in Lebanon. Certain men of faith feared that, by raising their demographic presence, the Sunnis would also eventually gain greater political power. Guterres often crossed paths with these bickering factions: "In Lebanon, I never had problems with the Sunnis and very few problems with the Shiites. I did have a lot of problems with the Christians."

Lebanon and Jordan, along with Iraq, Turkey and, on a lesser scale, Egypt, hosted 97 per cent of Syrian refugees, hence the repeated and public praises from Guterres for the generosity of these communities and for keeping their borders open when faced with "the biggest displacement crisis of all time."[17] When Guterres said that, the number of Syrian refugees had just broken the two million barrier.

The biggest crisis of all time arose precisely when Guterres was most prepared. After conflict broke out in Syria, the High Commissioner was spending more time at the United Nations than Secretary-General Ban Ki-moon. By 2013 he had been head of the UNHCR for almost ten years and this experience had made him, according to the Assistant High Commissioner for Operations, "the most knowledgeable person you have in the organisation." Janet Lim adds that, "In those years, he became much more hands-on and we were always saying nobody could beat him in terms of grasping the overall picture."

Similarly, Dominik Bartsch, the current UNHCR representative in Germany, explains that, "I have never seen anyone who was able to match Guterres in terms of detailed knowledge and understanding of the political dynamics of what was really going on." He adds, "It was not just knowledge but the ability to apply it in a wider context as a predictor to be able to say, 'This is likely to go in this direction.'"

However, this did not mean that the UNHCR's performance during the war in Syria was beyond reproach. An internal report concluded the agency "did not provide effective coordination in the earlier stages of the emergency,"[18] adding that, in the field, "there had been a perception that the UNHCR was at times more preoccupied with managing its own operations than coordinating the overall refugee response." A later evaluation referenced a perhaps overly close relationship between the High Commissioner and the Jordanian government: "While the UNHCR should be lauded for the relationship it has built to date, it cannot let the safeguarding of that relationship impede the need to advocate and lobby on behalf of refugees."[19]

Nevertheless, for the time being, this internal criticism remained in-house. It hardly infringed upon the external reality where events on the ground only served to highlight the High Commissioner's role.

In fact, the Syria crisis threw Guterres into the international spotlight.

Henceforth, he ceased to be just another official at the United Nations. He became the most newsworthy leader of any of its agencies; perhaps too newsworthy for the Secretariat's taste.

He was no longer just heard annually at the General Assembly's Third Commission, as befitted his High Commissioner status, but instead was regularly summoned by the Security Council.

He was no longer managing a budget of $1 billion and 6,000 officials; now, he was responsible for the UNHCR's largest ever budget: $5.3 billion.

The war was costly, requiring vast expenditure, and this was one facet that consumed the most time and energy. At the beginning of each month, Guterres held a meeting with the organisation's accountancy officers. He carefully analysed balance sheets with the trained eye of an engineer, reconciling debits and credits and calculating additional costs. He studied fundraising forecasts and updated the amounts allocated to large operations with respect to any funding gaps, all the while checking any savings generated through the

Budapest restructure. This X-ray analysis completed, he made decisions, asked for adjustments and launched new initiatives with the twofold purpose of controlling the functioning operations and perfecting a narrative line capable of attracting donors.

In Geneva, Guterres also attended regular meetings with those states contributing the most to the UNHCR's budget, the so-called "Twenty Million Club". Despite its annual contribution being less than $20 million, sometimes China would also sit at the table.

The club's ambassadors organised these closed-door meetings on a rotational basis, which could also happen at Guterres' special request. "After going on any important mission, he would come back and call for a meeting with the Club where he would work his magic," recalls Sophie Muller, his assistant who attended several of these events. "He would never really talk about money and would rather make them feel privileged by sharing very strong political analysis of the conflict, based on what he had seen in the field, and this helped him gain a lot of credibility."

In contrast, the High Commissioner refrained from voicing political concerns in public. He lobbied and engaged in fundraising for countries like Jordan and Lebanon. He always insisted that what these countries desperately needed, far more than humanitarian aid, were development projects in areas such as health and education, and he correspondingly called on the international community to come up with a "New Deal" for Syria's neighbours.

In spite of all the High Commissioner's efforts, there was still a lack of money. Hence his journey, in January 2014, to Kuwait to attend the Second Donor Conference on Humanitarian Aid to Syria. While a third of the donations promised a year earlier at the inaugural conference were still outstanding, the United Nations was once again urging the West and the Gulf States to dig into their pockets.

The UN was forecasting that 22.4 million Syrian refugees and displaced persons would need help in 2014.[20] To this end, the UN asked for more funding than ever before in their history: $6.5 billion.[21]

The new Secretary of State John Kerry led the US delegation, which included Guterres' principal interlocutor in Washington,

Anne C. Richard, Assistant Secretary of State for Population, Refugees and Migration.

Just before the conference's formal opening at the Bayan Palace, the official residence of the Emir of Kuwait, Kerry had scheduled a meeting with the event chairman, the UN Secretary-General.

They sat next to each other at the back of a carpeted room in the sumptuous palace. Kerry, unlike Ban, had a dossier open on his lap. They were not alone. The heads of UN agencies and members of the Secretary of State's team followed the conversation, but remained silent.

"Kerry was steeped in Middle East policy issues and proceeded to discuss Syria and other crisis situations with the Secretary-General," says Richard. "He laid out various actions Ban might take or ideas he could endorse. Ban was non-committal and did not say much. I looked across at Guterres and I saw how he could barely sit still and seemed ready to jump in at any moment. My sense was that he would have been eager to engage Kerry and discuss various policy options if they'd been meeting one-on-one."

The Arc of Instability

It was early in 2014 when, during the usual social engagements at one of Lisbon's functions, Portugal's head diplomat was startled by an unknown figure. This foreign emissary reached out his hand, introduced himself and, without further ado, delivered his message. "He said he was from the Norwegian diplomatic service," reveals Rui Machete, then Minister of Foreign Affairs, "and told me that, if the government agreed that António Guterres could take on the role of UN Secretary-General, then the Scandinavians would be ready to support him."

Machete took advantage of a trip to Geneva, in March 2014, to share what had happened with Guterres: "I told him that our government was completely willing to get behind him as a candidate if that's what he wanted. He thanked me reticently."

Guterres had refused to give any sign whatsoever to the Minister and, within the UNHCR, the High Commissioner's position was adamant. "Whenever people—Athar among others—

whispered in his ear about a possible candidacy for Secretary-General, he would always reject it in a very firm way, saying, 'Don't talk to me about that,' or, 'Absolutely not,'" says his former assistant, Sophie Muller.

Did that mean he was not thinking about succeeding Ban Ki-moon? Or that it was simply too early to take any position on the subject?

Or was that same meticulous politician, who had spent decades preparing himself for the role of Prime Minister, considering whether or not to run?

Was that "absolutely not" merely tactical, the response of someone who deemed it counterproductive to make his personal ambitions official while dealing with humanitarian crises? Was Guterres simply condoning this speculation, hoping to be called for a job he really wanted?

Among the UNHCR directors, there were some who—behind their boss' back—accused him of being calculating. "He has been preparing for ten years for this candidacy, manipulating us, outsmarting us for his own benefits," some commented in Geneva.

These same judgemental eyes saw him return to Africa in early 2014. Even though Syria was still absorbing nearly all of the High Commissioner's attention, the rest of the world was hardly letting him rest. For example, in the Central African Republic, the most recent wave of assault and retaliations between Catholics and Muslims had forced 300,000 people to flee to Cameroon, Chad or the Congos.[22]

And "Republic" in this case meant anarchy; "Central", paradoxically, meant far away from everything. Members of the peacekeeping forces deployed in the country, in a Security Council-approved mission led by the African Union, referred to the country as the "end of the world." They also said that often on the ground it was two words, rather than gunfire, that brought the enemy militias to their senses: "The Hague." The Dutch city that hosted the International Criminal Court, a body empowered to judge war crimes, was particularly attentive to events in Africa.

Guterres met with several of these men, many of whom were Portuguese, during his twenty-four-hour visit to the Central

African Republic in February, long enough for him to remember that visit as one that caused him the most anguish: "It's a total tragedy. There's extreme poverty, a complete lack of any kind of capacity: for security, for education, healthcare—zero. There's no state: beyond the capital, it simply doesn't exist."

On an expedition outside the capital, Bangui, Guterres came across a local farmer, a depiction of a country trapped in the past: "I saw a man digging a hole with a stick and throwing a seed into it. There was no plough! I saw it with my own eyes! 'What's this? What are you doing?' Poke a stick, put the seed in, poke again with the stick, another seed."

A few weeks later, his next trip took him to South Sudan. Instead of stabilising the country and fostering development, the independence process since 2011 had rapidly deteriorated into warfare. Guterres remembers his meeting with President Salva Kiir and how his warnings fell on deaf ears: "The elites there— both governmental and the opposition—don't care about the people. They're all the same; all bad; it's general corruption. They have done nothing in South Sudan after all these years. There's no investment. They bought a lot of war material; but roads, schools, hospitals... almost none."

Out of all the emergencies the UNHCR was responding to in East Africa, perhaps the most worrisome, and certainly the longest, was the one Somalis were facing in Kenya. The country hosted the world's largest refugee camp. In reality, it was not one camp but five. Some 400,000 people were estimated to live in the Dadaab complex, the overwhelming majority Somalis escaping war, hunger and extreme drought in the Horn of Africa.[23]

Nevertheless, Kenyan political life was being shaped more by a lack of security than by the humanitarian drama. Dadaab, the local authorities insisted, sheltered terrorists and had morphed into a recruitment centre for al-Shabaab extremists, a group opposing the Somali government who had sworn allegiance to al-Qaeda.

Each time they embarked on a killing spree—they killed seventy-one people in the September 2013 terrorist attack on the Westgate shopping mall, for example—the Kenyan government brought back the plans to close Dadaab and publicly gave the

UNHCR just a few months to deal with the issue, which demanded a particular political balancing act by the High Commissioner.

Given the size of Dadaab, Guterres kept Ban Ki-moon's office updated on the state of affairs, especially Ban's new chief of staff, the Argentinian Susana Malcorra. One feasible solution was to align the UNHCR's interests—to keep the camp open—with the needs of the Kenyan government—a need for investment in its security forces—while coordinating with the United States—who were publicly claiming to be invested in combatting terror in the region. If Washington could beef up support for Kenyan military training, and provide more equipment under existing bilateral programmes, this would certainly help soothe the mood.

However, on any number of occasions, the head of UNHCR had to improvise solutions of his own accord: "This was worse than it was with Pakistan. I went there various times just to speak with the President of Kenya. 'I completely understand, you have public opinion up in arms. It's a serious problem. Let's find a way out of this.' They announced a return scheme for the Somalis, the first began to leave, the plan went on slowly and, in the meantime, the pressure was lifted… it was a constant back and forth."

To win at this game, Guterres needed to reach beyond Nairobi. He made occasional returns to the Horn of Africa to meet with other capitals equally worried about Dadaab. In August 2014, he flew to Addis Ababa where the UNHCR had put together a regional ministers' meeting on Somali refugees. Why Ethiopia? "Because we had to work with the interest of all parties; the Ethiopians helped us contain the Kenyans because, as they said, 'If the Somalis are expelled from Kenya, they'll all come to Ethiopia.'"

Dissecting African conflicts was a recurring theme in conversations with a friend renowned for his understanding of the continent's power plays, the Executive Secretary of the United Nations Economic Commission for Africa, who was visiting Geneva to participate in the 2014 annual meeting of the UNHCR Executive Committee. Carlos Lopes was scheduled to give a talk during the African segment where, along with long-standing problems, new and alarming threats had emerged, such as an uncontrolled outbreak of Ebola.

As September drew to a close, there was plenty more filling the executive committee's agenda. In overall terms, the global humanitarian panorama was gloomier than in previous decades:

- For the first time since World War II, the total of refugees, those seeking asylum and the internally displaced had surpassed the 50 million barrier.[24]
- Of these, 16.7 million were formally recognised as refugees—the largest number since 2001.[25]
- The number of refugees returning to their country of origin had fallen to its lowest level in a decade.[26]
- The number of internally displaced persons had peaked at an unprecedented level: 33.3 million.[27]

The ExCom, as it was known, took place in the Palais des Nations Assembly Hall. Sitting at the podium's central table, Guterres was not a passive participant. He intervened to clarify various aspects of the agency's undertakings, to promise cooperation or to commend already-made commitments. Though geographically distant, many of the world's conflicts were, according to the Portuguese, part of the same Arc of Instability.[28] "In the end," says Guterres, "I began to use this expression because we're facing a group of problems—Nigeria, Mali, Libya, Somalia, Syria, the Palestinian Question, Iraq, Afghanistan, Yemen—which are all interlinked; fighters move between conflicts and all are in some way related to the rekindled and global phenomenon of terrorism."

Between public appearances and bilateral commitments, Guterres was so overwhelmed he was unable to be at the Palace's gate to welcome the UN Secretary-General, that year's guest of honour. The task fell to Sultan-Khan, who led Ban to the meeting in the Assembly Hall, where Guterres was presiding.

On the way, Sultan-Khan and his guest briefly stopped to view an exhibition in the corridor featuring a refugee house designed and developed by the UNHCR in partnership with IKEA. The "Refugee Housing Unit" was 17 square metres, divided into living and sleeping areas, with rigid plastic walls and ceilings high enough so that an adult could stand up inside. The building had a five-person capacity and could be assembled in six hours. It included a locking door, a solar energy-powered LED light and windows covered with mosquito netting. Ten thousand units were soon due for delivery at a unitary cost of $1,150, plus transportation and storage. It was designed to last three years, perhaps longer if reinforced with local materials.

The house was a key reason for the UN Secretary-General's presence in Geneva. Refugee camps had increasingly become permanent homes for millions of families, and the ExCom presented an opportunity to deal with this and other pressing topics that the United Nations General Assembly, held a few weeks earlier, hadn't found the time to discuss.

> Good morning. [...] Over the years, the UNHCR has been bestowed with the Nobel Peace Prize—not once, but twice. Today, you are at the centre of action and assistance for tens of millions of people in need. [...]
>
> I thank the High Commissioner for your decade of delivering for the UNHCR and the people it serves. I really thank you and highly commend your leadership.[29]

Similar to Guterres, Ban was nearing the end of his second term. Shortly after the former ceased his functions as High Commissioner, the post of Secretary-General would become vacant. There was another important parallel to consider in this looming chain of events: whoever succeeded Ban would begin work around the same time as the next President of the United States, then assumed to be Hillary Clinton.

It was still early for Guterres whether to go for the Secretary-General position, but he had an interest so he began exploring his prospects. With this in mind, the head of the UNHCR took advantage of Lopes' visit to Geneva to reflect on the future: "We had already talked about it, but it was more on the terms of, 'There are people who think I could be a candidate,' or, 'There are certain reactions from certain people at the UN because they think I'm going to be a candidate.'" Now, at that ExCom meeting, Guterres was adopting a different stance: "If I were a candidate, do you think I have any chance?" "Should I go for it, or not?"

Soap Bubbles

Volker Türk, in February 2015, had just been promoted to the troika, the Russian term Guterres liked to apply to the group comprised of the Deputy High Commissioner and the two UNHCR Assistant High Commissioners. It was also the Austrian's 50th birthday and that was the real reason for the celebration—and why he was far from Geneva, trying to enjoy a much-deserved holiday. But these were extraordinary times, so even during leave, he was still receiving four calls per day from his boss.

"Once [Guterres] called me sounding quite desperate," recalls Türk. "I think he was on his way to Dubai and, of course, during the flight he couldn't take calls. So, when he landed, he had missed calls from twenty heads of government. Suddenly, he was on the phone with Hollande, with Chancellor Merkel; all these European leaders wanted to engage, they were discovering the refugee issue, which they had never had to deal with in the same way before."

Türk knew all about the European resistance to admit refugees. Along with Guterres, he had attended various meetings with European Union justice ministers and interior ministers. He would invariably return from Brussels with bad news, or rather no news. In order to keep unwanted foreigners out of their countries, the ministers shielded themselves behind the so-called Dublin regulation. According to this law—originally ratified in 1997 at a summit that Guterres had attended as the Prime Minister of Portugal—the responsibility to handle an asylum seeker case fell to the European Union country of entry.

If, for example, 170,000 reached the shores of Italy after having made the voyage from Libya or other African ports—as happened in 2014, representing a nearly 300 per cent increase on previous years[30]—then Italy, and only Italy, had to deal with the issue. Should any such persons then cross the border into another European state, they risked becoming illegal and being deported... back to Italy.

Since Guterres' trip to Lampedusa, the situation in the Mediterranean had deteriorated so drastically that the new Pope had chosen the Sicilian island for his inaugural visit. On this small

Italian island, Pope Francis celebrated mass with a shipwrecked boat as an altar. During the service, he criticised "the culture of comfort, which makes us think only of ourselves, makes us insensitive to the cries of other people, makes us live in soap bubbles which, however lovely, are insubstantial; they offer a fleeting and empty illusion which results in indifference to others."[31]

Nevertheless, the exhortations of the Pope and the UNHCR's campaigns fell on deaf ears. According to the UN, crossing the central Mediterranean was the world's most dangerous route for migrants. The statistics—in all probability underestimating the real numbers—pointed to 2,300 deaths between January and September of 2014, ten times the figure registered on the Mexico-United States border.[32]

This data represented only one facet of the unfurling calamity as the humanitarian plight on the shores of the Mediterranean stretched beyond the Strait of Sicily. At the eastern end of the sea, the war in Syria was moving into its fourth year and the number of refugees was heading towards four million.[33] Inside the country, tallying the dead was no longer feasible. Even deploying its most top-level negotiators, such as Kofi Annan, round after round of political discussions sponsored by the UN and Arab League ended in deadlock.

Meanwhile, after exiting Iraq and resisting a new deployment in Syria, President Obama authorised air strikes against the Islamic State in both countries. Financed by discount oil sales, the extremist group had proclaimed a caliphate in the region and its gruesome propaganda in Arab, English and French, which included web pages and videos, such as the decapitation of the American journalist James Foley, attracted young people carrying European passports.

Guterres followed these events from a distance as he refused to set foot in Syria: "It was on purpose that I never went there. I sent emissaries to negotiate things and they sometimes even spoke directly with Assad. I decided not to go because I didn't want to be exploited as a tool. Several of my colleagues did go and this later created problems. For the UNHCR to be able to continue to protect refugees outside of Syria, on the one hand, working closely with the countries that surrounded it, and on the other hand, to continue to give some support to the internally displaced and still avoid playing the government or the opposition's game, I didn't go back to Damascus."

He continued to visit Jordan, Lebanon and Turkey, where the daily lives of Syrian refugees, painful and arduous from the beginning, had become unsustainable. "Their economic situation deteriorated as our funding went down, they even lacked food and a lot of them were evicted from their rented rooms," explains the UNHCR's regional coordinator, Amin Awad. "They were jobless, in debt, and the fact their children didn't have a school yet was killing them. So, they started marching towards Europe—I call it the Great March in the sense that you had one million people on the march for a whole year."

The number of refugees arriving in Eastern Europe started to increase in early 2015. In less than an hour, the truly lucky ones landed on one of the Greek islands, the beaches already littered with life jackets left behind by earlier arrivals. It might have been Lesbos or Chios, Samos or Kos—everyone felt the same pain as others had felt when reaching Lampedusa.

Once in Greece, another stage of their pilgrimage began. Macedonia was easily reached by public transport. From there began a long walk north. Wearing backpacks, carrying bags in their hands and children in their arms, they followed paths running alongside the northbound railway line until crossing the border into Serbia. Camps were set up along the way, and for long days and nights they dreamed of reaching Hungary, another crossing point to their final destination into Austria or Germany—two of the richest countries in the European Union, places many migrants imagined would be a happy ending to a months-long nightmare.

The dangers of this odyssey were widely known—to governments, international organisations and the general public. They were chronicled in the media, in reports issued by European institutions, in feature articles, and in the UNHCR's statistics.

With the Syrian exodus dramatically impacting the West, it was deemed wise to extend the term of the High Commissioner for Refugees. No one wanted to switch admirals in the midst of that storm. Ambassadors applied pressure, Guterres agreed, and the

UN General Assembly approved a six-month extension until December 2015, on the recommendation of Ban Ki-moon.

At this juncture, after ten years dealing with refugees and nearing the end of his mission, the last thing on Guterres' mind had been the organisation of a new operation in Europe, the world's richest region after the United States. "In spite of everything, the situation was manageable," says Guterres. "We are talking about integrating a million people into a population of 500 million in the European Union. What we needed was a robust reception machine, with adequate facilities, security screening systems and finally a way to distribute people over the various countries. All those people came to Greece, then they moved on from border to border… and the idea that people got from watching this on television was that the whole thing was out of control, and that, 'They come here and ruin our villages and cities.' There was panic and everything closed up."

These images were repeatedly broadcast on various television stations, including the Hungarian state-run channels under the control of Viktor Orbán's government, whose rise to power in 2010 represented a sharp change in the political climate from when the Socialists had convinced the UNHCR to set up operations in Budapest. The nationalist Prime Minister was running a concerted campaign against everything Guterres represented. He campaigned against the activities of foreign NGOs,[34] associated immigrants with criminality[35] and promised voters "to keep Hungary as Hungary"[36]—meaning, white and Christian.

In September 2015, the European Union attempted to impose refugee quotas on member states to alleviate the burden on Italy and Greece, but Orbán peremptorily refused. And on the same day, he walked arm-in-arm with other leaders during the Republican March in Paris, following the 7 January 2015 terrorist attack against the satirical newspaper *Charlie Hebdo*, that had been committed on behalf of the Islamic State after the publication of a caricature of the Prophet Muhammad. Orbán expressed his hope that "a composed, calm analysis of the recent events will guide European leaders and Brussels towards a tough policy restricting immigration."[37]

Orbán, at the time a member of a group of European conservative parties that also included the Presidents of the European

Council, the European Commission, and the German Chancellor, had been able to consolidate his power on the complacency of his European partners and the lack of American input. Although Hungary—once a member of the Warsaw Pact—was a member of NATO, the United States had taken eighteen months to send a new ambassador to Budapest, and Obama's choice to fill the post, a television producer who had contributed to the Democratic campaign, led to a good deal of controversy. "Hungary is on the verge of ceding its sovereignty to a neo-fascist dictator, getting in bed with Vladimir Putin," Republican Senator John McCain protested, "and we're going to send the producer of *The Bold and the Beautiful* as the ambassador."[38]

Throughout 2015, Europe hosted summits, conferences, special meetings, put an initial package of measures out for debate, and then another one, worked up agendas and plans for action and distributed statements to the press. In truth, Guterres maintains, "A European political agreement was never reached that would ever be able to create a serious mechanism for receiving and distributing refugees. They made some ridiculous attempts at relocating people that never really functioned." According to him, "The problem wasn't even the European Commission, they were actually on our side. The problem was the member states, especially the Ministers of Home Affairs. Purely and simply, they didn't want there to be any Europe-wide response."

Guterres' response was to denounce the regional imbalance, patent in the fact there were ten times more Syrian refugees living in Turkey than in all twenty-eight European Union member states. He also criticised the lack of European cooperation, stressing that Germany and Sweden alone were sheltering almost two-thirds of the Syrians who sought protection in the Union, and highlighted the benefits that immigration could bring to a continent with an ageing population. "Look, you don't have enough children, your people don't want to do all the jobs, and you don't want migrants. How are you going to live?" he inquired, during a dinner with European leaders.

Guterres continued his regular contacts at the highest level. But even those European leaders open to refugees, such as the German

THE GREAT MARCH

Chancellor, sometimes disappointed. Contrary to her party's conservative wing, Angela Merkel, who had grown up on the eastern side of the Berlin Wall, was open to the idea of taking in 500,000 refugees a year, hence the reason for calling the High Commissioner.

"Do you have tenses?"

With Sultan-Khan at his side, in his Geneva office, Guterres missed the meaning of Merkel's question and looked to the Pakistani for clarification. "Tenses?" Sultan-Khan was also lost.

"I am sorry, Madam, would you mind repeating the question?"

Merkel, who rarely spoke English in public, repeated the question, again leaving Guterres in the dark. This time Sultan-Khan grasped the meaning, scribbling onto a notepad: "TENTS." The Portuguese could not believe Germany, the all-powerful surplus economy, was asking him for help. "They need tents from the UNHCR?!" Guterres whispered to his chief of staff, before picking up the telephone again:

"No, we don't have tents, we have houses."

The Chancellor was in a hurry, so Guterres promised to send a "Refugee Housing Unit" within the next twenty-four hours. The equipment would be unloaded in a German airport, so that government technicians could perform the required inspection. Everything went according to plan, until the German response turned out negative: the house would catch fire too easily.

Without any indication that the European situation would stop deteriorating, the head of UNHCR went ahead with a decision that he never thought he would take: "Suddenly we found ourselves faced with the need—and I'd say very reluctantly—to set up an operation in Greece and be present in Serbia. We also ended up distributing food to thousands of people in Bulgaria, which was completely absurd. Didn't Bulgaria have the capacity to do that? I really have to say that one of the greatest surprises that I have dealt with in my life was having to run humanitarian relief inside the European Union."

Yet, some were also surprised at the UNHCR's inability to persuade Europe to take in more refugees. One of those pointing her finger directly at Guterres was Sylvana Foa. The former UNHCR Communications Director during the 1990s bluntly states that,

HONEST BROKER

"Guterres is not a humanitarian, but a politician who plays the humanitarian card. The entire time he was at the UNHCR, he dropped the protection ball. There were a lot of platitudes and cutesy refugee videos, but when it came to directly confronting governments over violations of the Refugee Convention, it didn't happen." Foa, who also served at the United Nations as the spokesperson for Secretary-General Boutros-Ghali, maintains, "He should have been pounding the table publicly over what Hungary was doing with the Syrians, about the way Bulgaria was treating the Syrians. He wasn't. Why? Because you don't upset governments, particularly not the big five, if you want to be Secretary-General."

Some UNHCR officials agree with Foa. They thought that Guterres, himself a former European Prime Minister, should have been more vocal and less calculating. Even if dealing with a mixture of economic migrants and refugees, the Agency should have spoken out louder and on more occasions, especially towards governments. This was not just bad-mouthing around the water cooler. These were opinions openly expressed in internal working meetings, of which Guterres was aware.

Guterres feels he made "increasingly more aggressive declarations in relation to this" and that "the UNHCR did what it could." He also insists there was a lot of pushback coming from the European states: "Those in the east were against it. Britain was complicated, very complicated. France *comme ci comme ça*. Denmark was also difficult. The most positive were, at the beginning, Austria, Germany and Sweden. The Netherlands, Belgium and Luxembourg pretty much cooperated. They were still tolerating us, but during my last two or three months the thing was… the system collapsed."

Adopting broadly the same words, Hollande, the French President at the time, asserts: "Guterres did what he could with an organisation that lacked the means to convince states." He also points out that "public opinion showed itself to be extremely reticent over accepting huge quantities of refugees," and that this helped "the extreme-right to grow in Italy, Austria, Germany and France, where it was already quite strong."

Within the team working closest to Guterres, the notion prevailed that the Agency's profile and reputation had been boosted by

226

the Syrian crisis. So much so that on the morning of 9 October 2015—the last day of Guterres' ExCom—there were expectations of a fairy-tale ending for the High Commissioner: "Melissa and I were both very carefully monitoring the Nobel Peace Prize announcement," remembers Sultan-Khan. "We were ready for it and some journalists had even approached us beforehand so that, if we got the award, they could be the first to the Palais for an interview."

When the announcement came, all eyes were glued to the screen.

"The Norwegian Nobel Committee has decided the Nobel Peace Prize for 2015 is to be awarded…"

Expectation was huge. The doors of history seemed to be opening.

"…to the Tunisian National Dialogue Quartet[39] for its decisive contribution to building a pluralistic democracy in Tunisia."[40]

Instead of the anticipated jubilation, the decision triggered ripples of disappointment among senior UNHCR staff.

With his term reaching its end, Guterres received his final visitors in Geneva. As he finished packing, he wrote thank-you letters to ambassadors, heads of partner organisations and others deserving of such gratitude. There was also the matter of cleaning out his office and ending certain personal arrangements, such as donating the furniture from the apartment that had been home for over a decade.

On the UNHCR's official statements it could be read that those ten years had been the most tumultuous in the history of the Agency. Even for someone like Guterres, more invested in tending to the future than revisiting the past, taking stock was inevitable. In a period punctuated by so many and such serious crises, was there any one error Guterres blamed himself for? "I think it was not being able to sufficiently alter the rules of personnel management, which have more repercussions on people's morality and the efficacy of the organisation."

One might also inquire: Did such catastrophic humanitarian realities in some way stain his vision of human nature? "No. Human nature is capable of the best and the worst, and I saw the best and the worst. But I already knew that. It was like that in the Socialist Party, in the shanty towns of Lisbon. Before I came to the UNHCR, the Rwandan genocide, the Khmer Rouge… they had already taken place. I can't say it was a surprise. It was a confirmation."

227

Rules of Procedure

Even with the curtain rapidly falling, the daily affairs continued to demand the attention, presence and words of the High Commissioner for Refugees.

On 12 November, Guterres publicly praised the choice for his successor, the Italian Filippo Grandi, who would be visiting Syria within the very first weeks of his tenure.

On the night of 13 November, Guterres and the world were rocked by a terror attack in Paris. Not even the city's current state of alert, due to the imminent United Nations Climate Change Conference, prevented an Islamic State group from assassinating 130 people and wounding another hundred.[41] They struck the freedoms of those sitting in cafés and restaurants, of people wandering the city's avenues, and of the concertgoers at the century-old Bataclan theatre. The target was clearly the Western way of life.

Young French and Belgian citizens, of Moroccan and Algerian origin, were identified as the leaders of the attack. And, in what was believed to be a strategic lapse, one attacker had left behind a Syrian passport that registered him as a refugee in Greece. While the truth was still being determined, and the terrorists at large were tracked down, the will to take in refugees, already practically non-existent, shrank even further.

Guterres played his part. He condemned the attack and drew attention to how "the first victims"[42] of terrorism had been the refugees. Retrospectively, President Hollande—who classified the attacks as an act of war and declared a national state of emergency—recognises that, "The attacks created—and legitimately so—a certain worry with respect to what would become of this huge influx of refugees and whether terrorists were infiltrating; and, in fact, some of the attackers had been in Syria." Nevertheless, Guterres still maintains, "The majority of refugees, if not nearly all of them, came because they had no other solution."

The candidates seeking their party's nomination in the race for the White House were asked for their reactions to the news. On the Democrat side, the favourite Hillary Clinton was asked to account for her time leading the State Department [2009–13]. The host of the CBS show *Face the Nation* asked her: "Seventy-two per cent of Americans think the fight against ISIS is going badly. Won't the legacy of this administration, which you were a part of, won't that legacy be underestimating the threat of ISIS?"[43]

Over on the Republican side, the media's growing appetite for the unorthodox and grotesque turned the spotlight on the response of a candidate who few took seriously, and who nearly everyone thought had no hope of winning his party's nomination, let alone the presidency. Speaking directly to the French public during a campaign rally in Texas, the businessman Donald Trump claimed, "You can say whatever you want, but if your people had guns, it would have been a much different situation."[44]

With the end of the year approaching, and of his tenure, Guterres travelled to the United States. Secretary-General Ban Ki-moon was keen to honour the outgoing High Commissioner with a lunch at the UN headquarters. Everything Guterres had to do felt inevitably like saying goodbye. This was the feeling at his final appearance as High Commissioner before the Security Council. During the last ten years, he had appeared in person, in writing, and via video conference before this vital organ—and not always in the best of moods. "Re-reading what I said in my last intervention," he declared at one of many briefings as the crisis in Syria was deteriorating, "I am almost tempted to limit my present statement to just ten seconds. Everything I said last time is still true, but it has all got much worse."[45]

That early afternoon, he knew practically everyone sitting with him at the table in the Security Council.

For France, Ambassador François Delattre, who President Hollande had transferred from Washington to the United Nations.

For the United Kingdom, Matthew Rycroft, newly installed in the job, only 47 years old, and arriving with a reputation of being a faithful custodian of Whitehall's instructions.

To represent Russia, Ambassador Vitaly Churkin, completing eleven years in that position, sent his second-in-command.

In China's chair, another of the P5 members, the Chinese Ambassador was also absent and replaced by another diplomat.

And for the United States, which was presiding that month, the Democrat Samantha Power. Before giving the floor to the Portuguese, Ambassador Power, on behalf of all, and for the record, bid him farewell, wishing Guterres "would stay involved in caring for people who have benefitted so much from his leadership."[46]

A few days before departing on this final trip, in the midst of the bustle of leave-takings, Guterres was able to find a few minutes to pick up the telephone. The international call was to New York, but the objective was not to talk with any diplomat in the Security Council, nor even with the Secretary-General's office. This time, Guterres asked to be connected with the Ambassador of Portugal to the United Nations:

"Mr. Ambassador, how are you? I'm calling because I will be in New York for a few days. I'd really like to have a word with you."

PART III

NERVES OF STEEL

18

AFTER MALAYSIA

Eighteen years had passed. Hairs had turned grey and wrinkles had spread. Some had survived potentially fatal diseases. Many had seen children and grandchildren being born. Almost all had quit politics.

Jorge Coelho. António Vitorino. Guilherme d'Oliveira Martins… Just a dozen close, personal friends were invited to the ceremony that brought together Catholics and atheists.

Eighteen years had already passed since Zizas had died and Guterres continued, always at the end of January, always in the church where they had married, to evoke the memory of his wife who had demised while he was still Prime Minister. There were years when the High Commissioner for Refugees would travel to Lisbon specifically for this event, and would spend only the necessary time to attend the mass celebrated by Melícias.

On this occasion, however, Guterres no longer had any international commitments forcing him to dash to the airport on his way to Geneva, or to any of the other destinations common to UN senior staff. Having formally completed his mandate at the UNHCR, the former Prime Minister had time again for personal projects and was even accepting invitations to participate in conferences in Portugal.

At the start of 2016, he was the keynote speaker at a public seminar for the refugee cause, attended by hundreds of diplomats,

233

academics, NGO representatives and journalists. However, his main intervention that day was due to take place later.

Dinner was served at the sumptuous palace housing the Portuguese Ministry of Foreign Affairs but the menu could not have been more frugal. The age of austerity still very much prevailed in Portugal and not even this dream team, urgently summoned for the secret meeting, found more than some last-minute sandwiches spread alongside the work tables.

Far from the spotlight and under the discreet cloak of nightfall, Guterres set his next plan into motion.

"I was certain that was it," says Ambassador José de Freitas Ferraz. "I had kind of already suspected that he might become a candidate" The former diplomatic adviser to Guterres was one of the few invited to this first meeting.

Lined with beige and blue wallpaper, the room had a long meeting table at its centre. Augusto Santos Silva, the Minister of Foreign Affairs, was sitting alongside two of his predecessors, the Secretary of State for European Affairs and a handful of former UN ambassadors and senior in-house diplomats strategically selected for the purpose.

"The Minister made a brief speech," Ferraz explains, "in order to announce that we were there because the government would be supporting the candidacy of António Guterres for the position of Secretary-General of the United Nations."

A round of comments followed, with each guest providing their analysis on the prospects for a successful campaign and the strengths, weaknesses and potential obstacles.

In addition to both the foreseeable and the unpredictable barriers, two monumental hurdles needed to be overcome from the outset. The first was the preference for a female candidate, which was almost unanimously supported by the international community. The second, following the unwritten rule of the United Nations regarding regional rotation, was that the next Secretary-General should come from Eastern Europe.

On that night, Guterres ranked his own chances of success as no better than 20 per cent. A modest estimate according to Silva: "We knew he'd go down very well inside the UN structure as his mandate at the UNHCR had earned him a great deal of prestige, and he would not encounter hostility from the machinery." Silva also points out that, "He had built bridges with practically every country in the world, in a position that came with a very strong advantage: at the UNHCR, he was not able to do politics in the strict sense and, in practice, he hadn't been an irritant to any of the main powers on the Security Council or to any other country."

The same meeting chose the members of the task force responsible for supporting the candidacy. A weekly meeting schedule was agreed, with sessions taking place every late Tuesday morning. However, the best timing to officially announce the candidacy divided opinion. Some argued it should be announced immediately, others later on, after other candidates had already thrown their hats into the ring. Over several weeks, no consensus could be reached. But at least one big doubt had now been cleared up: Just what did Guterres intend to do after leaving the UNHCR?

Indeed, despite the wide speculation that had entertained politicians, diplomats and UN staff, he managed to keep his plans a fairly well-kept secret. Even in his own country, very few were aware of his true intentions. Guterres had only planned to unveil his plans when the deadline for submitting applications drew near.

Given that only states can propose candidates for the position of Secretary-General, he needed the support of the Portuguese Prime Minister and the Minister of Foreign Affairs, whoever they were—and to whatever party they belonged.

It just so happened that, in late 2015, his Socialist Party had made its return to power, the new Prime Minister a previous Minister of Justice in Guterres' government; and the new head of Portuguese diplomacy was another socialist veteran, who had been a Minister of Education and Culture, also under Guterres.

Providentially placed in key places in the national political framework, both had been separately contacted to dine on different occasions with the still serving High Commissioner, speaking in private and with their phones turned off. After long conversations, they had both confirmed they would throw the weight of the government not only behind launching his candidacy, but also throughout the entire election process.

However, the ratification of the candidacy by the Portuguese government was the culmination of a long process of reflection and behind-the-scenes political manoeuvring. A path that had crossed Malaysia and the Vatican, via Addis Ababa and Paris, via Geneva and, of course, New York.

We Can Play this Game

"I'll be in New York in the next few days. I'd really like to talk with you."

During the short phone call, in December 2015, the Ambassador of Portugal to the UN did not need to ask Guterres what the subject of that conversation would be. "I wasn't aware of any obvious refugee-related issue that was under discussion in New York nor anything particular that he might need." Hence, Álvaro Mendonça e Moura concluded that, "This could only be about one thing and so I told him, 'Come and have dinner.'"

Face to face with the diplomat in his official residence, Guterres placed his cards on the table and confirmed his intention to advance with his bid to become Secretary-General, before requesting the diplomat's assessment on the likelihood of his victory. For three hours, they dissected his potential rivals and their respective trump cards.

They talked about the Bulgarian Irina Bokova—a woman from Eastern Europe, who met the two main unwritten criteria in this process. Furthermore, as Director-General of UNESCO, she was well known within the UN system and had already publicly announced her candidacy.

They discussed Kristalina Georgieva, another Bulgarian, Vice President of the European Commission, whom Guterres had already worked with at the UNHCR. Contrary to Bokova, Georgieva shared the same political colours as her ruling party in Sofia.

They perused the likelihood of a bid from Michelle Bachelet, another woman, a former President of Chile, but who would end up not running.

They analysed Malcorra, the powerful chief of staff to Ban Ki-moon, who was due to take office as Argentina's Minister of

Foreign Affairs, thereby potentially representing a region that had hitherto nominated only one Secretary-General.

They also ran the ruler over figures with influence over the process, including the New Zealander Helen Clark, Director of the United Nations Development Programme (UNDP), and the Serb Vuk Jeremić, the former head of the UN General Assembly.

"The stars are aligned against you, but this is not impossible," said Moura. "You have substantial international prestige among the ambassadors here. So, if you do want to go ahead, we have to start out as an underdog. But we can play this game."

But the fact was that the race had already started and Guterres was setting off at a disadvantage…

Malcorra had a window out onto the world. From her office on the thirty-eighth floor of the United Nations headquarters, the right-hand woman to the Secretary-General since 2012 had taken advantage of the preceding four years, building up her experience and contacts, gaining profound knowledge into the workings of the machinery driving the United Nations, and perhaps most importantly, establishing relationships with the permanent members of the Security Council. From her position of control, the Argentinian held access to a great deal of information.

Regarding Guterres' candidacy, Malcorra herself maintains, "I knew well before any announcement. I don't recall the exact moment but I think that, from the moment there were discussions around the final renewal of his mandate at the UNHCR, I already knew that António Guterres would be a candidate."

In fact, following the six-month extension that covered the period from June to December 2015, the UNHCR Executive Committee decided to once again request the High Commissioner to remain in his position—only on this occasion this would be for a one-year period, until the end of 2016.

Guterres affirms that he never sought this second extension: "There really was this movement of ambassadors for me to stay, but I confess that I had very little interest, even to the point of saying, 'It's enough for one country or somebody in New York to think that I should not be staying, for me not to accept this at all. If everybody were to come and tell me, without any exception, from the Secretary-General downwards, that I have to stay for another year, I would certainly consider doing so, but this is not what I actually want.'"

In the end, this was something that Guterres never had to consider. That exception, the certain somebody who thought he should be moving on, emerged at a top level within the United Nations. The extension of his mandate did not receive authorisation by explicit instruction from Ban Ki-moon's office.

"They interfered in the decision and that really did not go down well," remembers Sultan-Khan. Guterres' former chief of staff even argues that New York had no legitimacy over blocking the decision: "The mandate of the High Commissioner has total and utter independence. He does not fall under the Secretary-General; he's not supervised by the Secretary-General. He is elected by the General Assembly, he reports to it and that's it. So the Secretary-General's office doesn't have any reason to interfere."

UN Ambassador Moura agrees that this was no innocent decision, but does not grant a great deal of importance to the situation: "I am convinced that Susana Malcorra did not want to see the mandate of António Guterres extended in the belief that this might favour him and I believe she played a role in this as [Ban's] *chef de cabinet*. Is that pretty? No. But I don't think it was that serious."

What is certain is that this veto proved to be providential. Guterres reveals it was precisely after being released from the duties of High Commissioner that he felt enabled to fully dedicate himself to the campaign: "It ended up being ironic; all that to avoid me pursuing it. They all thought I wanted to continue as High Commissioner in order to run for the position. Today, I recognise that if I had spent another year at the UNHCR, I would not have been able to be a candidate because that was a year of great conflict with Europe and I would not have been in a position to get elected. But that was all luck."

In fact, at various stages, Guterres felt there really were adversaries determined to obstruct his path. The blocking of a new extension to his mandate at the UNHCR was but another piece in the puzzle.

Even prior to the summer of that same year of 2015, the High Commissioner had been chosen as the recipient of the annual Path to Peace Foundation award, one of the most important charitable organisations set up to support the work of the Vatican with the United Nations. For a potential candidate, the prestige and visibility of such an award, which had already been bestowed on two former Secretaries-General, and which would be delivered in person by Pope Francis, was truly a blessing.

From his Geneva office, Guterres told Sultan-Khan to respond, to say that he would be delighted to accept the award and, complying with internal UN protocol, requested that he also write to the Secretary-General's chief of staff to request formal authorisation from his office. "As is always the case, when there's no conflict of interest or whatever," explains Sultan-Khan.

Guterres was fully aware of the norm preventing senior UN staff from accepting awards but, used to accepting such honours as he was, he equally knew there was a solution that was commonly adopted—yes, you could accept as long you received it on behalf of the organisation and not in an individual capacity. "I had already received various distinctions and always after duly requesting authorisation from the Secretary-General. And so, I asked again and was entirely convinced that this would be accepted. This was very prestigious; a peace award from the Vatican."

And it was with this conviction that the High Commissioner set off for his summer holidays in Malaysia with his wife and some friends.

However, upon his return to Geneva and after resuming work, going through the pending issues with Sultan-Khan, he was caught by surprise:

"How is the Vatican thing going?"

"The Vatican? We've already said that you're not accepting."

"Not accepting? Why am I not accepting?"

"The Secretary-General did not authorize it."

"He didn't? But that really is most unusual…"

According to Carlos Lopes, who at the time was the Executive Secretary of the UN Economic Commission for Africa, the response from New York did not come as a surprise: "I thought he didn't have a chance of getting elected based on my internal knowledge of the machine, knowing how it would act to ensure that his candidacy would not be successful." According to the Bissau-Guinean, "The strings inside the system were getting pulled so as to prevent him from advancing with certain types of influence or gaining access to particular information. There were attempts to undermine the profile of some of the things that he might be doing during that period, precisely in order to stop him from gaining visibility. We forecast this and this was exactly what ended up happening."

Guterres even wrote to Ban Ki-moon to express his dissatisfaction at the decision. He argued that both the Secretary-General and he himself had already received similar awards, some very recently, and he was unable to perceive any conflict of interest that justified the negative response.

The episode with the Vatican emerged after the final decision to put forward his candidacy had been taken. Nevertheless, it served as an additional motivation for Guterres to press ahead. This was so much the case that, immediately in September, on the eve of his last ExCom, the High Commissioner decided to let his closest staff in on his decision. It was over lunch in a private room at the UNHCR restaurant with Sultan-Khan and the troika that brought together the Deputy High Commissioner and assistants.

"So, when he returned from the holiday, he formally told us that he'd decided he was going to be a candidate," recalls Sultan-Khan. "Then he slowly started to tell some of the member state ambassadors. He did not make an announcement because he didn't want it to look like, you know, campaigning on the job."

It Would Be Nice if It Were Both You and I Winning

Back in the now distant year of 2008, Thomas Stelzer had just taken on his new position. The Austrian diplomat, recently nominated Assistant-Secretary-General of the United Nations, was participating for the first time in a Chief Executive Board—the biannual meeting where the UN Secretary-General sits down with the leaders of the various agencies in order to best coordinate the ongoing political activities in the international system.

In the Greentree mansion outside New York, the meeting had gathered together the heads of all the different funds and programmes that made up the United Nations universe, from the World Health Organization to UNICEF and the World Bank, to the IMF and, of course, the UNHCR.

"We were the most senior leaders of the international system, all twenty-eight were highly interesting personalities making extremely solid contributions," remembers Stelzer. "And the contribution made by António Guterres was at a far higher level than all others. To me, that came as a great surprise."

Sultan-Khan points out that, by the time of his second term, the High Commissioner had become the most senior figure at these sessions. When holding Chief Executive Board meetings, it became common practice for Ban Ki-moon to participate only on the first day before requesting Guterres chair the rest of the working sessions: "This is to say, he was automatically becoming the de facto number two of the United Nations. He spoke all of the languages extremely quickly, without any written notes, and all of these facets drew the attention of those around him."

The voice of the Secretary-General that Sultan-Khan heard when he was sitting behind Guterres was not merely the fruit of his imagination. The favourable opinions backing the candidacy of the Portuguese politician multiplied and, especially from 2014, there were various states, as well as regional groups, that openly expressed their willingness to back him—when, or if, the time came.

In Geneva, the first group of countries to consensually state this position had been the Arab League. During a 2014 lunch at the residency of the Ambassador of Yemen, at which Guterres was the guest of honour, the diplomats in attendance had made a point of stating, without any reservations, that they would be most satisfied were he one day to become Secretary-General.

"Don't forget that the Arab League is usually represented by one seat on the Security Council," explains Nasser Judeh, then Minister of Foreign Affairs of Jordan, who goes on to say that, "We were at the Security Council 2014–15 and then it was Egypt, at the time of António's candidacy. So, he met with individual countries of the Arab League. So, you know, at the end of the day the support was there."

Shortly afterwards, it was the turn for the Organisation of Islamic Cooperation—which brings together states from all over the world, regardless of geography or ethnicity—to openly convey its support. This already accounted for almost sixty countries.

"On various occasions during my time at the UNHCR," Guterres says, "especially towards the end, various ambassadors and other people would tell me, 'You have to run for the UN,' but I didn't pay a great deal of attention."

Thus, the earliest encouragement came not from Europe, where he had made his mark as a head of government, nor from Africa, where he had maintained excellent relationships ever since his time in the Socialist International, but rather from leading Islamic actors with whom he had only begun interacting during his time at the UNHCR.

However, winning this race involved a great deal more than informal expressions of support. Despite the new election process promising greater openness, transparency and participation from the UN's General Assembly and from wider civil society, Guterres never lost focus that the priority was to convince each of the five permanent members of the Security Council. And so, he acted accordingly.

Ever since its first edition, Guterres had been a regular presence at the Clinton Global Initiative, an annual conference staged by the foundation set up by the former US President, and which attracted leaders from all around the world. Outside the scope of the meetings, where he would announce and explain the ongoing UNHCR programmes, there were fundraising campaigns involving partnerships with multinationals, such as Microsoft and PricewaterhouseCoopers.

And it was at the September 2015 meeting that Hillary Clinton, herself already a candidate for the White House, entrusted Guterres with her expectations given the rare coincidence between the timing of the elections for the next UN Secretary-General and the next US President, both due at the end of the following year.

During a lunch held by the Initiative, Hillary Clinton sat Guterres at her side and inquired whether he would be in the running to become the next Secretary-General. "I only said, 'I don't really know; nothing has been properly decided yet,' and she answered, 'It would be nice if it were both you and I winning.' It was that type of conversation," Guterres recalls.

However, no promise was made and Guterres considers that having received public backing from Hillary Clinton might even have been counterproductive: "She was not President; that was Obama. And she was not in a position to give the support of the United States, she did not have any direct influence. Those who mattered in this regard were Samantha Power or Susan Rice"—the Permanent US Representative to the United Nations and the National Security Adviser to Barack Obama, respectively.

Power recalls how, in late 2015, Guterres sought her out to inquire about how the United States would perceive his candidacy: "The first time that he came to see me and told me he was going to run, he told me something like, 'Look, I want to tell you that I'm going to be a candidate and I need to know whether the United States will oppose this. If that's the case, I don't want to run. I'm not in this to humiliate myself.'"

And in fact, the world's largest military, nuclear and economic power did not have Guterres down as their first choice. The country that would first take up the Portuguese candidate as their own, and that would lend their best efforts to get him elected, was on the other side of the Atlantic, in his own Europe.

Hollande, the President of France at that time, had known Guterres since the 1990s and recognises that "the idea of a socialist, a former President of the Socialist International, becoming the UN Secretary-General... what a fine ambition!"

However, the former French head of state affirms that the alignment in their political thinking was not the main motive that led him to support Guterres: "His deep capacity for analysis, the fact that he speaks various languages, his government experience, of coming from southern Europe, a region recognised for its presence in Latin America and in Africa... he was a good candidate. There were various factors that led us to support him as well as encouraging other countries to do the same."

Hollande also adds: "There was, furthermore, a feeling that an increasing number of countries wanted a weak UN, with a weak Secretary-General, in order to be able to pursue their own interests."

Indeed, Guterres confirms that, "The people who most insisted with me were, in fact, Hollande and his Minister of Foreign Affairs, Laurent Fabius. That was already in 2015."

In practice, this support from Paris, more than from any other capital, would be decisive to the entire campaign. But it could not be excessively overt: no candidate wants to run the risk of appearing to be a stooge of one of the P5.

Therefore, throughout all of this coordination of contacts, operations and manoeuvres made by the French, there would be constant discretion: from the surgical movements of the Ambassador in New York to the efforts—direct and personal—of the country's head of state.

Low-cost and Low-profile

"The first instruction that he gave us was to lead a positive campaign and not to talk anybody down: 'We have to affirm our candidacy in our own right and not in function of others.'"

David Damião, a journalist by profession, was acting as press officer for the campaign. This was his third stint, as Guterres had first invited him to join his government team back in 1995. Two decades later, he was the choice of the task force to take responsibility for contacts with the media.

Rule number one, the "Positive Candidacy" rule, as pointed out by Damião, meant that no public statement should ever make reference to the other candidates. Furthermore, not only would there be no direct criticism of a rival, they were also not authorised to engage in any behind-the-scenes conspiracy to harm the image of others.

Official responses, articles in the press, subliminal replicas of insults thrown at Guterres—everything was forbidden. The campaign for the position of Secretary-General was to rest on promoting his own track record as a politician and as a humanitarian, without any attacks, controversies or deliberate antagonism. The core factor was to portray Guterres as a man able to prevent conflicts and avoid hostilities.

Rule number two—"Low-Cost Candidacy"—was derived from both the vision of the candidate and from the prevailing circumstances in the country that would be paying for the campaign, which continued to suffer the hangover of the financial crisis, and the IMF's and European institutions' bailout.

"Comparing the cost of the António Guterres candidacy with what the others spent is truly unbelievable," claims Santos Silva, the Portuguese Minister of Foreign Affairs.

Guterres would mostly travel on his own, whenever possible in economy class, and would preferably stay at the residences of the Portuguese ambassadors in the various countries that he would visit. The campaign would also draw exclusively on national resources with all expenditure covered by the Ministry of Foreign Affairs budget, with a total cost that would not exceed 200,000 euros.

Even if throughout the campaign Guterres was able to count on sporadic support and the discreet help of friends, the strategy and the outcomes resulted only from the contributions made by himself and his task force, which was made up exclusively by half a dozen diplomats nominated for this purpose and accompanied by advisers to the Prime Minister and the President of the Republic.

Additionally, it was public knowledge that Guterres called for—and, to any possible extent, had undertaken—structural reform within the United Nations, arguing that it was necessary to make the organisation more closely oriented to its results and manage its resources more efficiently, adapting them to a new cost structure. In summary, this involved applying to the wider organisation a strategy identical to that which he had implemented at the UNHCR, with the Budapest reform.

Therefore, there was no tender to award the campaign to a major international lobbying firm, nor to hand any lengthy list of specifications to public relations companies. There was no contracting of even a single communications consultant, political strategist or marketer.

This led to rule number three which, as far as Damião was concerned, was certainly the greatest burden: the "Low-Profile Candidacy".

Guterres was to avoid any unnecessary public declarations. All interviews were carefully chosen, and opinion pieces, posts or videos uploaded onto social networks were a matter of careful assessment over the course of the campaign.

Despite being the first election in which the candidates for Secretary-General could campaign, Guterres knew that he had to win over the heads of state, not public opinion. That is why all appearances and media exposure required a cold and strategic approach.

According to Melissa Fleming, who had been Guterres' spokesperson at the UNHCR, "He wanted to do media very strategically, he wanted to be extremely low-key. He thought that too much media attention in a thing like this could backfire and he wanted this to be behind the scenes; it was a state selection. When he did meet with the media it was off the record, like with the *New York Times* editorial board. He didn't want to be too much out there, looking too desperate or too hungry."

Guterres thought it would not help, perhaps even unadvisable, to take up too much news time, already coveted and fought over by the presidents and ministers whose vote he would need.

This approach was also designed to portray him as somebody who preferred to work directly with the stakeholders, off the public stage, and that he would not be entering into any permanent competition with heads of state for any of the increasingly dispersed media attention.

Finally, rule number four: a "National Candidacy".

Guterres had to appear as a mobilising and capable actor, able to bring together political forces from different sides of the fence. The projected image was of someone able to reach understandings and bring together actors who would normally perceive each other as opponents around common causes.

These efforts started at the beginning of 2016 when the President of Portugal was one of Guterres' longest-standing political rivals: Cavaco Silva, the former Prime Minister from whom he had taken over in 1995 amid numerous political disputes. But the then head of state, who was just a few days away from finishing his term in office, proved entirely willing to lend his support to the candidacy and, to this end, on 27 January, he publicly bestowed upon Guterres one of the highest national honours that protocol permits.

In general, all the political parties and their respective factions proved both willing and able to unite around Guterres' campaign, regardless of past ideological differences or particular tactical circumstances. The cohesive movement that emerged from this cross-party arrangement turned out to be particularly relevant given its sharp contrast with ongoing events with one of the Portuguese candidacy's main rivals.

On the other side of Europe, Bulgaria was experiencing strange days. The nomination of their official candidate, a socialist, was not to the taste of the conservative government that had taken office.

In June 2014, when Irina Bokova publicly launched her candidacy, her country was ruled by a left-wing minority government, which would fall from office in the following month. The right-wing party that would win the subsequent elections, also without a majority, would equally be hostage to a fragile coalition. Under the threat of the socialists bringing down his government, the new Prime Minister, Boyko Borisov, had agreed to keep Bokova as a candidate—begrudgingly and without proper support.

In the meantime, even with all these circumstances running counter to her aspirations, Georgieva had not given up on displaying her own interest in succeeding Ban Ki-moon.

After all, this conservative belonged to the same party as her government. And, through her powerful position as Vice President of the European Commission, where she held responsibility for the entire community budget, she had direct access to two permanent members of the UN Security Council: the United Kingdom and France. Likewise, Georgieva displayed all the conditions to count on Russia's support. Not only had she represented the World Bank in Moscow and spoke fluent Russian, but she also belonged to the same regional group.

What happened, despite nobody knowing exactly how, or even when, was the unprecedented possibility that Bulgaria would put forward not one, but two candidates.

In Guterres' headquarters, these incidents were being thoroughly tracked. On the very day that the Bulgarian government dispatched the candidacy papers for Bokova to New York, the Portuguese Secretary of State for European Affairs, Margarida Marques, who had a lead role in Guterres' task force, met in Brussels with the European Commission's Vice President—Georgieva.

Marques read in the newspapers that morning that, following Bokova's formal submission of her candidacy, Georgieva would withdraw her bid. However, this did not correspond entirely with the truth: "I was going there to speak with her about an entirely different matter and, prior to bidding farewell, I happened to say, 'Well then, I've seen that you said you're not interested in the UN Secretary-General position this time around'—this was because Guterres had asked me to try and sound her out. And she answered, 'It was not me who said that. Nobody has heard me say that. You heard the government of my country say that on my behalf. And that's really not pretty.'"

Simultaneously, the Portuguese presidential elections would only deepen the contrast with Bulgaria and bring further good news for Portugal's national candidate. The future Portuguese head of state would be another long-standing contact of Guterres. Dating back to his earliest days in politics and the times of the Luz Group, Marcelo Rebelo de Sousa—a friend who had become an adversary, and a rival who had enabled the survival of his first government—won the January election to become the next President of the Republic.

Task force coordinator José de Freitas Ferraz explains how the inauguration in March of the new President was leveraged as an act of campaigning: "This was the occasion when Mr. Guterres had his first contact with some of the attendees at the ceremony. He also held meetings with the King of Spain and with the President of Mozambique, for example."

However, not even the fact that his candidacy drew support from every side of the domestic political spectre was sufficient to ensure a greater allocation of resources. At some point, Guterres had an office at his disposal in the palace housing the Secretary of State for European Affairs. But whenever he was in Lisbon, he spent most of his time in his office at the Calouste Gulbenkian Foundation where, since 2013, he had been a non-executive director.

It was there he would receive guests, hold meetings, prepare his travel plans, and coordinate the drafting of his dossiers following the same method he had previously applied to his tours of Europe when he was Prime Minister: calling in specialists and evaluating just what he might do for the various stakeholders, while always retaining focus of his own objectives. Only now, it was no longer the fifteen members of the European Union, but rather the fifteen members of the UN Security Council he needed to woo.

Guterres would have to visit each of them individually, both the five with veto power and the ten non-permanent members, in order to take notes on their respective strategic priorities and set out his vision of how the UN would work better under his leadership. This effort was particularly important for countries whose diplomatic alignments ran counter to his own.

Guterres knew that it would be very difficult for Uruguay and Spain not to support Malcorra from Argentina. He knew that New Zealand would necessarily have to support their former Prime Minister, Helen Clark—just as the United Kingdom, their partner in the Commonwealth, and Malaysia, their neighbour in the Asia-Pacific region would. He knew that Russia and the Ukraine would always prefer a candidate from Eastern Europe, while the United States were strongly campaigning for a woman to take over. For each of them, he needed to weave tailored arguments.

Simultaneously, securing bilateral audiences, especially with the P5, required realistic and complex planning, and perceptive timing was an essential factor for these discussions. This was due not only to the advanced scheduling of these meetings, but also, and above all, to the tactical considerations of the candidacy—in particular, the moment when to announce his own bid. Should Guterres throw his hat into the ring before the others or wait until more, and potentially more dangerous, names go ahead and make the first move?

In fact, the letter from the UN in which the Security Council President and the President of the General Assembly invited the member states to submit their nominations had been sent out on 17 December. The race was already more than fully on.

Looking for a Woman

> Convinced of the need to guarantee equal opportunities for women
> and men in gaining access to senior decision-making positions,
> Member States are encouraged to consider presenting women, as
> well as men, as candidates for the position of Secretary-General.
> We note the regional diversity in the selection of previous
> Secretaries-General.[1]

Any doubts that might still be lingering were swept away by the
letter. For the election of 2016, the United Nations finally declared
in writing that they intended to have a woman as the next
Secretary-General.

On the date the official letter was sent out to member states, the
Security Council was chaired by the United States—represented
by a woman. "The fact that it had been seventy-one years and no
woman running the organisation was ridiculous and absurd,"
declares Samantha Power.

Obama's Ambassador to the UN was one of the strongest drivers of the feminist dynamic, and her agenda from the moment she
arrived in New York was well-known. "There was a big lobby by
some of the female ambassadors in New York run by Samantha
Power and some other female ambassadors about the next
Secretary-General being a female," contextualises Sultan-Khan.
"Nobody could say no to that argument because everybody sup-
ports gender non-discrimination."

An organisation known as the Group of Friends in Favor of a
Woman Candidate for Secretary-General was set up inside the UN
General Assembly. Coupled with the mass efforts of NGOs, to a
greater or lesser extent multiplied all around the world, but especially in the United States, the initiative swiftly drew support from
practically sixty countries… but not from Portugal.

Álvaro Mendonça e Moura accompanied this movement without any enthusiasm, but with a great deal of attention. He knew
very well there were only two names that made sense for his
country to put forward for the position… both of them men!
Hence, the dynamic driving the preference for a female candidate
was against the interests of Portugal, whose hopes of successfully
nominating a candidate fell on the then President of the European

Commission, Durão Barroso, or the High Commissioner for Refugees, António Guterres.

"We were not able to find a woman in Portugal with the prestige and the CV to become Secretary-General," Moura explains, "and therefore did not embrace this movement that was then beginning to take shape. Our work was to prevent the idea of a woman for Secretary-General from becoming unstoppable. I was always saying, 'For this position, I will always choose the best person, do not ask me to be shackled down by saying that this has to be for women.'"

Thus, were Portuguese diplomacy to hold out any hopes of electing a Secretary-General within the foreseeable future, it would have to strive, not necessarily against the female gender, but certainly inflexibly in favour of another great change that was already underway.

Based on concepts foreign to the UN machinery, such as openness and transparency, the method for selecting the Secretary-General was undergoing a historical transformation, promising to attribute a more active role to the General Assembly and even to civil society, thereby counterbalancing the weight held thus far by the Security Council.

The major objective involved the reconfiguration of the entire process to ensure that the successful candidate was not necessarily the preferred option of the five permanent members, but rather the most capable. Or at least, the candidate who could turn the best performance during the public evaluation process, even though the rules for this phase of the process were yet to be defined.

Therefore, should the Portuguese maintain any ambition for electing a Secretary-General, supporting the democratisation agenda was very much the horse that required backing.

A New Methodology

Number 633 on Third Avenue in New York City is just a ten-minute walk from the UN headquarters. Its twenty-ninth floor happens to house the Permanent Mission of Switzerland which, in turn, hosts a large proportion of the meetings of the working group known only by its acronym ACT: Accountability, Coherence, Transparency.

251

Fed up after many decades of having been condemned to a merely decorative role and without any real power to intervene in the choice of the Secretaries-General, and effectively limited to ratifying whatever names the Security Council put forward, in 2016 the member states represented in the General Assembly began to meet in different working groups. The goal was to reach a shared position in order to make substantive alterations to the status quo, in a powerful statement that they were no longer willing to accept a subordinate role or the secrecy of the past.

"The ACT group is highly influential and very serious," explains Moura. "This is a group of countries that really do work and with which we [the Guterres team] have been involved right from the outset."

Even those lobbying for a woman to be made Secretary-General tried to convince this group to adopt its cause, but their initiative immediately ran into a barrier: "What we told them was, 'No, no, you have to be patient but this is not a working method. This is a political consideration that is very valid, but it is not for discussion here and far less for approval here,'" remembers the Portuguese Ambassador.

Effectively, this forum of twenty-seven countries from all continents was designed in order to rethink the very architecture of power within the United Nations and the way that the Security Council worked. The institutional structure of the UN had been set up seven decades earlier and placed the five permanent members at the centre of all relevant decision-making processes. This had long since ceased to reflect the prevailing geopolitical, economic or even demographic realities of the contemporary world.

As such, the desire to impose a set of best practices and introduce more democratic working methods to the United Nations in general, and the Security Council in particular, was shared by the majority of the permanent representatives—and their governments—in the General Assembly. However, despite having started in the late 1990s and dedicated serious efforts to this cause, there had been very few practical results to show for all the work.

Dissatisfied with the inertia prevailing throughout the structure, the Danish politician Mogens Lykketoft was taking advantage of the powers he was endowed with as the President of the UN General Assembly for 2015/16 to attempt to push through reforms of what he deemed an obsolete legacy. And since his mandate coincided with the election of the new Secretary-General, he was left with the responsibility for approving and implementing the change that so many member states had been campaigning for.

According to the rules that would now finally come into effect, for the first time in the history of the United Nations the General Assembly would begin to have a say in this process, granting its President the power to put forward a privileged view over the value of each candidate. Lykketoft would argue, "There have been good Secretaries-General but they have not been known before and they have not been selected de facto by the membership of the United Nations."

Nevertheless, these transformations were only possible due to the joint efforts of various movements: from the diplomacy work undertaken by the Ad Hoc Working Group for the Revitalization of the Work of the General Assembly, constituted by permanent representatives of UN member states; the political pressure of the Elders, an association founded by Nelson Mandela that at the time was presided over by Kofi Annan and that includes in its ranks almost twenty former Presidents and Nobel Prize-winners; the constant advocacy of the 120 states in the Non-Aligned Movement; and, in particular, the diligences of the initiative 1 for 7 Billion: Find the Best Leader for the UN, a conglomerate of almost 800 NGOs and civil organisations gathered "according to the premise that the Secretary-General represents the aspirations of everybody in the world and that an open and transparent election process, which involves every member state and civil society, would help in producing the best candidate, revitalising the United Nations and strengthening the overall authority of the organisation."[2]

Indeed, the already famous 15 December letter sent out by Lykketoft and Power conveyed symbolic content with political messages for various governments. For the first time, it was signed not only by the Security Council, as would always have been required, but also by the General Assembly. It also made reference, in the very first paragraph, to "transparency and inclusion,"[3] in addition to providing for the staging of "informal hearings"[4] of the candidates.

From now on, the decision would not remain exclusively reserved to the corridors of the Security Council, but would be opened to the General Assembly, who finally gained some relevance in the process.

This wave of change, which proved able to take advantage of the social networks as a means of amplifying the message, sought to gain credibility for the United Nations, while making it more appealing to both the member states and to the rest of the world.

For those following these events from Lisbon, Guterres could only benefit from all of these ongoing transformations. The then Foreign Minister Santos Silva believed that the greater the clarity for the citizens-electorate-taxpayers of the various countries and the visibility of the entire process, with more open debates and more stage time for the candidates, then the better would be Guterres' chances: "It's enough just to know him to be sure that he would steal the show in any public hearing and it would be difficult for any of the others to keep up with him. That talent that allows him to switch from French to English and then to Spanish, always improvising and putting forward consistent ideas, would be an almost unbeatable strength."

Guterres and his team hoped that the expected good performances during the public examination process might offset the gender dynamic. However, there still remained another problematic issue: regional rotation.

Despite it not having been written down in any resolution, let alone in the founding United Nations Charter, this rule was designed to symbolise the UN as the house of everyone and where every region has a voice. This rule had been applied ever since the early days, and it was already known that Russia, with its veto power, perceived this 2016 election as an opportunity to elect a Secretary-General from within its sphere of influence for the very first time.

Recalling how the letter he himself had signed drew attention to the regional diversity of the preceding Secretaries-General, and that the UN system formally included the group of countries from eastern Europe, the sitting President of the General Assembly considered that this pressure shaped the entire campaign: "In the beginning of the process, all the expectations were on eastern Europe and we had a lot of Eastern European candidates."

In fact, the first candidates to officially declare all came from this region—the only region never to have nominated a Secretary-General in the history of the United Nations.

In just two months, between December 2015 and February 2016, Macedonia, Croatia, Montenegro and Slovenia had all confirmed their candidates. Three men and just one woman.

And with each nomination, Guterres became increasingly impatient. Declaring too late incurred a series of risks. On the one hand, this might give the image of being calculating. On the other hand, he could not allow too much time for another candidate to build up steam and win popularity, which would add to his already natural disadvantage.

Therefore, that same January, he went to the office of the Portuguese task force leader and demanded, "The letter has to be sent. The letter needs sending and has to be sent by the end of this month."

The Letter

Just to the north of the equator, in the warm waters of the African Atlantic, there are ten small islands. Located off Mauritania and Senegal, the Cape Verde archipelago manages to be simultaneously barren and volcanic.

Despite being home to just half a million inhabitants, the archipelago is one of Portugal's most important partners in Africa. After all, Cape Verde is a former Portuguese colony, with whom they share a language, and a specific mechanism for political affirmation: the CPLP—the Community of the Portuguese-Speaking Countries. It is therefore common for the highest representatives from each country to visit one another. What is less common is to use such visits to make major public announcements.

It was during an official visit to Cape Verde in late January 2016 that the Portuguese Prime Minister confirmed to journalists that the government would be putting forward Guterres as a candidate for the office of UN Secretary-General. The decision was finally public and would travel the world in just a few minutes. The next step was primarily one of administrative nature: sending the papers to the UN headquarters.

Due to the surgical precision with which it was written, with each and every word picked following careful assessment, the letter took weeks to prepare. Thus, with Guterres yet to formally submit his bid, another hat was thrown into the ring, on 6 February: Danilo Türk, from Slovenia.

A few days later, and finally in an official manner, came Irina Bokova, on 11 February.

And in the following week, it was the turn of Natalia Gherman from Moldova, on 19 February.

There were already six other candidates in the race, three women and three men, and all from Eastern Europe.

Guterres was of the opinion that he would benefit not from being the first, but for being among the first to submit his bid. He believed it would be an advantage if he were among those ready and willing to be called for the first public audience that would inaugurate the campaign. Nevertheless, it was only on the final day of that month that he formally submitted his candidacy. His letter arrived in New York on 29 February, the same day when Angola— one of the Portuguese-speaking African countries—was taking over the Security Council's Presidency.

The document, signed by the Portuguese Prime Minister, constituted a political statement in itself, designed to effectively convey the core ideas of the candidacy, a taster of Guterres' position towards the United Nations in general and the election process in particular.

Thus, the letter, which took an argumentative and convincing stance, highlighted the strengths of the Portuguese candidate and skirted around his two great weaknesses. The text described the characteristics that a good Secretary-General should possess as those that coincided with Guterres' image, and thereby, from the very outset, seeking to persuade those who would be his constituency:

> It is indispensable for candidates to have previously demonstrated
> leadership and managerial abilities, as well as an extensive experi-

ence in international relations and strong diplomatic, communication and multilingual skills.[5]

His career at the UNHCR was held up to demonstrate not only Guterres' commitment towards reforming the UN, in keeping with the wishes of the majority of the states, but also, and most importantly, that he did not have issues with any of the stakeholders:

> He maintained excellent cooperation with member states and developed strong partnerships with civil society and the private sector. At the same time, the Office of the High Commissioner went through a period of continuous and intense reform and innovation, allowing it to triple its annual activities.[6]

The topic of "women" could not be entirely ignored. The letter highlighted the work done by the Portuguese candidate and guaranteed he would always attribute "special attention to the protection and empowerment of women and girls, as well as to the promotion of gender parity in its workforce."[7]

There was no mention of his region of origin. But the letter contained a clear message targeting the member states of the General Assembly, one that would certainly be more to their liking than to the Security Council's: his expression of support for the new election rules. What might have appeared to be a mere diplomatic elegy, shorn of content but which would always go down well in a letter of this nature, was anything but innocent:

> The Government of Portugal is also mindful of the other aspects referred to in your joint letter, specifically the opportunities that will be offered to the candidates for interaction with members of the General Assembly and of the Security Council, which we very much welcome.[8]

By this stage, the various new and revolutionary phases in the Secretary-General election methodology were already known. After decades of discussions, writing of reports, negotiations and controversies, the following procedures had been set out:

– Informal hearings, that would take place during three days in April, where all candidates would set out their visions for the future of the UN and be subject to questioning. All of the countries could question the candidates on their plans for dealing with some of the most serious problems facing the world and, time permitting, civil society organisations would also be able to participate. These audiences, which would last for two hours, would also be broadcast live through the streaming service of the United Nations website.

— A set of public debates among the candidates, organised by the Association of the United Nations in the United Kingdom, by the British newspaper *The Guardian*, by the New America think tank and by the project FUNDS—Future UN Development System.

— One major debate with all candidates in the General Assembly Hall, also broadcast live to the world by Al Jazeera, the state television channel of Qatar.

— The holding of informal straw polls, where there would be no distinction in the colours of the ballots of the P5 and the ten without veto power, in order to determine the viability of candidates prior to the decisive voting round.

With this framework in place, the candidates felt effectively compelled to participate in public initiatives: interviews, debates, conferences in think tanks and, of course, meetings with the member states.

All of these innovations, which might appear merely procedural, were a true revolution in the UN operational paradigm. In his memoirs about his experiences as President of the UN General Assembly, Lykketoft recognised that, "For the first 70 years, the General Assembly's election of the SG has basically been rubber stamping a difficult birth in the Security Council."[9]

By 2016, all of these transformations seemed to point to the idea that the larger, symbolic objective was to take a decisive step in reforming the United Nations and its traditional source of power. Lykketoft: "It has been criticised that the Security Council deliberations took place in secret. Other UN member states and the world public often didn't even know whom or what the Security Council discussed in the formerly smoke-shrouded back rooms. Even less known were secret agreements on the consecutive distribution of top posts in the UN system [...]. Only afterwards was it obvious that such agreements existed."[10]

In confirming the dilution of power amongst a larger number of actors, the General Assembly emerged into a stronger position while the Security Council was apparently weakened. Lykketoft also provides insights into the reactions of the five permanent members: "France and Britain thought it was a brilliant idea. The United States, under the Obama administration, didn't oppose it. China was very silent. Russia was more or less against. The difficult thing was to find a way to get the approval from Mr. Churkin."

In effect, only after various insistent efforts did the Russian Ambassador, Vitaly Churkin, acquiesce and allow Lykketoft to seal the model for the informal hearings. The Danish politician recalls that, "Vitaly left the office saying that if this was really so important to me, then fine. No one would be interested in the procedure anyway, he said, implying that, as always, anything of importance would surely take place in the Security Council."

However, Russia was not the only one with reservations. The US displayed a certain scepticism in relation to all these new developments and did not believe such a process would serve to enhance Guterres' chances: "We were brutal supporters of Guterres from the start, but we thought it was highly unlikely that a man from Western Europe was going to get through," recognises Samantha Power. "And also, the idea of somebody so qualified and so independent like this to get through... that's not what normally happens in the UN, right?"

However, the Ambassador insists that the Obama administration got along with Guterres' positions even when running counter to direct American interests: "He used to come into my office and criticise the US policy on Syria. I got word from Barack Obama and Barack Obama was okay with him being critical."

Guterres was the seventh candidate to join the race. That timing allowed him entry to the first set of public audiences held on 12 April. The next step would be to prepare for the informal dialogue in which the candidates would be bombarded with questions from the 193 delegates to the General Assembly. The audience in attendance: the entire world.

19

BACK TO CAMPAIGNING

Robert Sherman is a successful lawyer. His name first came to prominence in 2002 when he participated in a legal case against the powerful Archdiocese of Boston. Sherman was part of the prosecution team that accused a set of influential Catholic priests of child sex abuse. Years later, the paedophilia scandal that shocked the United States would be portrayed in the film *Spotlight*.

In addition to his legal expertise, Bob—as almost everybody called him at home and at work—was also a lifelong Democrat. The role that he played in financing Barack Obama's second campaign was recognised to such an extent that the President decided to honour him, as is fairly common practice in the case of leading and trusted fundraisers, with an ambassadorship.

When he was offered the opportunity to choose the country in which he would like to represent the United States, Sherman guarantees he answered immediately: Portugal. According to his memoirs,[1] during his childhood spent in Brockton, Massachusetts, he developed close ties with the local Portuguese community that, similar to his own parents, had migrated to the United States.

Thus it was in Lisbon, the European capital geographically closest to the United States, where Sherman got his motorbike licence and purchased his first Harley Davidson. It was there where he celebrated the victory of his New England Patriots in

261

the 2015 Super Bowl and won the hearts of his hosts by publicly supporting the Portuguese national football team on several social media publications.

And it was also there that, in 2016, his diplomatic responsibilities came to include interviewing the country's best-known politician who had recently declared his candidacy for the position of UN Secretary-General.

Bob Sherman, as the US Ambassador swiftly became known to the small Lisbon diplomatic circle, had clear instructions about which topics to raise in his private meeting with Guterres: "We spent a lot of time talking about his management style because, for us, you needed to lead an organisation such as the UN but you also needed to manage the organisation. So the question was: How would he be, not only as a leader, but also as a manager? What he thought needed to be done in the position of Secretary-General, as well as in terms of trying to consolidate, to prioritise and to really make the UN mission more effective, not scattered or bloated, but conscious of budgets, conscious of allocating resources based on priorities. And I was incredibly impressed with him on that subject."

During the conversation, which lasted over two hours, Guterres interrupted the formalities of the job interview to pick up a pen and a piece of paper. He began sketching a set of diagrams to explain some of the reforms he had implemented at the UNHCR and that he believed could be replicable in New York. In particular, shifting the focus of the work—and the money—away from the UN offices and onto actions in the field.

The Portuguese candidate knew very well that all of his words and gestures would be subject to microscopic analysis not only by the Ambassador, but also by the State Department diplomats. "My reports went to Washington as part of our due diligence process," explains Sherman. "Given what we were looking for within this context, within this moment in world history, it was also a value-driven determination: the values of inclusiveness, of tolerance, of concern for the people who don't have access to the process and to the decision-makers. It was about the values we were looking for in a leader."

However, before taking an official position, it was New York—not Lisbon—to which Secretary of State John Kerry was paying a great deal of attention. It was there, at the UN mission, that Samantha Power conversed in the corridor with diplomats from every country and gathered information.

Power states that the values of the candidates in this election were subject to examination and, during their conversations, Guterres never promised positions or any type of favouritism: "We got into this process looking for the best possible candidate, not the person who was going to be bought off."

However, nobody could ignore how the historical backdrop of the eight preceding elections had cast a blanket of opacity, very well sewn up throughout seven decades of exchanging favours, attempts at manipulation and bargaining, and that the Secretary-General would be called on to align with the interests of the powers that control the Security Council.

And naturally, this election was not going to sweep away the institutional memory of the UN nor the survival instincts of the candidates. Without mentioning names, Malcorra confirms that in 2016 there were candidates selling themselves to countries on the Security Council in exchange for their votes: "I have absolutely no doubts. The answer is yes."

As a result of the role played alongside Ban Ki-moon and the internal knowledge that she had acquired, Malcorra's analysis is perhaps the most well-founded of any of the candidates. Hence, even with the new methods for choosing the Secretary-General, the Argentinian still retains a pragmatic interpretation: "The process of the Security Council was totally equivalent to the traditional historical process in which everything was decided behind the curtains, behind closed doors. It does not seem to me that there was any real change in the decision-making process. Yes, there was an alteration in the process, but it does not seem to me that this had any impact on the way the permanent members of the Council made their decisions."

Thus, candidates might indeed present themselves as displaying bulletproof integrity, be a woman and come from Eastern Europe, put on outstanding performances in the public audiences and interviews… and, in extremis, they might even have the support of 192 UN countries. But all it took was a Security Council veto to ensure the candidate did not have a shadow of a chance.

5 + 10

There was at least one thing that united the P5. They all had dealt with Guterres at length, whether in bilateral negotiations or over multilateral crises, in purely political questions or on humanitarian affairs. So, the permanent members of the Security Council knew very well what they could expect from him.

Another sure thing that Guterres could count on was having won, if not the preference, at least the sympathy of the United States: "He wasn't like an abstract Western European," says Power. "Abstraction is the enemy of cooperation and Guterres was not an abstraction. He was just a guy with whom you have to figure out how many refugees we're going to take, or a guy who a lot of people in my administration had worked with on the East Timor crisis. And similarly with China."

Indeed, the Beijing central government also had good memories of Guterres. "The Chinese don't show their cards," recalls Sultan-Khan, "but they told me something like, 'We don't know the High Commissioner well, but we'll never forget what António Guterres did in China as Prime Minister.'"

Right from the outset, Guterres could count on the support of two permanent members of the Security Council, China and France.

On the opposite side, Russia would be the most difficult to get, at least in theory. In those first months, the perception in Lisbon that the number-one priority of Moscow was not so much a matter of gender, but rather one of regional rotation, was getting stronger. The Kremlin's point of view was that having a representative of their geopolitical bloc installed on the thirty-eighth floor of the UN building would not only be a political triumph, but would also enable a better understanding with the Secretary-General—and even a greater input. And so, Guterres' team began drawing arguments to which Moscow might be sensitive.

In order to get the Russians to cede the opportunity to put one of their own into the office of the Secretary-General, the messages from Lisbon emphasised the equidistance of Guterres in regards to the other powers. Ensuring that the Portuguese politician did not raise any unsurmountable obstacle for the Putin administration, these efforts sought to demonstrate that no candidate from the East would be able to safeguard the Russian position better than an independent without any bond of obedience to Washington or any other capital. Guterres was not a regional product, but a global one.

However, the Portuguese candidate had few doubts about Moscow's stance: "Russia maintained the same position right from the beginning, with a great deal of coherence. The Russians told me, right on that first day, 'Our position is that it should be a candidate from Eastern Europe. But we have nothing against your candidacy.'"

This left only one P5 member.

London and Lisbon are bound by the oldest international treaty in the world, dating back to 1386,[2] and still in force today. These were two European Union capitals, allies through centuries, across different international conflicts and causes. However, for this election, the preferences of Conservative Prime Minister David Cameron were, in all likelihood, already defined.

On 4 April, the former Prime Minister of New Zealand joined the race, presenting some heavyweight credentials. Not only could she count on the likely support of the United Kingdom and the majority of the fifty-four members of the Commonwealth, she had also served seven years as the head of the United Nations Development Programme, the UN agency with the greatest presence in the field.

Therefore, Guterres embarked on his campaign knowing from the outset that he was not the candidate of the Americans, the Russians, or the British. Nevertheless, Lisbon did not see any motives for London to veto Guterres.

In regards of the remaining ten members of the Security Council, the Portuguese analysis was as follows:

— Angola, also a member of the CPLP, shared with Portugal a language and 500 years of history, as well as being an important political and economic partner. Guterres was the only candidate who was personally hosted by President José Eduardo dos Santos.

- Egypt—a member of the Arab League and the Organisation for Islamic Cooperation—belonged to the group of countries that had long encouraged Guterres to run. The country was not an automatic ally of Portugal, but was also far from being an adversary. Furthermore, the events surrounding the Sudanese demonstration in Cairo, during the first term of Guterres in the UNHCR, did not seem to have left any lasting effects.
- Spain, despite its proximity to Portugal, Madrid had a political duty to support Malcorra. The strategy here was to explain that Portugal understood their need to support the Argentinian candidate, but that would not prevent them from giving Guterres a positive vote too. After all, Spain was the only overland neighbour of Portugal, its main commercial partner, and Madrid was but 600 kilometres from Lisbon. In addition, this was a country where Guterres had always maintained good and important friendships, to such an extent that it was Spain that had launched his candidacy to the UNHCR a decade earlier.
- Japan was historically one of the main financiers of the UNHCR, which meant that Guterres had had an active working relationship with the country throughout the preceding ten years. Furthermore, despite the geographic distance between the two countries, the team played with the deep-reaching historical and cultural affinities that they share. The Portuguese were the first Europeans to arrive in Japan in the sixteenth century where they introduced firearms, influenced the cuisine, engaged in important commercial exchanges that are still apparent today, such as the dozens of Japanese words that derive from Portuguese.
- For Malaysia, the natural candidate would be Helen Clark from neighbouring New Zealand. The Malayan government took the longest to respond to Guterres' request for an audience, which raised serious doubts about their position.
- With their own candidate, there would not be any arguments that would secure a vote for Guterres from New Zealand. However, Álvaro Mendonça e Moura praises the New Zealand stance throughout the campaign process: "They always played a

fair game even to the extent of questioning, within the Security Council, if they should actually be able to vote given that they themselves had a candidate involved."

- Francophone Senegal was one of the first to confirm its support. Since his time as a co-leader of the Africa Committee of the Socialist International, alongside the then President of Senegal, Abdou Diouf, Guterres had kept close friendships and personal relationships with key actors in power in Dakar.

- Ukraine would be one of the most complicated given its Eastern European location. However, the task force was confident of the good relationship established with Portugal, partly due to the good level of integration of many Ukrainian migrants in the country, but especially after the denunciation of the occupation of Crimea by Lisbon, and its support for the sanctions decreed against Russia by the European Union.

- Uruguay had the same problem as Spain, with the aggravating factor that Malcorra was from a neighbouring country, over the River Plate, with which they shared a language, as well as countless cultural references and still a significant part of their respective histories. Furthermore, Argentina was a major economic partner of Uruguay. Margarida Marques explains that, "Were the final decision down to either Guterres or Malcorra, this would be a problem."

- Although from the same region as Malcorra, the geopolitical context in Latin America had seen the governments of Venezuela and Argentina grow steadily apart. Hugo Chávez had passed away three years earlier, there was a full-blown economic crisis sweeping Venezuela, and Nicolás Maduro's government had already embarked on an authoritarian turn that would only worsen the relationships with the neighbouring countries, especially those that had recently elected liberal presidents, as was the case of Argentina. Furthermore, the presence of an influential community of Portuguese migrants in Venezuela and the existence of good bilateral relations led to the belief that a positive vote might be possible.

Having concluded the diagnosis of each state, Guterres' team could now bring together the various individual arguments and present the Security Council with a true candidate of the world, to which none of the fifteen members could raise any reservations. This was exactly the same formula formerly tested out during his bid for the UNHCR, only now, with a far more extensive network of allies and supporters than in 2005, Guterres had effectively turned his name into a global reference.

The time had come to prepare for the first major test, the unprecedented informal dialogue scheduled for 12 April. Guterres knew very well that before him lay a once in a lifetime opportunity: this was the first time that the General Assembly of the United Nations—and international public opinion—would hear him speak as a candidate for Secretary-General.

Furthermore, according to Lykketoft, "Not everyone was keen on the idea of being scrutinised in the General Assembly, with cameras rolling. A few of them—Irina Bokova from Bulgaria and Srgjan Kerim of Macedonia—tried to excuse themselves in order to avoid the very public dialogue. Considerable pressure on their advisers and their countries' permanent representatives in New York made them change their minds and participate."[3]

Any errors made by the candidates in those two hours would be held against them during the campaign. However, for Guterres, this remained the very best occasion to exhibit his talents and begin winning further support. Ever since entering political life, he had been perfecting his techniques for public speaking and means of persuasion. For the last four decades he had participated in election campaigns and debates. He would be like a fish in water.

He could not have asked for anything better.

Secretary or General?

"God has given me the opportunity to access a wide range of opportunities difficult to match, but that creates an obligation for public service."[4]

The tie was made of silk, red with small white lines. Guterres was positioned behind a set of papers that he did not bother to look at.

"When the root causes of problems become increasingly inter-linked, the priority of prevention requires a holistic vision. An understanding of the great global trends of our times is needed, as well as strategies and policies able to respond to them in a coherent manner, and in parallel with the three pillars of action of the United Nations [Human Rights, Peace and Security, and Development]."[5]

Lykketoft presided over the informal dialogue between the candidate and the UN General Assembly. On his left, Guterres hardly paused as he switched between different languages.

"It is the responsibility of the Secretary-General to mobilise the entire UN system—in cooperation with other regional and international organisations, civil society and the private sector—in order to support the states that are the true protagonists in this process. This support must be total: it is what guarantees the success of implementing the 2030 Agenda."[6]

The Portuguese candidate, who had once earned the nickname the "Talking Pickaxe", set out his vision for the future of the UN over the course of ten closely timed minutes.

Surrounded by the gaze of 193 countries seated around a hemicycle facing him, Guterres argued that, "Prevention must be not only a priority, but the priority in everything we do," while maintaining steady eye-contact with his interlocutors throughout the entire interview.

Determined not to waste any time, he recognised right at the beginning of his speech that, "The UN must be at the forefront of the efforts of the international community for gender equality, and let's be honest, it was not always exactly the case."

His hands were constantly engaged in gestures, but his body language remained controlled. While explaining the official text of his vision statement, he either interlocked his fingers in a sign of convergence or left one of his hands patiently open over the table. He then advanced with his reasoning for running: "The best place to address the root causes of human suffering is at the centre of the UN system, and that's why I am a candidate for Secretary-General."

The wider framing shots by UNTV, which broadcast the session live online, showed how packed it was in the wood-panelled Trusteeship Council chamber. Close-up shots showed the attentive gaze of François Delattre standing out above the diplomats flanking him, taking notes with their heads down. The French Ambassador was hanging on the candidate's every word.

Guterres continued: "My experience in the High Commissioner for Refugees shows that, by working together with other states, we can go a long way in simplifying with a win-win reform strategy, making the UN more effective and cost-effective, more able, more flexible, more decentralised and more field-oriented."

Opening up the debate, the former High Commissioner took the first wave of questions: fifteen in rapid succession. Inaugurating the hostilities, the Non-Aligned Movement countries inquired how Guterres intended to avoid the historical pressures of the all-powerful permanent members on the Security Council.

His response triggered a wave of complicit smiles around the room: "I cannot say that I'll be able to avoid pressure, what I can do is to resist pressure."

In regards to the Israeli-Palestinian conflict, Guterres was adamant about the need for a two-state solution.

He argued that UN forces who have committed acts of sexual violence should be severely punished.

He continued to place the recruitment of young people by terrorist movements at the top of his concerns and defended the need for development policies capable of keeping them away from radicalisation: "An idle mind is the devil's workshop and I think it is absolutely essential to support, in development cooperation policies, youth programmes as an absolute priority."

At the end of thirty-five minutes, the first round was completed. The questions that followed required responses concerning his plans on counterterrorism…

The future of peacekeeping operations…

Antisemitism…

Reform of the Security Council…

The functioning of the UN…

Bureaucratic efficiency…

The results and not the processes…

"What is essential is to have mechanisms that allow for decentralisation of decisions, for field empowerment to be possible […] decentralisation, I must say, is always the best way to make sure we make the best use of our resources."

At the end of ninety minutes, forty-eight questions had been answered.

However, there were still France and Spain, Colombia and Angola to come… along with two NGOs, one representing New Zealand Maoris, and the other from Burkina Faso, as well as another twenty countries. In total, there were still almost eighty questions to address.

Before concluding, Guterres made a final clarification disguised as a diplomatic promise: "Sometimes there is a question of whether one should be a secretary or a general. I would like to say that I won't be a secretary and I won't be a general."

At the end of two hours and fifteen minutes, Lykketoft's gavel finally came down on the table. Three short raps brought the session to a close.

With a smile, Guterres removed his glasses and placed them in a black case. He took a quick gulp of water and began tidying his papers. He calmly put the A4 sheets, that served mostly for taking note of the questions, in order and added them to the small stack of paper cards with his talking points, just like he had been doing ever since he entered politics.

Positive Signs

Guterres' performance in the informal dialogue managed to simultaneously portray him as a humanitarian—with the experience to respond to the concerns of the General Assembly—and as a politician—with the ability to work with the Security Council, especially on dossiers that call into question the direct interests of the permanent members.

In Lisbon, the Minister of Foreign Affairs, Santos Silva, was following the performances of all candidates and considers that, "The first hearing made clear the enormous difference there was between António Guterres and the general level of the other candidates, whether in terms of linguistic fluency or in regards to their knowledge about the issues, or even from the point of view of the level of ease that each of the candidates displayed."

Freitas Ferraz also recognises that, "The first time we made a highly positive assessment came after that first hearing." According to the task force coordinator, "We were not the only ones to

271

understand that he had turned in a performance far better than the others. These were also the echoes coming out of New York from the permanent representatives, who were delighted."

Lykketoft, who chaired the entire round of informal dialogues from a neutral perspective, later confided that, after hearing a total of twelve candidates without the chance to give any opinion, "Guterres was the man that convincingly presented the strongest experience, the best results, the best vision and also the best ability to explain to the world what the UN is all about. And also that he was under no special influence from major powers".

The strategy of taking advantage of the new characteristics of the process seemed to be working, and therefore should be maintained. The first straw poll was scheduled for 21 July and, with practically three months to go, there was still a great deal of meetings, trips, audiences and votes to win… but there was also still the opportunity for further adversaries to declare their intentions of running for the position.

In fact, on the very same day of Guterres' public hearing, another candidate joined the race. Vuk Jeremić was not only from Eastern Europe, but also had particular influence over the UN system: he was a former President of the General Assembly and a former Minister of Foreign Affairs of Serbia.

Several weeks later, at the end of May, it was finally Malcorra's turn to launch her campaign.

During the years she served as chief of staff to Ban Ki-moon, the former Argentinian minister had followed closely all of the pressure groups demanding that the next Secretary-General be a woman, as well as those calling for regional rotation. Therefore, she did not think that the public performance of Guterres was enough to turn him into a serious contender: "I was totally convinced that it would be a woman and, as I always said, in this selection process there was always a first filter, which was implicit—this should be somebody from Eastern Europe."

Malcorra officially declared her candidacy on 23 May—the same day when dozens of leaders were inaugurating the Humanitarian World Summit.

On the premise that the international community was experiencing the highest levels of human suffering since World War II, this event was a red alert issued by Ban Ki-moon.

In effect, the simultaneous emergence of crises such as those in Syria and Libya, the dramatic plight of the Rohingya, who were only just beginning to receive global media attention, the war and hunger in Yemen, terrorism in Nigeria and Mali, the systematic violation of human rights in the Central African Republic and the Democratic Republic of the Congo, and the looming catastrophe facing Venezuela, had motivated the sitting UN Secretary-General to convene the international community for two days of working talks in Istanbul.

At a time when the seeds of isolationism were beginning to germinate, the appeal was heard by almost sixty heads of state and representatives from over 170 countries and around 700 NGOs.

In full campaign mode, Guterres could hardly let such an initiative pass him by and, in order to capitalise on all the networking opportunities that such an occasion could provide, he accompanied a heavyweight national delegation led by the Prime Minister of Portugal.

Indeed, one of the core duties of the task force was to define a precise schedule of the major international conferences the former High Commissioner should attend. In fact, a fundamental part of the due diligence process consisted in ascertaining with appropriate notice the list of people who would be at these events—and who most needed to be approached.

As a first step, the courting of international leaders took place through the official diplomatic network. However, the persuasive efforts, at the decision-making level, had to be taken on directly by the Minister of Foreign Affairs, or even by the Prime Minister whenever justified. According to the Secretary of State responsible for the team, "Yes, this did involve a great deal of coordination, among our ambassadors in the countries and among the members of the government who would be participating in international meetings," explains Marques. "There were ministers who were clearly identified, and we would choose which of us would be meeting with them, in order to be able to schedule bilateral meetings. Sometimes this was also to discuss other issues, but they were above all about mobilising their support for the candidacy. And, to a certain extent, this structured our priorities in terms of scheduling bilateral visits."

Even so, Guterres undertook the majority of the trips and the diligences. In the dozens of intercontinental journeys that he went on during those nine months, he spent nights at airports just to be able to span the world in a few days.

"What is extraordinary," says Marques, "is that Guterres did all this alone, the tours that he had to do, I don't know how many flights in a row that would take him around the world. If he arrived at 2 am and had a flight at 6 am, he wouldn't even go to a hotel."

And, when he did, Guterres very much kept to his low-cost approach. Melissa Fleming, the former UNHCR spokesperson, recalls, "I couldn't believe when he showed me the hotel he was staying in in New York. I thought, 'He really stayed here?' It was a three-star hotel or something and it had a really bad breakfast."

For each flight, regardless of the destination or the duration of the trip, the Portuguese candidate would always arrive equipped with the same accessories: a single cabin bag and a suit carrier. The mathematical organisation of his clothing was a ritual that this trained engineer would not give up on, religiously following an almost scientific method: his shoes always tucked away in the same place, defining in advance what should be placed on top of each object, and what should go in one pocket or in each compartment. It did not matter what went into the cabin bag. At the end, it would all add up.

After all, he had many years of practice. He had spent thousands of hours on flights and in airports usually on work, but plenty of times leisurely. Travelling continued to be a hobby, and even that year spent campaigning, Guterres took holidays on two occasions in order to travel with his family.

For his first week of non-campaigning, he touched down in Lisbon on a Friday, after flying in from New Zealand via a stopover in South Africa, and was back at the airport the very next day with his wife and stepson to catch a flight to Denver, where he had rented a car to visit one of Colorado's national parks.

On the second occasion, he took off from Lisbon to Chile, visited Easter Island, returned to Santiago, and flew from there to Peru because his daughter had never been to Machu Picchu.

During these trips, Guterres' recent discovery of portable technology enabled him to access his team's work. On landing, he would call in or swap messages with Lisbon, always keeping in frequent contact.

The age of info-exclusion was over and, as his campaign press officer David Damião explains, this was what enabled him to overcome the lack of resources: "He would always make his calls via WhatsApp [while connected to Wi-Fi] so as not to spend money, as well as using his private phone. Few really do actually believe how his candidacy was built up. There were candidates with dozens of people working for them and with a great deal of resources available. The composition of our task force did not even amount to a dozen staff."

#SGDebate

The main auditorium in the Barbican Centre was packed with a multi-ethnic, global audience: from students to ambassadors, the famous and the unknown awaited the beginning of the performance.

This was not another concert by the London Symphony Orchestra, nor a play by the Royal Shakespeare Company, nor even an extravagant contemporary ballet.

The warm, yellowish lights lit the centre of the stage where the three performers took up their places.

Both those in the audience and those watching via the live stream could see Guterres sitting on the right. Once again in his red tie with small white stripes, he was the oldest participant on the stage. To the left, Igor Lukšić, the former Deputy Prime Minister of Montenegro, and at the centre, Vuk Jeremić. All three were there to participate in the second public debate in UN history for the election of the next Secretary-General.

Of all the candidates, Guterres remained the only one who didn't fit any of the two pre-established selection criteria. Even the last man to have thrown in his hat, right after the Istanbul Summit, was at least born in the right place—Slovakia, where he had served as Minister of Foreign Affairs. At the end of May, Miroslav Lajčák had officially become the eleventh candidate.

However well the public hearing in the General Assembly might have gone, Guterres still very much needed to score points. So he sought out the best opportunities to shine.

A quick analysis had led to the conclusion that the two debates organised by the United Nations Association in the United Kingdom and by *The Guardian* seemed very much worth his time—in conceptual, media and political terms.

The first of these debates was held in New York immediately after the last day of the public hearings. Now, with the calendar reading 3 June, it was London's turn to host the Secretary-General candidates who would respond live to questions posed by citizens from around the world, as well as civil society organisations.

In total, over 30,000 questions were submitted. The model for the debate had very simple rules: a moderator would ask the questions or invite someone in the audience to do so, while also giving voice to the Internet—especially since the debate was open to participation via Twitter by using the hashtag #SGDebate.

Sat in front of the Barbican Hall audience, almost 2,000 in capacity, Guterres started out by proving his commitment to becoming Secretary-General through his experience at UNHCR.

"You can't imagine what it is to be at the service of the most vulnerable of the vulnerable, to see levels of suffering that are absolutely unimaginable and to feel the frustration that there is no humanitarian solution for their plight. The solution is political."[7]

However, there was also recognition that the organisation he was seeking to lead needed urgent change.

"We need to overcome the paralysis [the UN has been in]—from a political perspective—in many key issues, such as Syria or many others [...]. I don't think the UN has grown too much. Probably there is a lot of fat that needs to be cut."

The greatest divergence among the candidates emerged when asked how they were going to hold the permanent powers responsible at a time when they were engulfed in competition. Guterres played it safe and opted for the traditional diplomatic approach.

"There is a basic lack of trust between the key powers. Power relations [have become] less clear and the role of the Secretary-General in this regard is to be a convener, to sit together with all the parties. The challenges are so interlinked that their differences are smaller than their common interest—and that interest is peace."

During his turn, Jeremić adopted a far more assertive position: "He or she will have to be a very powerful loudspeaker and should not shy away from using this loudspeaker. It should be a person with a spine."

However, the Portuguese candidate was the first to win the public's applause. In order to demonstrate how he intended to unblock political deadlocks among leaders of states or factions, he drew on an old lesson that he had learned from his deceased wife: when there are two people alone in a room, there are not really two but rather six people—the two who are in fact there; what each of them thinks about themselves; and what each one thinks about the other.

"That is true for people and that is true for countries and for organisations. One of the roles of the Secretary-General when dealing with the different members of the Security Council, or with different key actors in each scenario, is to make sure we bring these six into two; to make sure that this misunderstanding disappears, that the false perceptions disappear—perceptions are essential in politics; and to make sure that people are able to [in the end] overcome their differences and be aware of their dramatically needed perception of a common interest."

When challenged, Guterres declared himself a feminist. He proposed concrete objectives and a rigorous timetable for obtaining equality between men and women across every level of the administration. And he stressed that, "Parity is not sufficient. The central question is empowerment."

After having led one of the largest agencies in the system, and after having participated for years in meetings with organisms across the UN, he knew only too well the rivalries and divergences between them. Thus, he promised greater coherence between the three fundamental components of the United Nations actions—Human Rights; Peace and Security; Sustainable Development—through what he described as a continuum of peace: prevention, resolution, peacekeeping, peacebuilding, long-term development.

"It is this capacity to see things together and to act [on] the different fronts at the same time with coherent strategies that has been lacking. The UN has been too fragmented, dealing with different things in different ways and not being able to connect the dots."

Guterres thereby attempted to position himself as an aggregating candidate; as the mediator best prepared and best positioned to manage, bringing together divergent parties; and as the greater defender of inclusion and diversity.

Undeniably, in a city with the characteristics of London, such a stance contained everything necessary to be impactful. The British capital, ranking among the five richest in the world, is also the city that has taken in the most immigrants, with over a third of its population born abroad.

For similar reasons, just twenty days after the Barbican debate, when Londoners were called upon to decide whether their futures should be inside or outside of the European Union, they chose to stay.

However, many parts of the United Kingdom, ethnically more homogeneous, but economically poorer, opted to head in the opposite direction. In the 23 June referendum, a majority of British voters voted for a political earthquake called Brexit.

Feeding off the mantras of the new nationalist tribalism, which stood at the opposite end of the spectrum to Guterres' messages, the Leave campaign managed to effectively harness the prejudices, fears and disillusionment of the British people.

Those within the campaign who were responsible for the surgical dissemination of nativist slogans and factual lies about the European Union knew especially well how to correctly read, and astutely leverage, that political moment to gain a victory that left the world incredulous—in addition to hiring the services of an analytics company that collected data from social media in order to better target their propaganda.[8]

It seemed that people distrusted the politicians that the traditional party system chose, shaped and finally presented to them.

Frustrated by the inability of liberal democracies to respond to their insecurities and expectations, voters backed a campaign that promised to put their interests before those of others.

In this context, the campaign to split from the European Union decided to turn its sights on migrants, deeming them the enemies of the British. A poster, which would duly attain notoriety, showed a long column of people queueing to enter a refugee camp under the ominous slogan: "The EU has failed us".[9]

In fact, new leaders began to emerge across every continent, promising to restore the lost grandeur of their nations. Leaders born after World War II who, often with more charisma than content, despised the complexity of the politically correct, affirming their role as the sole legitimate interpreters of the popular will and the only ones able to stand up for the people against the crony elite. They were leaders committed to dividing and segregating, who preferred to decide unilaterally than be held back by tiresome democratic mechanisms for controlling their powers, who survived cloistered away behind the walls of their identities and self-proclaimed exceptionalism.

Thus, the relationships of power set down in the liberal order were becoming increasingly unable to respond to the fears and anxieties of citizens, and the discourse of openness and multiculturalism, which was the brand image of the United Nations, seemed to be losing support in a growing number of the states whose votes Guterres needed. According to Freedom House, the American watchdog, in 2016 over fifty states displayed democratic decline, not through any coup or unexpected violent actions, but rather as a consequence of a rising generalised sense of distrust towards their model of governance. This seismic shift was effectively symptomatic of the end of an era that so many leaders and observers had already forecast.

In London, Prime Minister David Cameron resigned the day after the referendum, leaving the path of succession open to his Home Secretary, Theresa May. The British government needed a reshuffle and, to obtain the essential vote of the United Kingdom in the Security Council, Guterres would have to win over the next Foreign Secretary.

All of the rumours and backstage talk that were emerging from Whitehall corridors pointed to one of the key instigators of the United Kingdom leaving the European Union. His name was Boris Johnson.

Silence Is Golden

Fidel Castro had once spoken for four and a half hours without any interruption.

Benjamin Netanyahu had displayed posters depicting the designs of bombs, or maps of secret Lebanese posts, and photographs of Iranian nuclear storage facilities.

Colonel Gaddafi had ripped a page out of the United Nations Charter and threw it over his shoulder.

Robert Mugabe had clarified that, "We are not gays," as an argument for justifying the homophobic laws of Zimbabwe.

Hugo Chávez, the day after a speech by George W. Bush, had declared that the devil had just been in that same place. After a dramatic pause, he had made the sign of the cross and complained there was still a lingering smell of sulphur in the air.

The magnificent room hosting the General Assembly of the United Nations, with its bottle-green wooden panelling, had already seen its share of great performances.

Despite its daily mission of witnessing endless and obscure technical-diplomatic meetings, of rather questionable added value, the unmistakeable logo of the UN that sits proudly on the golden coloured wall at the back of the auditorium has also presided over history-changing events.

This was certainly the objective on 12 July 2016, when Al Jazeera held the first live debate for the position of Secretary-General. The Qatari state news channel both broadcast and moderated the session that brought together ten of the then twelve candidates. Indeed, there were now twelve because a few days earlier another hat had been thrown into the ring. Despite not coming from Eastern Europe, Christiana Figueres would be able to argue that her regional group had only ever nominated a single Secretary-General. The Costa Rican, Latin American woman would also be participating in the second round of the debate with Igor Lukšić, Danilo Türk, Helen Clark and Irina Bokova, but only after the first round had pitted Guterres against Vuk Jeremić, Vesna Pusić, Natalia Gherman and Susana Malcorra.

The Portuguese candidate maintained visual consistency—a dark suit and white shirt with that same red silk tie with discrete white lines—and kept with his style—again talking without any papers. However, he was not able to give a convincing response when asked how he expected to use the new digital media to communicate the UN's message.

Guterres did recognise that communication "is a serious problem that we have in the UN."[10]

He then limited his reply to vague considerations about the need to "translate the many important initiatives the UN has, the many important things the UN does for the world, into a language that everybody understands."

It was either that or launching generic appeals for the utilisation of clearer language: "We need to make people understand, we need to speak with a language that everybody uses."

This was a topic in which Guterres was not, and had no intention of ever becoming, a specialist. Responsible for campaign communication, Damião explains that, "We wanted to do much more and Mr. Guterres was always very resistant. I remember when we were presenting the website to him and he asked, 'But what's it for? It's not necessary.' It ended up as a page that essentially presented the candidate, produced internally at no additional cost."

In order to add contents to the website, Damião himself carried out the research and trawled through the digital and physical archives, seeking out all the information and highlights in the candidate's CV, choosing the speeches he gave while in the UNHCR, speaking with Fleming to request photographs from Geneva of his time as High Commissioner, and sorting out the special authorisations needed so that the page might contain some relevant information.

The official documents in support of his candidacy were available online, such as a brief page of information useful to the media with photographs, articles and videos. But nothing else.

"Contrary to what the other candidates were doing," Damião points out, "with very active Twitter pages, with interactive sites and Facebook pages, he never accepted any of this. Even the website was highly institutional."

Guterres' objective was to proceed as unnoticed as possible in everything that was not an essential part of the process: the meetings that might directly influence the representatives or leaders of the states, or events with an international visibility where he might intervene personally.

Silence was part of his strategy, and the Portuguese candidate made a point of keeping his movements discreet, especially so that it would not be publicly known just who he was being received by or who might be promising their support.

Whenever his travels did not receive any local media coverage, this was good news for the candidate. Especially in Latin America and Eastern Europe, it was important that the neighbouring governments of those with whom he had an audience did not get to see Guterres splashed all over the newspapers. This might generate difficulties for the candidates in that region, and therefore perhaps negatively affecting Guterres' campaign as well.

"In diplomacy," stresses Damião, "what very often happens is that you get promised support that in the end is not delivered. The votes are secret and it is very difficult to forecast the alignments emerging so this discretion was always very important."

Hence, the focus of the work remained very much on preparing for the debates and the content of the message.

Whenever he was in Lisbon, Guterres arrived at campaign headquarters burdened with bundles of papers, sheets, notes and dossiers. He explained to his team the topics he had been preparing for each hearing and audience, the key issues for each of the countries, and what he intended to achieve in each phase.

Marques sets out that, "We had the task force, but working the strategy, what needed doing on a day-to-day basis, it was Guterres who determined that. We all had our opinions, but the strategy was that of Guterres."

Given that a high media profile had been classified as counterproductive, and that the bulk of attention should be concentrated on the candidate's interventions, dossiers on dozens of topics were prepared for the Al Jazeera debate. The debate would be open and could indeed involve delicate issues for Moscow, Beijing or Washington… not to mention London, so recently overwhelmed by the outcome of the Brexit referendum.

Guterres decided to approach the British issue in his first intervention: "We see people, common people, more and more alienated from national political establishments, but also international organisations. See, for instance, the European Union."[11]

Not only did the preparation for this debate span the priority themes for the P5, it also had to reach further. After all, the questions would be asked by the moderators, but also by any country or even special guests.

The Senegalese Minister of Health, for example, wanted to know what the candidates intended to do to change the negative perceptions prevailing about the actions of the International Criminal Court, considered selective and discriminatory in relation to African states.

Hardly imagining that, just two years later, the United States of America, one of the most solid democracies and leading powers in the world, would explicitly threaten the independent investigations of the court, and would go as far as to question the Court's legitimacy and even defending its abolition, Guterres called for the strengthening of its credibility: "It is necessary to make a major effort to expand the number of states able to accept the jurisdiction of the Court."[12]

Regarding the reform of the Security Council, the Portuguese candidate managed to draw smiles from those sharing the platform amid generalised applause: "I would like to clarify that I'm not here as a candidate for the Security Council but as a candidate for Secretary-General […]. The reform of the Security Council will only be possible if the membership wants that reform. I think that the Secretary-General would welcome anything that would move in that direction and would be very happy to support it, but there is no way the Secretary-General can replace the membership on this issue."[13]

Each section of the rigorously timed debates lasted twenty-five minutes, and throughout Guterres was again able to convey a positive image. According to Damião, the very opening of this process served as the best communication strategy: "We did not need to invent anything or to create media events. The historical decision of making the presentation of the candidates public and the consequent debate in the General Assembly of the United Nations was extremely important. This allowed the quality, the preparation and density of the candidacy of António Guterres to shine through. Our strongest card was him."

On that day, Theresa May officially replaced David Cameron as the British Prime Minister and Boris Johnson would take up office as Foreign Secretary.

By then, they had less than a week before the first straw poll.

20

THE STRAW POLLS

Moscow was backing Irina Bokova.

London had Helen Clark in the ring.

Paris was putting forward Guterres.

Beijing was also betting on the Portuguese candidate but, since they had been behind Ban Ki-moon's victory in the previous selection, this was not a campaign in which China would want to play a determining role.

Washington had not quite decided, but was leaning toward Malcorra as their first choice.

In addition to the backing of the United States, and being a woman, the Argentinian also held another enviable credential: just like Guterres, she was well known to each of the P5 members.

Her years as the Chief Operating Officer of the World Food Programme, as the Under-Secretary-General in charge of Field Support for Peace Missions, and afterwards, the cherry on the cake, as Ban Ki-moon's chief of staff, had enabled her to sit down face-to-face, on countless occasions, with the leaders of the five permanent member states and their representatives. This afforded her insight into their sensitive issues, helping them overcome problems, while simultaneously having the time to win over their confidence.

However, of the five Security Council states with veto power, the Portuguese Minister of Foreign Affairs testifies that it was the

Americans who were most enthusiastic about the Argentinian candidate: "They were subject to a great deal of pressure in the sense
of backing a woman." Santos Silva accepts that, "Samantha Power
was assumed here as the main instigator of the idea, 'Now, it's the
time for a woman.' Therefore, they always greatly supported
Susana Malcorra."

This was also the understanding of the team that worked behind
the scenes on Guterres' campaign. The information that they had
access to indicated that the Americans preferred a woman and that
their preference went to the then head of Argentina's diplomacy.

However, Malcorra is categorical that she never had the support
"in those definitive terms, of any permanent member of the
Security Council. None of them gave me such explicit support as
was then being stated, not even the United States."

The fact still remained that, with or without Washington pushing
her forwards, Malcorra had a good set of characteristics. Mendonça
e Moura, the Portuguese Ambassador to the United Nations, closely
monitored her work up on the thirty-eighth floor and ranked her as
"a magnificent chief of staff; Ban Ki-moon owed her a great deal as
she ran the house and efficiently controlled the Secretariat."

Just a few days before the first informal voting, the team had
decided which were the most serious contenders. Bokova was, of
course, on that list.

All the information gathered by the task force seemed to confirm
that the Bulgarian, despite being poorly cherished by the government
of her own country, and having failed to turn in good performances
in the public hearings, was still Russia's top preference.

However, in Sofia, the conservatives continued to hope for a
poor result from Bokova in the straw polls in order to justify their
nomination of the candidate most to the liking of their party:
Kristalina Georgieva. But, since the Vice President of the European
Commission was still not officially a candidate, there remained the
twelve already announced candidates in the running.

On the Portuguese list of the main contenders, there were also:

— Slovenia's Danilo Türk was the only former head of state and had
  served as Assistant Secretary-General under Kofi Annan.

— Vuk Jeremić, who had an ambitious 80-page policy paper on reforming the United Nations,[1] had also delivered solid performances in the public debates and was making regular use of social media to share new developments in his campaign, as well as maintaining good contacts with the American media.
— Miroslav Lajčák, was positioning himself as a candidate of both the East and the West. On the one hand, the Slovak had studied in Moscow and spoke fluent Russian. On the other hand, he had been the special European Union representative for the independence of Montenegro in 2006. Hence, his name might easily crop up as a suitable compromise between Washington-London-Paris and Moscow at a time when the interests inside the Security Council seemed otherwise irreconcilable.

In effect, of all the prevailing evaluation criteria, the single most important factor for the fifteen countries on the sitting Security Council, and even more so for the P5, was understanding how the candidates would work with all of them collectively, and with each one of them individually. For that reason, they accepted yet another unprecedented event in the history of the UN: to meet individually with each candidate.

The objective here was not simply to repeat the format of the informal dialogue, held with the majority of states in the General Assembly, but rather for the Council to build up a deeper image of the profile of each candidate—and their specific plans.

These audiences took place behind closed doors and the contents of these extended interviews were never released.

Presenting to the Jury

They had to be alone. No adviser could accompany them and there was to be no debate with the other candidates. This was a private meeting, where the candidates had the right to make a brief initial intervention that was not to exceed ten minutes. After that, candidates had one hour to answer questions put to them by the ambassadors.

"This was something that never got talked about very much," admits the task force coordinator, Freitas Ferraz. Guterres' plan was not to give a detailed explanation of what reforms he had planned for the United Nations, nor to share more detailed analysis of the devastating conflicts afflicting various regions of the world, nor even how he expected to contribute to possible solutions. Instead, the plan was to describe how he would navigate the turbulent waters of the Security Council were he to be elected.

In the headquarters of the French mission, Delattre was able to stage the first three audiences, but since *pro tempore* presidencies of the Council last for only a month, he then handed over the rest of the proceedings to Japan.

In July 2016, the permanent Japanese representative organised the interviews with the nine remaining candidates, and Ferraz once again saw Guterres fly off to New York.

On this occasion, there were no exchanges of messages, no WhatsApp calls. The Ambassador only heard back once Guterres had returned to Lisbon: "He is not an optimistic person and not the type to say, 'It's in the bag.' But he did come back satisfied. And for him to be satisfied, then it must have been an absolute riot. He thought they loved the conversation."

However, there remained a series of doubts. What real effect would these interviews actually have when it came down to the decision-making? Could some other candidate have given a better performance? Or might one of the others have simply been more persuasive, making promises of greatest interest to the countries? There, far from the cameras and without any witnesses, it would just have taken some negotiation skills to go down well with the most important players and transform this hour-long conversation into an auction, trading favours and promises for the most sought-after positions in the UN.

Guterres did not make any such offer, on this or any other occasion. The French Ambassador, Delattre, argues that, "You need to know him to understand. He is not the type of person who makes such promises."

Nevertheless, however wonderfully the interview might have been, the election was yet to begin. The straw polls—the sequence of informal votes that had paved the way for the election of the Secretary-General ever since 1981—needed to start so that a clearer image of the electoral dynamics could take shape.

The inaugural round took place with the Japanese delegation still holding the presidency. Seven months after the beginning of this process, there would finally be the opportunity to sound out the different positions cohabiting within the scope of the Security Council.

This was a non-binding vote, where every member of the Security Council, permanent and non-permanent, had identical ballot papers. And none could veto a candidate. However, it had the power to boost or end the chances of a candidate.

1st Round

Everyone was already seated. Uncomfortably seated. The political distances that separated the permanent representatives made the large round table seem even bigger. The number of resolutions approved unanimously so far by this Security Council was at the lowest level since the 1990s and, with hints of Cold War revivalism, Russia and the United States exchanged accusations and vetoes, especially in regard to Syria.

Mistrust was mirrored in the gazes and gestures of the ambassadors. Far more than reflecting a fragmented global order with new power relationships still under construction, the Security Council had become a strong means of blocking international initiatives.

The mass shedding of blood, destruction and violations of human rights had been splashed across newspapers and television screens, Facebook posts, Twitter and YouTube videos. Yet the positions of Obama, Putin, May, Hollande and Jinping remained irreconcilable.

And now, as if it were business as usual, in New York the representatives of these leading powers had to meet and embark on a purely political process in which their interests would certainly clash once again.

This was not about peace in Yemen, hunger in Somalia or the ongoing conflict in South Sudan, but rather about electing a mediator for all these conflicts. Or at least one that would not create more tensions. It was about arriving at a consensus over a name able to please all parties—or, at the least, that would not particularly irritate any party—and who would put forward plausible solutions—or who would simply not make the situation worse.

On 21 July, the ambassadors received twelve blank ballot papers—one for each candidate. Each paper had the name of the candidate written on top, followed by the same options:

Encouragement
Discouragement
No opinion

The vote was secret and, at least formally, no ambassador would have any means of identifying the choices of their colleagues. The information circulated at the end of this two-hour-long straw poll would only show the votes each candidate had obtained in each of the columns.

These initial rounds would serve to measure the depth of support or the level of rejection for each candidate. This was a way for the members of the Security Council to grasp, slowly but surely, the level of consensus that the candidates were or were not able to rally.

And, as this information had the key objective of supporting—and influencing—the sensitive decision-making process of the governments, the outcomes were only available to their own ambassadors.

The non-publication of the results was a common internal procedure since secrecy was deemed to be in the interest of the candidates and the members of the Council.

Thus, outside of this circle, it should not have been possible to know that Malcorra had gathered seven votes of encouragement in this first round.

Traditional media and social media alike should not have been able to write about the support that nine countries gave to Jeremić and to Bokova.

And the General Assembly was never supposed to learn that Türk had attracted eleven expressions of encouragement.

Outside the Council, Guterres' result should have remained absolutely secret: twelve votes of encouragement, three without opinion and none expressing open opposition. On the contrary, his opponents had between one and five votes of discouragement.

The Main Challenger

Despite the formal commitment that the voting results would remain secret, the information was immediately leaked.

After the first straw poll was completed, UN correspondents from the main media outlets quickly went on Twitter, posting complete tables, some filled in by hand, others simply photographed on their smartphones, and others already computer formatted. A little later, NGOs from all over the world were sharing digital graphics, bedecked in colours and logos, to illustrate the outcomes of this voting process.

"This clearly indicates that one or more Security Council members intentionally or inadvertently gave away the information,"[2] the Japanese Ambassador later set out in an internal report.

The contradictions between the initial transparency of the process, the secrecy of the Security Council and the clandestine disclosure of the results led to calls from some of the actors who had long defended the need to modernise the method of selecting Secretaries-General.

On that same day, Lykketoft used the official Twitter account of the Presidency of the General Assembly to launch an appeal to the Security Council:

> #UNSC should communicate results of 1st informal straw polls on #NextSG to #UNGA to live up to transparency. Letter: http://ow.ly/ ThJn302trXg.[3]

Lykketoft argued that, "Limiting the communication to the fact that the informal straw poll has taken place, without any further detail, adds little value and does not live up to the expectations of the membership and the new standard of openness and transparency."[4]

This discussion was again reopened in the Council. Various ambassadors came out in favour of releasing the results, including Samantha Power: "I thought we should make the results public of our voting because they were getting leaked anyway, and I thought it was just silly."

Bequeathed by an anonymous source and received with mixed feelings, this leak showed the world how the Security Council had evaluated the different candidates. Rightly or wrongly, the differences between the candidates were in the public domain and this immediately shaped perceptions in regards to who was best positioned.

Observing the result from Lisbon, US Ambassador Robert Sherman states that, "From my perspective, António emerged very early on as the candidate to beat. Nobody was blocking him, nobody had anything negative to say. So that was helping cement or crystalise the US view that he was in fact a strong candidate and potentially could be a consensus candidate for everyone down the road."

The same assessment was immediately made by Santos Silva, the Portuguese Minister of Foreign Affairs: "I recall having thought, 'Well, this is truly a game changer, from here on it is clear that he is the candidate.'"

At the precise time of the first straw poll, Santos Silva was participating in an international meeting in Latin America and so he was unable to follow the voting. However, at the other end of the table, there was a member of the government of Spain who, at that time, occupied a non-permanent seat on the Security Council, having immediate access to all the information about what was going on in the room.

Suddenly, the Spanish politician got up and approached his Portuguese counterpart, confiding that Guterres had come out in front, highlighted, ahead of all the other candidates. According to Santos Silva, the numbers from these first results were so clear that they could only receive one interpretation: "He had immediately become the main challenger."

Spread the Word

From the moment Guterres became the one to beat, the very first concern in Lisbon was to identify the three countries who had not voted for him.

New Zealand had their own candidate so were certainly one of the abstentions. It could also be predicted that, as Guterres had now clearly demonstrated he was the strongest adversary, this vote would turn to discouragement in the subsequent rounds.

In regards to the other two countries that had not expressed an opinion about Guterres, the information gathered up until that point led to the assumption that one of them would likely remain neutral, while the other might well change and either vote in favour of rejection or of support.

However, as this process had only just begun, it was essential to continue along the right path with the other twelve Council members, as with all the regional groups represented in the General Assembly.

The African states, which Guterres knew extremely well due to his years at the UNHCR, the Socialist International and the CPLP, the group of Portuguese-speaking nations, were particularly united and participated both directly and indirectly throughout the entire campaign.

"Above all," states Carlos Lopes, "they held the role of convincing others, trying to ensure that on the African side the support for candidate Guterres was that of the entire bloc, without any hesitation, to make it fully clear to other interlocutors that there was an African preference." The former political adviser to Kofi Annan explains that, "We had to make sure that the African members of the Security Council—three in total: Angola, Senegal and Egypt—strengthen this opinion, but also going beyond these three. Guterres and I made an entire web setting out how these relationships might be consolidated."

This web spanned the Atlantic and Indian Oceans, reaching from Suez to Cape Town. On the African east coast, the lead anchoring these efforts was the former Portuguese colony of Mozambique.

Pedro Comissário, who had been Ambassador to Lisbon at the time of the founding of the CPLP, explains that, "In the region of East Africa, they would always be coming to ask us, 'But is this Secretary-General worthwhile? Do you know him?'—and many people expected us to say, 'Ah, no, not the Portuguese coloniser, no way!' because that is the type of relationship that they have with their former colonies and we don't have any of that.[5] We would respond by saying, 'This is an excellent candidate to run our organisation, the United Nations.'"

The Mozambican diplomat, who reencountered Guterres in Geneva and who would later serve as President of the UNHCR

Executive Committee, also declares there had been complete unity across the CPLP around the candidacy, "from the outset, unanimously and without any reservations. With perhaps a far more prominent role of Angola due to its seat on the Security Council, but I may tell you that in terms of lobbying, approaching countries, et cetera, Mozambique and the other countries played an equally important role."

Over in West Africa, Guinea Bissau assumed responsibility for expanding the level of support throughout the rest of the sub-region, especially to neighbouring Senegal, which also held a seat on the Council. Hélder Vaz, a former Bissau-Guinean minister, remembers, "I myself spoke with the Ambassador of Portugal in New York and with the Ambassador of Senegal on the Security Council and, from then on, we did our work raising the awareness of Ghana along with all the others."

Vaz even defended that Guterres could present himself in his campaign not just as a European, but also as a man from the African continent: "He was the candidate of Guinea, the candidate of Angola, he was the candidate of us all, and that had a sort of a multiplier effect."

The role played by the small community of Portuguese-speaking countries, only nine in total, scattered across four continents, without any territorial continuity, is likewise highlighted by the former freedom fighter and President of East Timor. According to Xanana Gusmão, the geopolitical interests in Asia-Pacific, which should have conditioned Timor to vote for the New Zealand candidate, were worth less than the shared language—and, of course, recollections about the role played by Guterres' government in the liberation of his country: "We knew that we were not going to be the decisive factor, but yes, I did go about making various contacts, also as an eminent member of a group of fragile nations called G7+. We did what was possible to contribute. To us, as members of the CPLP, Helen Clark was not acceptable. If it had not been for the CPLP, perhaps, I don't know... but first of all came the CPLP."

Along with the efforts of these international allies—on occasion quite public, on other occasions far more low profile—there were also other reserved channels among those with skin in the game.

At one point, Guterres was contacted directly by American members of the Freemasonry: "There were some gentlemen who wanted to talk with me and so I did. Freemason friends of mine in Portugal were involved almost certainly, as others were as well, from various other organisations. If there had been a Mason campaign against me, that might have been very inconvenient, but there wasn't."

2nd Round

Alarmed by the results of the first straw poll, the New Zealander had no alternative but to up her game. Helen Clark had only eight states on her side and had notched up five negative votes. It was necessary to do the utmost to undermine the support for Guterres, beginning with New Zealand's own vote that had been neutral. But this would not be enough.

In this second round of voting, and in order to make up the lost ground, Helen Clark needed to mobilise more support. On the other hand, she needed to guarantee that her allies took stronger positions against the Portuguese candidate, downgrading the votes they had entrusted in him in the first round. Of course, if she were able to win over some P5s to this anti-Guterres movement, even better.

A week before the second round of voting, Russia's UN Ambassador, Vitaly Churkin, revealed Moscow's plans. Despite having their own candidate, and their priorities clearly known to all from the outset, the Ambassador declared to the media that there were no motives to discourage Guterres: "Why should I? He's such a good man."[6]

Churkin took advantage of an interview to send out a message to clarify the role he intended to play in this process. Anticipating that, at a later phase, the United States would veto candidates from Eastern Europe, Russia lifted the veil on the way it would seek to condition the election. Timings are as fundamental to politics as they are to diplomacy, and Churkin decided to warn at that moment that he was under no pressure to decide on the next Secretary-General: "It is not going to be resolved on Friday. This is my gut feeling."[7]

Indeed, nothing did get resolved on 9 August.

Firstly, because two straw polls would seem too few, especially in comparison with the four rounds needed to elect Ban Ki-moon, ten years earlier. Secondly, and most importantly, in this second round, the front runner was about to lose ground: Guterres picked up two discouragement votes and saw one supporter disappear. From 12–0–3, he dropped to 11–2–2.

Despite having finished again as the candidate with the most indications of "encouragement", there was speculation that Guterres' negative votes included not only New Zealand, but also a P5. The ballot papers of the permanent members might still be the same colour as the other members of the electorate, but the rumours seeping out of the Council's room strongly pointed in that direction.

The problem was that, assessing the individual positions of those countries with veto power, it was still unclear who was the dissenting voice.

It could not have been France—they were among the key supporters.

China would not make any sense—Beijing was on the Portuguese side.

The United States were surely encouraging more than one candidate, but Guterres was one of them.

The United Kingdom had declared to be an ally and there were no reasons why this would not be true.

And Russia had stated that it would not stand in opposition. However, a vote against the front runner would run in favour of the game of patience suggested by Churkin.

Without consensus among the permanent members, the Council would not advance with any formal vote and the straw poll process would have to be extended. Furthermore, at this point, it had not yet been decided how many voting rounds would take place with unmarked ballot papers.

Diplomats in New York estimated that the Security Council would only be in a position to organise the first single-vote straw poll in September or October, but this was mere guesswork.

In any case, the second round served to corroborate Guterres' lead among the most threatening of his fellow candidates, and almost all others had also lost support.

Apparently, in the twenty days that lapsed since the first straw poll, the mood of various countries had changed. Despite having lost one vote of support, trailing right behind Guterres was Jeremić, with eight countries in favour, four against and three abstentions.

The best-positioned female candidate was Malcorra, who had made it into third place, but with six negative votes. Türk had dropped back abruptly and Lajčák was failing to make any progress, as was the case of Bokova and Clark—each with seven votes against.

On the eve of the second round of voting, Pusić had withdrawn her candidacy.

But Why Did You Come Here?

"They do not answer our calls, they don't give us any date. Purely and simply, this is because they do not want to receive us. They don't want to tell us face to face why they are not supporting us." Freitas Ferraz was pessimistic. Since announcing Guterres' candidacy, months had passed by and they persisted in pushing the Government of Malaysia to grant Guterres an audience.

Freitas Ferraz persevered. Insistently, he requested updates from the Portuguese Embassy in Bangkok. Nothing. The network of contacts of the Ambassador in Paris was deployed. In vain. They tried yet another triangulation via Beijing. Pointless. The phone calls from Ferraz himself, day after day, did not get any results.

This was the only non-permanent member of the Security Council that the Portuguese candidate had not been able to visit, and it was a much-needed vote. After all, the country's economic and political credibility gave it influence throughout an Asia-Pacific region that needed mobilising, especially since this was the group where Helen Clark naturally gathered more support.

The delay in the response was interpreted as a political message and, with each passing day, fears mounted that the vote cast might at best be "no opinion".

Until, finally, Kuala Lumpur gave the green light.

The official response set down a date after Ramadan, in midsummer. Then Guterres and the Malaysians would be able to talk face to face.

Once again, Guterres packed his bags and set off on the 12,000-kilometre journey before checking into yet another hotel. When it was time for the formal audience, the conversation took place not in a climate of distrust, but rather of surprise. On both sides.

"But why did you come here? We don't understand why you went to all the trouble... We did our analysis and we've been supporting you from the beginning. Did you have any doubts?"

Damião recalls how Guterres returned from Malaysia "with a great deal of enthusiasm, everything had gone very well, especially as they verified how well he knew the country. And the way in which, once again, he had prepared for the meeting, what he already knew about his counterpart who he was meeting with. This all helped a great deal."

The method with which he prepared all high-level conversations had changed little since his time as Prime Minister. He would meet with close members of his team and work to understand the host country of his visit in terms of migrations, internal or international conflicts, sensitive political issues, and convergent or divergent positions in the United Nations.

Marques puts it plainly: "He did not engage in any blah blah blah conversation. He would arrive and present his strategy, shaped in accordance with that country's specific issues. He would carry out this preparation work with us every Tuesday. For example, with Japan, he prepared the meeting around the theme of development aid donors because he knew that was a matter of great importance to them."

The Guterres world tour naturally focused on the fifteen members of the Security Council, but the campaign's agenda was structured in order to provide the candidate with the chance to harvest the produce of seeds planted decades ago in different countries across the globe.

During the summer, he travelled to states with regional influence, such as India. And the only reason he did not go to Brazil was due to the instability that the country was going through caused by an economic recession and the corruption scandal that was dragging down his friend, the former President of the Republic, Lula da Silva.

When he chose which capitals to visit, Guterres obviously took into consideration the network of contacts that he had cultivated ever since his days leading the Socialist International.

A former political adversary and Minister of Foreign Affairs of Portugal, Paulo Portas, often heard about Guterres' trips: "International party alliances aren't a deciding factor in the vote, but the Socialist International is important, especially in developing countries, and he made all those pilgrimages. He criss-crossed Africa and Latin America and did so highly professionally. Wherever I would go during those months, I would hear that he had been here and that he had been there."

Around this time, Guterres had already clocked up hundreds of hours of flight time, and Freitas Ferraz has no doubt that the accumulated tiredness was beginning to take its toll: "He has great resilience but by that time he was completely exhausted."

At the same time, the Portuguese government accompanied all these efforts and seized whatever opportunities might be good for campaigning. An initiative entitled "Women and Wine" in Denmark? What an excellent idea! There could be no better pretext to schedule a bilateral visit!

Having complied with the official protocol and highlighted the strategic importance of the wine cause through the presence of Marques, Secretary of State for Foreign Affairs, she headed to the Danish Ministry of Foreign Affairs.

The topic on the agenda was, of course, the candidacy of Guterres. According to Marques, "The Minister was accompanied by two people, one on either side and I told him, 'We know that he has two difficulties: he is not a woman but...' and he began writing everything down! It seemed as if I was dictating. This was quite impressive as nothing like that had ever happened before."

What particularly surprised Marques was the fact that it was the actual member of government, and not a member of his team, taking notes. "When I finished, he picked up the pen and said, 'As you might imagine, your arguments are so important to me because I need them.' It was to convince the other countries!"

Denmark, alongside its Scandinavian neighbours Norway and Sweden, is considered by the international community as a credible actor committed to the values of the United Nations Charter. Within the scope of the UN's work and the promotion of human rights, these three countries have a solid democratic history, a portfolio of humanitarian actions, and a global reputation capable of influencing other states. Plus, they often vote together.

While High Commissioner for Refugees, Guterres had maintained close relationships with them all, especially with Norway. Additionally, he was up to speed on the Scandinavians' 2014 approach to the Portuguese government, suggesting that he would be put forward as a candidate. Nevertheless, now that his candidacy was in full force, the Scandinavian support could no longer be taken for granted.

Their support was also coveted by other candidates, especially at a time of indifference and lack of response from the major powers to the brutal demonstrations of cruelty and flagrant violations of human rights that were continuously spreading across the world. In this context, Scandinavian support represented an important trump card in the election for the powerful diplomatic message it carried: not only did it embody the candidate's capacity to gather consensus, which deeply contrasted with the multipolar nature of the political wills prevailing internationally, but it was also testimony to their genuine commitment to the ideals of peace, combatting poverty, sustainable development and respect for the rules-based order.

In fact, success in promoting these values represented the cornerstone of the election campaign for the next Secretary-General and was considered by many in the UN system, and even by Guterres, as the antidote to the paradoxes and fractures that the wider world was experiencing.

In fact, in these early years of the new century, the voices inside liberal democracies that questioned their own model of development were multiplying, as were the numbers of citizens seduced by the apparent success of the new authoritarian regimes and their repressive tactics. Even within the Security Council, right there among the permanent members, those experiencing periods of extended internal convulsion were Western countries.

It seemed that much of the economic prosperity of those early decades was being generated in countries where citizens had foregone both their individual liberties and their collective rights in exchange for a formula that promised greater wealth at home, stability in the workplace, or security on the streets. The equation that millions of Europeans and North Americans had learned in schools about the unquestionable benefits of democracy and globalisation was starting to give room to widespread confusion and existential doubts.

The UN Is Not a Friend

A landmark of Soviet architecture, the colossal, almost 200-metres-tall ministry building stands in the centre of glorious and imperial Moscow.

Part skyscraper, part fortress of gothic inspiration, the Ministry of Foreign Affairs reflects not only the inevitable destiny of Russian supremacy, but also projects the venerable authority of the state over the city's structure.

The wings around the main tower appear to be two conquering arms, reaching out into the public space, creating a reception room under the open sky—an antechamber that provides guests with one last opportunity to contemplate the sheer power of their hosts.

At the top of the almost thirty-floor building, surrounded by a victorious crown of laurels, the hammer and sickle occupy the centre of a map of the world. Overseen by a red star, the communist coat of arms covers every country on Earth.

It was from here that Sergey Lavrov commanded the Russian diplomatic machine.

It was there that Guterres arrived in July 2016 accompanying a bilateral visit formally requested by the Portuguese Minister of Foreign Affairs. The main objective of the meeting was to confirm the official position of Vladimir Putin's government on the future leader of the United Nations.

After all the points in the initial working agenda had been discussed, Santos Silva ventured, "Now, we have another matter that I would wish to raise with you. That's the election of the Secretary-General of the United Nations…"

"The election of António Guterres," interrupted Lavrov.

For months now, Lisbon had known Moscow's perspective. Since the outset of the process, Guterres and his campaign team had worked on the basis that he was not Vladimir Putin's first choice. The information was correct. But now, this simple act of futurology, made by the man who had occupied the most senior position in Russian foreign policy for the previous twelve years, definitively set the conversation on the right track.

Santos Silva continued to pitch the candidacy, highlighting the reasons why the candidate, despite coming from the European Union and belonging to a NATO country, did not pose any insurmountable problems to Russia.

Lavrov dismissed the issue of gender that so excited the United States, but nevertheless insisted that this was the time for somebody from Eastern Europe. For that reason, they could not support Guterres.

However, as a way of concluding, the Russian let slip a sentence that summed up everything the Portuguese candidate needed to know: "But we can live with him."

There was also a tactical consideration that helps understand Moscow's position: Lavrov knew that the Americans would not hesitate to veto any pro-Russian candidates.

Furthermore, one could argue that this concession from Lavrov was in fact a more solid offering than a clearer, more positive affirmation might have been from a Western power. The institutions of the Russian state are fully loyal to the Kremlin's interpretations and positions, including on foreign policy. In other words, from the perspective of the Portuguese candidate, Vladimir Putin's regime could be relied upon. Having internal stability as a top political priority ensured continuity of decisions; and, since there was no foreseeable change in Moscow's power structure, Guterres could count on the fact that Lavrov's word would not be called into question later by some divergent-thinking government official who might suddenly appear on the scene.

The same analysis could also be made for the Chinese regime, where the most senior decision-making circles have proved impermeable to sudden shifts.

Ironically enough, the problems laid in the Western capitals.

28. First words to staff at UNHCR's headquarters in Geneva.

29. Guterres with his chief of staff, Athar Sultan-Khan, in their last meeting of the UNHCR Executive Committee.

30. At the border between Tunisia and Libya in the aftermath of the Arab Spring.

31. Guterres meets with Assad's Deputy Foreign Minister, Faisal Mekdad. Guterres never returned to Syria after the uprising against the regime.

32. The Za'atari refugee camp in northern Jordan suddenly found itself hosting 80,000 Syrians who had fled the war.

33. Visit to a camp of internally displaced persons in the suburbs of Baghdad, Iraq, in January 2011.

34. Guterres (centre) immediately flew to Kandahar, Afghanistan, after an attack involving suicide bombers and gunmen on one of the UNHCR guesthouses.

35. Guterres delivered a landmark speech on the theme of "Faith and Protection" during the 2012 High Commissioner's Dialogue on Protection Challenges.

36. Guterres in Kenya, 2015, shortly after the al-Shabaab attack at Garissa University College that left 148 people dead.

37. Private meeting in Geneva with Carlos Lopes, a close friend who was the Executive Secretary of the Economic Commission for Africa at the time.

HIGH COMMISSIONER FOR REFUGEES   SPECIAL ENVOY OF THE HIGH COMMISSIONER FOR REFUGEES

38. Next to Angelina Jolie, UNHCR's Special Envoy, during a Security Council meeting about the Syrian crisis.

39. Guterres (centre) with the European Commission's Vice President, Kristalina Georgieva (in red), in the suburbs of Beirut, Lebanon.

40. On World Refugee Day 2015, Guterres visited the Midyat refugee camp in Turkey, home to hundreds of thousands of refugees that had fled conflicts in Syria and Iraq.

41. Guterres on the Greek island of Lesbos, the first point of arrival for migrants fleeing to Europe, having risked their lives trying to cross the Aegean Sea.

42. Guterres with his mother, his current wife and stepson, after the Portuguese President Cavaco Silva publicly bestowed upon him one of the highest national honours.

43. The first-ever public debates between candidates vying for the UN Secretary-General post.

44. During his informal dialogue with the UN General Assembly, Guterres answered more than eighty questions.

45. Kristalina Georgieva, the current IMF chief, long rumoured to be interested in the role, entered the UN Secretary-General race too late.

46. Guterres finds out he is the next UN Secretary-General. The Portuguese Prime Minister António Costa rushed to congratulate him.

47. Guterres with Ban Ki-moon, minutes before being sworn in as the 9th UN Secretary-General.

48. 7 December 2011: Five years later, Hillary Clinton would unexpectedly lose the US presidential bid a month after Guterres' election as Secretary-General.

49. 3 January 2017: Guterres' first day of work as UN Secretary-General.

50. Guterres avoided addressing controversial issues in his meetings with US President Donald Trump.

51. Pope Francis and Guterres recorded a joint video message against religious intolerance at Christmas in 2019.

52. After Trump's term ended, the Covid pandemic became Guterres' main challenge as head of the UN.

France had elections scheduled for the following year, 2017, and Hollande was under pressure following a combination of personal scandals and government decisions highly criticised by wide sectors of society. By September, the approval rate of the socialist President stood at just 15 per cent[8] and it was almost certain that he would not be standing for re-election.

The United Kingdom was still dealing with the political after-shocks of the Brexit referendum: the internal fractures in the country, inside the Conservative Party, in government and in Parliament, foretold the difficulties in obtaining reliable commitments and coherent decisions.

The greatest uncertainty, however, loomed over the United States where, with just a few months to go until the presidential election, an anti-establishment candidate was riding a wave of dissatisfaction, sweeping key constituencies across the country.

Serving as an adviser to Guterres throughout his entire candidacy, especially in regards to the best way to approach the most senior decision-makers in each Security Council country, Lopes admits, "It was difficult for us to anticipate exactly what sort of influence we might have over specific players in a period when everybody was already positioning themselves for what would come next... everything was already in the post-phase... for example, the American administration and diplomatic machine were already preparing for change. Regardless of whether Trump or Clinton won, this was a shift, as the main interlocutors would be changing. We had therefore a set of turbulent contexts that made the Western leaders difficult to slot into any strategic framework."

Indeed, on 7 June 2016, Donald Trump, the real estate tycoon turned reality-show star, would clinch the Republican Party nomination to officially become the candidate for the Presidency of the United States.

Throughout the country, liberal voices and many media groups rushed to denigrate the candidate and announce his foreseeable defeat. However, Donald Trump's discourse was also gaining in popularity.

Fully aware of his own skills for inflaming and channelling the frustrations of other people, Trump was able to build a powerful image not of a politician, but of a man, white and conservative, who loved his country and who had the courage to stand in defence against all those who were attacking it: the foreigners, the liberals, the elites, the media, the entire system. He was the image of some-body who shared the suffering of the average American and who had the courage—and the resources—to say whatever he wanted.

It was above all Trump's offensive style that positioned him as a new product on a shelf full of old relics. Even though his content was essentially recycled old material, it at least appeared with a different type of packaging. And, to a growing number of clients, the Democrats, against whom Trump was running, appeared to be no more than undifferentiated antiques. They all staged broadly the same scenario, with the same promises, and all reflected the same heritage: that of liberal democracies, of globalisation, of multicul-turalism, of tolerance.

The strategy brought along by the Trump brand stood out in the political market for being the exact opposite of everyone else.

Treating the electors as consumers, he would present simple answers to respond to complex problems. For example, in terms of illegal immigration: "I'm going to build a big, big wall." He rejected the dogmas of political correctness, packing his speeches with straightforwardness and a provocative attitude: "The beauty of me is that I'm very rich." He made promises around protectionism and insulted those who defended free trade: "Crooked Hillary will sell us out, just like her husband did with NAFTA." He promised to restore the country's lost dignity: "Make America Great Again."

For some, Trump was the solution for everything. For others, he was at least an attempt to do things differently. Many voted for him because of what he was saying, while many others would vote for him despite what he was saying.

Hence, with the same isolationist rhetoric that had powered the victory of those behind Brexit, Trump knew how to win over the political and media void that so many other actors and observers pretended not to see. This was fertile, unoccupied ground ready for the taking, at the mercy of whoever had the foresight and the skill to take advantage of it. That abandoned territory contained millions of electors, starved of leadership and desperate for protection.

After all, that was what Trump's exaggerated promises offered: protection against threats—Mexican migrants, Chinese producers, Arab refugees... even the Europeans were competitors that needed beating and to be put in their places.

Within the universe of the Republican candidate, everything was a competition that America had not been winning for far too long—and, if it was not winning, then it must be losing.

For too long, the United States had fallen captive to a conspiracy of countless hidden socialists whose main objective was to strip average Americans of their guns and leave them defenceless before replacing them, the true Americans, with foreigners and invaders.

For too long, their America, the biggest and best country in the world, had been on its knees, focusing its energy on problems abroad. Indeed, so much money and time invested in standing as the guarantor of the international system, which allegedly places justice and dialogue at the heart of its functioning, but which brought no benefit whatsoever to such a great nation.

For far too long, Washington had been permissive towards distant and abstract entities such as the World Trade Organization or the International Criminal Court, and overly generous to NATO and, of course, the UN.

"The United Nations is not a friend of democracy, it's not a friend to freedom, it's not a friend even to the United States of America,"[9] Trump proclaimed.

"The UN isn't doing anything to end the big conflicts in the world,"[10] he would also announce.

In this reality, in which the foreign policy of the world's largest power would be bulldozed under the slogan "America First", the UN was portrayed as a bureaucratic monster, inefficient, ineffective and wasteful, to which the Americans were the largest contributor and that, on the good days, did not serve any purpose.

Dollars and Biscuits

While half of the international stakeholders were conspiring around the future UN Secretary-General, the human suffering that Ban Ki-moon had been signalling seemed to spread beyond walls and borders.

From Myanmar came alarming reports about the cruelty and efficiency with which state authorities were persecuting the Rohingya minority.

In Syria, the civil war was entering a new phase, with the number of innocent victims rising in tandem with the speed at which the government in Damascus was recovering ground lost in recent years, whether to terrorist forces or to the non-radicalised opposition.

In Yemen, the conflict between the Iran-backed rebels and the government forces supported by Saudi Arabia and the Western powers was beginning to turn into a humanitarian nightmare, notching up almost 10,000 dead, with an estimated two million children suffering from extreme malnutrition.

Moreover, just as the UN's response capacity was being seriously called into question, right in the midst of the campaign, there were new public reports about shocking sexual abuse committed by members of peacekeeping forces deployed for the very purpose of protecting the most vulnerable.

Guterres had visited the Central African Republic in April 2014, weeks before the deployment of MINUSCA was confirmed—an international mission for maintaining peace, under the mandate of the Security Council, made up of African Union military forces supported by French armed forces.

The operation had barely got under way when the first rumours had surfaced.

A sporadic case here.

Another alleged report there.

In the initial months of the mission alone, thirteen children had been victims of sexual exploitation by soldiers from France, Chad and Equatorial Guinea: all peacekeepers in the service of the United Nations.

According to an internal report made public in April 2015,[11] the acts of paedophilia forced upon the children of the Central African Republic had been "paid for" with five dollars—and a few biscuits. As shocking as the acts themselves were, half of the scandal revolved around accusations that the UN system had connived in a cover-up, ignoring whistle-blowers and punishing them rather than the alleged perpetrators.[12]

And, with the campaign to take over from Ban Ki-moon very much under way, it now came to light that the number of children abused in the Central African Republic greatly exceeded the original thirteen. In March 2016, a further ninety girls had complained that they had been victims of sexual exploitation, detailing the cruelty they had been subjected to. In July, forty more cases emerged.

Inflamed by the proliferation of films, reports and documentaries about figures such as Julian Assange and Edward Snowden, the topic encroached into the campaign and forced the candidates to take positions. With global public opinion divided—between those who considered the whistle-blowers to be authentic liberating heroes of the digital era and those who perceived them as sinister figures, traitors to their cause, motivated by personal agendas or criminal objectives and, in some cases, even financed by obscure sources—the candidates had to clarify on which side of the barricade they stood.

In the debate held in June, in London, Guterres had guaranteed that his priority as Secretary-General would be to protect those calling out such crimes: "To punish whistle-blowers that denounce serious violations of human rights is totally unacceptable and must completely stop."

Those on Guterres' side of the argument saw the question of how to handle such cases as part of a wider existential struggle for the survival and primacy of the UN itself. In order to guarantee that the political leaders remained committed to supporting the UN, civil societies could not have any doubts about the importance of the organisation's work, and far less so about the nobility of their actions. The perception that the United Nations still serves as a moral compass in a dangerously complex world was a vital tool for the next Secretary-General, but the global theatre in which the organisation was striving to maintain its leading role was an already crowded stage disputed by a growing number of competing actors: financial development institutions, bilateral/triangular/multilateral cooperation programmes, wealthy states, supranational and intergovernmental organisations, NGOs… and even major private corporations increasingly committed to a framework of social or environmental responsibility, even if only for cosmetic purposes.

Aware that their profits were impacted by market perception, which values the image of corporations as committed members of their respective communities, multinational oil companies rebranded themselves as energy companies. Car production companies were now calling themselves mobility service providers. Investment funds made a point of publicising their sudden allocations of capital to the preservation of the environment. There was some serious jostling in the race to secure the hearts and wallets of consumers, the approval of shareholders, praise from political leaders and the media, all while contending for the same emotional territory as the United Nations.

Hence, the UN had to strive more than ever before to justify its relevance and, in extreme cases, its very existence. The organisation desperately needed to uphold its reputation as champion in combatting the inequalities and injustices of the world. Its good name needed to stay immaculate and the legitimacy of its actions could never be called into question by the kind of reports that had come out of the Central African Republic—especially since the overall efficacy of the mission was far from being an acceptable example.

With the Security Council so deeply split, there was little hope that the organisation would be able to generate political solutions to bring an end to conflicts, whether new or old, that afflicted so much of the planet.

Without any consensus in its main decision-making structure, the external actions of the UN were amputated from the outset and, with the five permanent members disagreeing, the next Secretary-General would need to find a mobilising cause, an idea that would enable the peoples of the planet to come together and render meaning to a UN held hostage by the tensions prevailing among the great powers.

3rd Round

"John Kerry told us, 'António Guterres is our candidate. At least, one of our candidates.'" The revelation comes from Santos Silva.

The Portuguese minister confirmed that the American Secretary of State had personally committed support to Guterres by August, even though he was quite aware that there were other candidates receiving encouragement from the United States. According to Santos Silva, the pressure to elect a woman remained high right until the end of the process: "The US themselves internally experienced this contradiction. However, Kerry told us, 'Don't worry, this is going to work itself out.'"

Six days prior to the third straw poll, Igor Lukšić, the candidate from Montenegro, abandoned the race. That left ten candidates, five men and five women, simple mathematics that only strengthened the duty of the United States to continue supporting the female candidates.

Guterres confirms that, "The Americans told us, 'We would prefer a woman, but we are voting in favour [of you].' And the Americans don't lie about this kind of thing."

With the summer holidays in the northern hemisphere almost over, many permanent representatives had yet to make their way back to New York, but there was a schedule to comply with and the next round of informal voting needed to commence.

Guterres still needed to find out just who might be accompanying New Zealand in his discourage column, while continuing to follow the trends in the results of his adversaries.

Indeed, it was precisely in this third round of voting, held on 29 August, when a warning sign appeared from one of the candidates identified as a danger: Miroslav Lajčák. Somehow, in the twenty days since the second straw poll, the Slovak had managed to add a score very similar to that of Guterres.

The Portuguese candidate had been unable to attract more encouragers, leaving him with four unsupportive countries: the innocuous abstention column still registered a single vote, but the number of votes against him had increased from two to three. The question was, who had changed their opinion from neutral to negative since the early August round, and why? And what were the chances that this country was one of the P5? Finally, which other states might follow this trend for rejection and how could they stop it?

"It took us a while to understand who the cheeky blighter was, which country had been with us but wasn't any longer," says Álvaro

Mendonça e Moura. The then Portuguese Ambassador to New York remains cautious in his revelations: "I cannot go into details, but when we understood just who it was, we were no longer overly concerned. This does not have any political logic of great international politics; this is related exclusively to personal motives. This was a small personal issue and we knew it would get resolved. This did not even need António Guterres' intervention, he had nothing to do with it, but he knew about it obviously. What we did was to make life a little more difficult for those who were complicating our own life… conveying how it had not even crossed our minds that this particular country would not be on our side on this."

The Portuguese Foreign Minister, Santos Silva, concurs that various theories were debated but that, in the end, there were no major doubts: "That vote against us appeared in August. It could be a country that had been one of the fastest out of the blocks in publicly supporting António Guterres, but whose ambassador was on holiday. It could have been something as ridiculous as that. This theory, which has a certain charm of simplicity around it, is supported by the fact that this lost vote was subsequently corrected."

Analysing the fifteen members of the Security Council one by one, as well as their respective expressions of support, there had been a lot more doubts than actual evidence. And, in order to get to the finishing line, it would be necessary to tie up some loose ends.

That the Egyptian Ambassador was on holiday and absent from New York that August is certain. As is the fact that this was the country that abstained in the second round and that voted against in the third. From that point onwards, the explanations vary.

Either the chargé d'affaires, who was filling in for the Ambassador, misunderstood the instructions and simply got it wrong when it came round to vote, or the personal friendships that this diplomat had with other internal UN candidates influenced the direction of his vote. Or still, perhaps a more far-fetched hypothesis, that the Cairo authorities wanted to send a message to the Western powers warning them that this matter was still far from closed, and took advantage of the absence of their ambassador to do it in a more discreet fashion.

In any case, even with three votes against and an abstention, Guterres remained in the lead and continued to be the candidate able to gain the greatest consensus amid the sourly divided Security Council.

The clashes between Russia and the Western powers were raising the probability of a block on any candidates from the East and complicating the game of negotiations between Samantha Power and Churkin—who were never to formally sit down together in order to discuss this subject.

The US Ambassador recalls that on every occasion she conversed with her Russian counterpart about the election it was either an informal or social event, and within an ambience of mutual distrust: "We talked about it but we never were transparent to each other, because each of us would have a responsibility to report back to our houses. If we told the Russian Ambassador who we were going to support, given the state of US-Russia relations, that would be very damaging for the candidate who we supported."

In addition, while Russia still assumed that the United States had decided to veto the candidates supported by Moscow, in Washington nobody wanted to get pushed into any such scenario. The fear was precisely that Russia would force the United States to formally cast its veto against an Eastern European country with which Washington had maintained good relations ever since these countries had engaged in NATO's sphere of influence, some even becoming members of the Alliance, after the collapse of the USSR.

However, of all the candidates from the region, the one who was probably closest to the United States continued on the sidelines. With three straw polls already completed, the name that might emerge as a solution capable of pleasing both the United States and Russia remained officially outside the race, but still widely considered a potential candidate.

In the run-up to the third round of voting, Andrew Mitchell, a former UK Secretary of State for International Development—a member of the Conservative Party then in power in the United Kingdom—had published an opinion article in which he argued, "If Ms Bokova receives so few votes she drops out, a new candidate should be put forward. Easily the best would be another Bulgarian, Kristalina Georgieva."[13]

21

CHECKMATE

Boris Johnson swore he was convinced. In September, just two months after having taken up the position of British Foreign Secretary in Theresa May's new government, the eccentric man who managed to disconcert rivals and allies alike with his demeanour constantly swinging between charm and haughtiness, seemed to have been persuaded by Guterres.

Marques, then the Portuguese Secretary of State, reports that in a private conversation her UK counterpart told her, "I'm totally won over by your former Prime Minister. He is extraordinary, he knows everything. I was quite stunned; I've never met quite such a man!"

Renowned for having built up a deliberately picturesque and contradictory public persona—which conciliated his education in the same elite school as children of royalty, having published books on Churchill, Shakespeare and the Roman Empire, with his relatable, "anti-establishment" persona and happiness to adopt popular left-wing policy ideas—Johnson's other famous characteristic was his accumulated track record of provocative, sweeping statements that would often turn out not to accord with the details of statistics or policies, including during the Brexit referendum campaign. This best-known minister of the new British government had swiftly accepted Guterres' request for an audience.

During their conversation, the UN candidate once again drew on his recipe for success that had helped him cultivate allies on so many previous occasions. In order to charm Johnson and persuade him of his capacity to lead the UN, Guterres made recourse to his knowledge of history built up over decades. He dissected political facts and spoke with simplicity about complex realities.

"You are a person who reads a lot of history," Johnson observed.

"I read, but you write."

"He melted his heart," vows Marques. "Boris was completely melted."

After personally having won over the person responsible for Her Majesty's diplomacy, the assumption was that the formal support of the United Kingdom would be duly forthcoming.

However, what was especially important was the timing of this conversation. The voting with coloured ballot papers, which would take place from the fifth round, was increasingly close and there was the corresponding need to clarify once and for all just who was hiding their cards and voting against Guterres.

4th Round

"Our big assumption was that truly one of those discouragements was coming from Russia or from China," says Power. "António told us something like, 'I think I'm okay with Russia,' but I thought it was quite likely that Russia was saying one thing and doing something else. Churkin saying that he was ok with Guterres didn't convince me in any way."

Power does not hide her scepticism. The external interests of the United States were increasingly clashing with Russian positions, and the Ambassador did not believe Moscow would simply accept a candidate from a founding member of NATO, and one so close to canonical Western thinking.

In turn, the French, still the greatest allies of Guterres, had a different view. Despite the growing divergences between Paris and Moscow, especially due to the Russian support for Bashar al-Assad, Ambassador Delattre still trusted Churkin.

"The Russians implicitly told us that, if at the end of the day he was clearly the frontrunner, they would go with Guterres," states Delattre. "And we believed in that, based on the good relationship we had. I think that other players in the Security Council didn't. And the key point of the election was here, in believing or not believing."

Voting on 9 September confirmed Guterres again as the front-runner, with a slightly improved tally of 12 positives, 2 negatives and 1 abstention. The mysterious country that had withdrawn its support in the previous two rounds had been reconverted and Guterres managed to snatch back the number of favourable votes obtained in the first poll. But this fourth round also confirmed the advance of the Slovak Miroslav Lajčák and his affirmation as Guterres' most dangerous rival. Lajčák continued to accumulate support. With a final score of 10–4–1, he became the only candidate, apart from Guterres, to receive more than the nine votes deemed necessary to win the election.

Right behind came Jeremić, with 9–4–2. Only the feminine cause continued to lack good news.

Bokova and Malcorra were the highest-ranking female candidates but achieved only seven favourable votes each.

With the election already heading towards its final stages, the Bulgarian Prime Minister Boyko Borisov felt the rising pressure from his European allies to replace Bokova with Georgieva, since his candidate seemed unable to move off fifth position.

At this time, no observer of this process had any doubts that one of the key drivers behind this movement was the European People's Party (EPP)—the group of conservative parties that had always perceived the socialist parties as their greatest rivals—involved in a game of power that sought to project their international influence and place one of their own as the head of the UN.

Just a few days prior to the fourth round of voting, German Chancellor Angela Merkel, the most powerful leader in the EPP, took advantage of the G20 Summit in Hangzhou, China, to drum up support and promote the future candidacy of Georgieva—in particular with Vladimir Putin, who continued to prefer a Secretary-General from the Eastern European region.

In what seemed to be another play of a concerted strategy, one of the EU's highest-ranking officials took to Twitter to announce to the world that Georgieva was going to step forward. On

10 September, the day immediately after Bokova's disappointing result in the fourth round, the German Martin Selmayr, chief of staff to the President of the European Commission, and considered internally as the lead puppet master within the European executive power structure, wrote:

> Would be great loss for @EU_Commission. But Kristalina would make strong UNSG, and many Europeans proud. + strong signal for gender equality.[1]

This tweet was even shared by a former European Commissioner also affiliated with the EPP.

The connections between Selmayr and the European People's Party were publicly known, as were his skills for behind-the-scenes manoeuvring. In the corridors in Brussels, the German went by the nicknames of "The Mentor", "Rasputin", or "the Prince of Darkness". The award-winning French journalist Jean Quatremer, who has over two decades' experience in Brussels' meandering power structures, wrote that, "The other chiefs of staff had such fear of him that they built up the habit of meeting regularly to discuss his psychology and organise their resistance, forecasting his whims and blocking his coups."[2]

However, in Sofia, Prime Minister Borisov was still hesitant. Contrary to Portugal, who had united in support of Guterres, Bulgaria remained politically divided. With presidential elections looming that November, the last thing the head of the conservative government wanted to do was to give the socialists excuses to attack him. He knew that such a decision would bring about inevitable consequences for the international credibility of the country and might seriously weaken his position. He also needed to maintain a delicate balance between its alliances with Berlin and Moscow, so Borisov continued to stall and avoided interfering with the pieces on the table.

The contrast in the positions assumed by Portugal and by Bulgaria may have been another factor valued by the US State Department. The then Ambassador in Lisbon, Robert Sherman, confirms the diplomatic cables sent from Lisbon highlighted that the different actors in the Portuguese power structure were all rowing in the same direction: "It was very clear, from the Presidency, the Prime Minister, from the different parties, it didn't matter. He was the consensual choice and it was not because he was a socialist candidate or something else. And that was actually something that I did report, that the Portuguese political system was aligned behind Guterres. It sent a very strong message."

Guterres had emerged victorious in all four voting sessions. However, the deciding stage would only begin when the P5 ballot papers were differentiated by colour from the remaining ten members of the Security Council. The methodology for the next phase was simple: the ballot papers with the names of each candidate to be delivered to the permanent members—and only to them—would be red. A vote of discouragement cast on these red papers would immediately indicate a veto.

However, there were diverging opinions as to how many straw polls should be held and when the coloured ballot papers would be introduced. Power confirms Churkin was the one dragging his feet: "I wanted to start the process earlier in the summer and he kind of slowed it down, so we had a lot of clashes on the process, there was a lot of tension in it."

Finally, the Council members decided to set the number of exploratory straw polls to five.

The Russian tactical decision to drag out the process was part of a political strategy that involved playing for time, but not as part of some secret plan to favour a particular candidate. The key factor here was simply the diplomatic calendar and the stipulated rotation within the Security Council.

By holding five straw polls—not four and not six—the first coloured ballot paper voting would be scheduled for the beginning of October, the same month when the Security Council would be presided over by Churkin.

Guterres explains that, "My interpretation today is based on the way the Russians led this matter, which was: there would be no decisive votes scheduled until it was their turn for the Presidency. They always opposed the holding of votes at an earlier stage so that they would have to undertake all of the subsequent rounds of voting."

As a result, Moscow would be the one to announce to the world the name of the next UN Secretary-General. For the history books, it would be Russia that had overseen the closure of this unprecedented selection process. At the centre of this precious democratic moment, Vladimir Putin's government took centre stage: the face of consensus among the great powers, the state most willing and able to find solutions for the fragmentation of global power, all while performing a positive leadership role in major multilateral decisions.

For Guterres, on the other hand, it was advantageous to begin the colour-coded votes as swiftly as possible. The longer this process dragged on, the greater the opportunity there was for his wave of support to dissipate, the more the chances his rivals would have to pull some rabbit out of the hat and render the election even more unpredictable.

Fake News

Ambassador Mendonça e Moura doubled down on his contacts. He would stalk the corridors and talk to every delegation he met along the way. He monitored newspapers from around the world and analysed all the reports that crossed his desk or his e-mail account. He made phone calls, pressured everyone around him, and then did it all over again with his fellow ambassadors in New York.

There were only a few short weeks until final decisions would be made and everybody needed to continue singing from the same sheet.

The microstates of the Pacific and the nuclear powers, the developed states and the emerging economies, nobody could be allowed to abandon ship—however seductive the siren calls and tempting the promises from other candidates might be, however effective the influence of political cycles or adverse media coverage.

In the midst of all this frenetic electoral activity, the Ambassador was interrupted by his phone ringing. The call was coming from Lisbon and, on the other end of the line, the member of the task force responsible for communications and media was not happy.

"So you set up an account for António Guterres on Twitter and I know nothing about it?"

CHECKMATE

"We what?"

"Yes, the Twitter account. How did that happen?"

"No, no. Look, I really don't know anything about it."

David Damião acknowledges that, "Somebody had set up a fake profile for Guterres and I had to talk to various people before understanding just what had happened."

What at the beginning was a fairly innocuous page, with just two or three posts "without any relevance at all", rapidly turned into a matter of great alarm.

Those behind the page began following the Prime Minister and President of Portugal, as well as various international figures, up until a point when the tables turned and the digital community, such as journalists, began to follow the account itself believing it was Guterres' official channel.

The red alert was only triggered in Lisbon when this digital Guterres published a post capable of bringing the whole candidacy crashing down.

"The tweet said, 'I've just been in Moscow with President Putin and I committed myself to doing… this, and this and that,'" recalls Damião. "A complete lie that set the alarm bells ringing!"

The team immediately contacted Twitter but the company was slow to provide a response.

With the clock ticking, and in order to control any damage that might already have been done, they decided to improvise: "We had to begin publishing warnings, in the comments on the posts and in the message boxes… this was the only way we had of highlighting the account was fake!"

With time running out and the Twitter account still active, their phones kept ringing demanding reactions. It was also impossible to foresee the potential international consequences of the tweet about Russia, as it was to ascertain who might be behind this attack.

Even worse, there was no response model for swiftly countering such an emergency and, as there was no legitimate profile of Guterres on the social networks, his team did not even have the means to fight back with the same tools. Aside from the non-interactive official candidacy webpage, they did not have any digital platforms through which they could unmask the impostor. "This took place right in the final phase and it was really complicated," admits Damião.

After almost twenty-four hours, the improvised reaction of flooding the comments section with warnings about the account's false nature proved effective and the actual author of the profile— later identified as a Swiss citizen—decided to go public. Damião remembers how, "After all of our denials, he did later issue a warning that this was a false account and justifying what he had done was to prove how easy it was for the media to create political facts out of nothing without ever having to verify the facts."

However, even in a post-truth era swarmed by fake news, in which information launched into circulation on social networks can easily shape public perceptions more effectively than reality itself, the opinion of the major newspapers continued to hold great weight.

In the run-up to the fifth and final blind straw poll, one of the most prestigious news outlets in the United States launched a vehement attack on Guterres. On 23 September, precisely three days before the poll, *The Wall Street Journal* (WSJ) declared its support for another candidate. In an article entitled "Who will run the UN?"[3] the daily newspaper known for being critical of the United Nations categorically stated that, "The best choice for reform... is Serbia's Vuk Jeremić". The *WSJ* characterised Guterres as a "life-long socialist who mismanaged a global humanitarian organization," adding that "the U.N.'s Internal Audit Division lambasted [Guterres] in April for failing to comply with rules, safeguard U.N. assets, provide accurate financials and conduct effective operations."[4] The article concluded, "That leaves former Serbian Foreign Minister Vuk Jeremić, who polled third."

Complying with his dogma of a positive campaign, there was no reaction—neither from his team, nor from Guterres himself.

When stating that there was no other eligible candidate, the newspaper was also ignoring the fact that there was another name that corresponded to all of the originally defined criteria and that, because she was not in the race at that point, had not been defeated by Guterres: Kristalina Georgieva.

Behind the scenes, the Bulgarian continued to sound out the situation and find a way to enter the race, even if she still did not have any guarantee of getting the official support of her own government. Right at this time, a rumour arrived in Lisbon that Georgieva was not only attempting to find a state to launch her candidacy, but the actual endorsement she was striving for was none other than one of the highly influential Scandinavian states.

The rumour had emerged from the diplomatic corridors of Paris, where a Norwegian representative of a multilateral organisation had confided to a Portuguese colleague that their country was considering the idea of supporting this late entry.

Only when this story reached Guterres did something click. At the Humanitarian World Summit that he had attended in Istanbul back in May, Guterres had casually approached his friend, the Norwegian Minister of Foreign Affairs, who was talking to Georgieva. When they noticed his presence, they had both subtly moved away to continue to talk in private.

In Lisbon, Guterres commented that the gesture had appeared strange to him, but he had not attributed it to any great significance. At least until these reports that the Bulgarian was fishing for support among the Nordic countries, making it clear that in the eventuality the Sofia government would not support her, Georgieva was working on a plan B.

5th Round

This was a real ultimatum. Either Bokova reached the end of the next round in the top two positions, or the Bulgarian government would withdraw their support. The Sofia government knew very well that such a result was mathematically impossible, so the threat was, in practice, prior notification.

This ultimatum triggered reactions across Europe and contributed towards an escalation in the verbal confrontation between Russia and Germany. The relationship between Merkel and Putin—always framed within the context of German energy dependence on Russian gas—had deteriorated noticeably following the Russian occupation of Crimea in 2014. But what had sparked the most recent exchange of accusations had flared up in China.

The Russian President considered the attitude of the German Chancellor during the G20 Summit in early September unacceptable in terms of how she had leveraged the occasion to campaign for Georgieva, calling on the leaders of the world's largest economies to support the candidate coming from the European Commission.

Putin must have seen this as an attempt to pressure him and ordered public denunciation of the German conspiracy that sought to force Bulgaria into backing Georgieva—an especially provocative stance from Moscow given it had supported the original Bulgarian candidate, Bokova, right from the start.

According to an official source at the Russian Ministry of Foreign Affairs, Putin had personally warned his German counterpart that, "The nomination of any candidate to the position of UN Secretary-General is the sovereign decision of a country and any attempt to influence this decision, directly or indirectly, was unacceptable."[5]

In turn, Berlin accused Moscow of spreading objectively false information and having engaged in hostile actions.

The then French President, François Hollande, who naturally maintained regular contact with the German Chancellor, explains that, "Irina Bokova did not convince Merkel. And, having good relations with Georgieva, Merkel wanted, even beyond the UN question, the Bulgarian to gain a more important political role. Nurturing a great appreciation for her, Merkel had already supported her for the European Commission; furthermore, in addition to the political relationship, there was also a personal bond between them."

Held on 26 September, the fifth vote confirmed what had already been predicted: not only did Bokova not make the top two, she dropped a place, ending in sixth position. To make matters worse, she received more discouragement votes. If doubts still remained, it was now more than clear that Georgieva was ready to leap into the competition.

In this round, Guterres emerged victorious again with the same result as in the previous round: 12–2–1. The Serb Vuk Jeremić managed to climb to second place.

By the end of the exploratory rounds, Guterres was heading to the sixth straw poll—the first in which the candidates could be subject to formal vetoes—with the following advantage over the second-placed candidate: four more votes in favour, 12 against 8; and four fewer rejections, 2 against 6.

The female pole position was held by Malcorra, whose result remained unaltered since the previous sessions.

As the months had passed by, and as the results had started to gain some consistency, the frustrations of all those who had campaigned to ensure that this was finally the time for a woman Secretary-General seemed to be justified. Out of the six who had hitherto entered the competition, not one of them had stood out as a leading candidate.

Simultaneously, the various appeals and lobby groups that had been set up to boost the transparency behind this process, continued to crash into the internal resistance of the Security Council. The new procedural architecture, designed and implemented to choose the best Secretary-General, had indeed imposed a revolutionary transparency on the process. This may even have shaped and influenced some of the votes of Council members to the benefit of candidates that had turned in the best public performances. However, according to the Japanese Ambassador to the UN, Koro Bessho, "There is no denying that the Security Council was unable to respond effectively to calls for transparency."[6]

The countless leaks that had made the voting results public stemmed more from the unilateral decisions of diplomats or their political masters than any formal intention of the Council to respond to its stakeholders. Hence, it was the individual agendas of the ambassadors—some against the expressed wishes of the Security Council—and not the existence of collective political will, that enabled public knowledge of the election results. In some cases, the results appeared on the Internet even before the actual candidates were informed by their respective governments.[7]

Despite the information leaks, the secrecy around who was voting for whom remained inscrutable, hindering the predictions for each of the candidates. Indeed, it was only around that time that Guterres and his task force were able to piece together which country had been keeping New Zealand company in the discouragement column.

In the end, the Russian pressure to hold five straw polls prior to getting on with the coloured ballot papers did not harm Guterres' candidacy. It actually provided another opportunity to see his leadership reiterated and more time to unravel the clues about who was voting against him.

It was around that time that Guterres' team learned of a meeting of European Union ambassadors in New York where the Permanent Representative of the United Kingdom had warned his peers from Eastern Europe that, if they did in fact wish to elect the next Secretary-General, they would need to come up with another candidate.

The message, which was actually an instruction, could only hold one real meaning: get rid of Bokova and put Georgieva forward.

According to this report, London was supporting the candidate who had been commissioned by the European power game—and who was deemed as the only way to turn the table against Guterres.

Sultan-Khan confirms, "There were rumours that some Europeans were behind her. The British were the big question: 'Are the British behind her or not?'"

In this regard, Santos Silva, the Portuguese Minister of Foreign Affairs, mentions only that, "The United Kingdom has a very peculiar and cryptic diplomacy."

A More Successful Nomination

It was 6 am and Robert Sherman was already up and about, ready to get to work in shorts, sneakers and a T-shirt.

The Ambassador's routines included morning workouts with a personal trainer in the palace that serves as the official residence of the White House representatives to Lisbon—that is known as "House Carlucci" in homage to its incumbent during the 1970s.

Shortly after his training session, just as the rest of the city was beginning to wake up and Washington was still asleep, Sherman's attention was drawn to his phone. At the other end, the familiar voice of the Director-General of Foreign Policy greeted him. The most senior diplomat in the Portuguese civil service was inviting him to make an urgent visit to the Ministry.

The early call did not come as a great surprise to the Ambassador, who had already guessed the topic of the conversation. Almost ten months on from the letter sent by Power and Lykketoft; after five straw polls, one round of informal dialogues in the General Assembly, countless public debates and private meetings; seven months on from Guterres presenting his bid, Georgieva had been announced as a candidate for the position of UN Secretary-General.

"My thinking at the time," admits Sherman, "was that they were going to be very upset by the fact that at the last moment there was this stunt, that there was somebody who was going to steal the votes and that it was completely unfair to the process."

However, when he arrived at the meeting, the message was very different: "I think the Ministry handled this masterfully. Never once did they say anything about that. We sat down and I started the conversation by saying, 'I assume you want to talk to me about Georgieva,' and they said, 'No, we want to talk to you about António Guterres.' They said nothing negative about either Bulgaria or Georgieva, and I think that had a very important and positive impact on our thinking as the United States."

The arrival of this second Bulgarian also triggered reactions from the other candidates. Malcorra recalls that, "She was clearly an excellent candidate. The fact that her country had first supported Irina complicated the situation and it seems to me that this created a dynamic with a real impact on the selection process. I do think that Kristalina entered the election at a very late stage."

The formal announcement was made on 28 September. The Bulgarian Prime Minister explained that Georgieva was now their official candidate, thereby withdrawing their support for Bokova: "We consider this will be a more successful nomination."[8]

The internal rivals of Borisov immediately turned their fire on the root of the problem: "We think that the sovereignty of Bulgaria and the Bulgarian government is at stake because [this decision] was obviously influenced by many foreign factors,"[9] complained a socialist MP from the opposition.

On the same morning that her candidacy was made public, Georgieva received unpaid leave from her position in Brussels, courtesy of the President of the European Commission. In the previous month, Jean-Claude Juncker had already taken the Bulgarian to a meeting with Vladimir Putin in Saint Petersburg in a gesture now interpreted as a display of endorsement.

The Luxembourger Juncker, who had been friends with Guterres ever since the 1990s when they were both prime ministers, was perceived by many as one of the main drivers behind this diplomatic power play, especially because he also belonged to EPP, the family of right-wing European political parties.

"I used to tell António Guterres, 'Your biggest support for Secretary-General comes from countries in the south,'" affirms Sultan-Khan. After all, the information gathered by the Pakistani diplomat led him to believe that the Portuguese candidate was most actively supported by African, Islamic and Latin American states, "most probably because of his popularity in those parts of the world. I told him, 'Where you have least support is in your own backyard, in your European Union.'"

In effect, even the bilateral ambassadors, in service of their governments and not the European Union, began to receive messages requesting support for Georgieva. These were not instructions issued by their own ministries but rather an attempt to wield pressure by senior members of the Brussels bureaucratic machinery. Confusion was installed to such an extent that the Permanent Representative of the European Union to Washington shared on his official Twitter account the tweet in which Selmayr had mentioned that the Bulgarian would be a very strong Secretary-General.

In truth, while these orientations came directly from the office of Jean-Claude Juncker, they were not coming directly from him. The influence that his chief of staff held over the various European structures of power managed to propagate the idea that the Commission itself was supporting Georgieva. And, as the connections between Selmayr and the office of the German Chancellor and the group of European conservative parties in the European Parliament were equally well-known, it was inferred that Germany and the EPP were sponsoring this late candidacy.

However, the then President Juncker maintains that his role was limited only to authorise the candidacy: "Kristalina Georgieva was a Vice President of the Commission at the time and has all the passion, drive and attributes needed for such a job. She wanted to run and was determined to become the first woman Secretary-General. The Commission unanimously granted her a leave of absence to run and I wished her all the best."

Santos Silva, the Portuguese Minister of Foreign Affairs, says that he had "never imagined that Germany and part of the European Commission would be either quite so hasty or so amateurish." Even at that time, the Minister suspected that the entrance of Georgieva would end up benefitting Guterres: "I was left with the idea that this would sort itself out faster than we were expecting. Just what good reason might there be for expecting Mr. Vladimir Putin to say 'yes' to Chancellor Merkel under such strange circumstances, as the approach that had been made on the fringes of the G20, which everybody knew all about? I really cannot understand it."

Nevertheless, Georgieva did stand out as the candidate with the greatest probability of emerging as a favourite should a deadlock occur.

If one of those two discouragement votes for Guterres turned into a P5 veto in the following round, the Bulgarian would have a very strong chance of rising as the favourite, simply because she was in the right place at the right time and could be portrayed as a compromise solution after every other option had failed. In case of no understanding between the Russians and the Americans, she might represent that third option who would resolve the matter. And all the victorious rounds notched up by the Portuguese candidate would have been utterly in vain.

But Guterres could still count on the assistance of a silent ally that was accompanying all these movements as an attentive observer: a former empire, discreet in recent decades, but with one of the most able and experienced diplomatic services worldwide; a country accustomed to behind-the-scenes manoeuvres, and fully aware that the major decisions are not decided on the front pages of newspapers but rather in private conversations in which only world leaders are engaged.

Marques confides, "It's quite unfair that nobody knows about the role of the French."

Late but Finally You Came

The circumstances were so bizarre that they were not even foreseen in the regulations. In seven decades of industrial-level bureaucratic production, the United Nations had never discussed, and far less approved, any resolution regarding the withdrawal of support from a candidate to Secretary-General.

There was no manual of best practice, no emergency protocol to regulate the administrative procedures that member states should adopt, and there were certainly no legal grounds for forcing the now orphan candidate to step aside.

Indeed, following a brief internal debate, the Security Council itself agreed to keep the name of Irina Bokova on the ballot papers and thus, for the first time in history, there were two candidates from the same country running for the UN's top job.

That decided, it was not only necessary, but also urgent to provide equal opportunities to the two Bulgarians, ensuring they went through the same processes, auditions and hearings.

Georgieva's candidacy had only entered the system on the eve of the sixth straw poll, leaving only three working days to convene all the member states and carry out the same evaluations that the other competitors had been subject to over the first half of the year.

With the first colour-differentiated voting due to take place on Wednesday 5 October, the week started off with an additional session of the informal dialogues held before all member states of the General Assembly.

On behalf of the African states, and a member of the Security Council, the Angolan Ambassador made a point of subtly heckling the Bulgarian: "Welcome back here... late, but finally you came."[10]

The permanent representative from Ukraine, also with a seat on the Security Council, was equally astute in his choice of words: "We were expecting you and I think your appearance will make the process even more intriguing."

At the end of two hours of questions, Georgieva recognised that, "I'm a newcomer, I need to learn more about the United Nations."

Russia sat by and attentively observed the performance of the European Commissioner but did not pose any question. The representative remained in silence throughout the hearing of the woman who, up until the previous week, had represented a European institution governed by the EPP and who had been responsible for the sanctions decreed against Moscow in the wake of the annexation of Crimea. After all, looming in front of Putin's diplomatic representatives was not just a simple candidate from a particular geographic region. She was a core conservative politician, supported by the same European Commission that was now Russia's competitor. Above all else, she was part of an institution that had spent decades attempting to dispel Moscow from the countries that belonged to Russia's sphere of influence.

On Tuesday, with the reins of the Security Council in Churkin's hands, the fifteen electing states welcomed the new candidate for her closed-door session. This was on the eve of the straw poll that could end up nominating the next Secretary-General.

In Geneva, Sultan-Khan continued to keep up with the rumours that swept the diplomatic corridors worldwide. He agrees that the arrival of Georgieva was the moment of greatest concern for him: "I was kept informed about the obstacles, so yes I was concerned. Mr. Guterres' chances were getting better as the straws went by, but I didn't trust the system that well. In the very end, something could happen and suddenly a veto comes in, so I was not so sure."

It was during those days, when the former chief of staff was on a train crossing the Swiss Alps, that his phone rang with a warning. "Some people at a very high level called me and said, 'Athar, you know this is a game changer.' And I said, 'Yeah, yeah, I respect your judgement, I know it's a game changer.'"

Such a message, conveyed to such a close ally of Guterres, and right in the run-up to the final vote, was clearly intended to target the candidate himself. Feeling the weight of the threat, Sultan-Khan decided to call his former boss.

"'Calm down, Athar. Nerves of steel,' he told me. 'Nerves of steel.'"

The Phone Call

Scenario: Russia vetoes Guterres.

The United States is forced to respond, subsequently vetoing all the candidates from the Eastern European region.

Russia thus manages to prove to all countries that were formerly under the influence of the Soviet Union that the Americans really can't be trusted.

At the end of the day, the true ally of these countries, who in recent decades chose to adopt the West and NATO as their political and diplomatic references, was still in the East.

This way, the election of the Secretary-General ends up as nothing more than a short chapter in the imperial narrative idealised by Moscow, in order to reaffirm its position as a superpower and to boot US influence out of Eastern Europe.

This had been the academic hypothesis sketched by Power earlier in the year, and it had seemed to be gaining credibility. Within a logic of bipolar confrontation, the pieces seemed to be falling into place and the messages put out by Churkin were only deepening the likelihood of this outcome. Power says, "He would say things like, 'All these countries from Eastern Europe… who work so hard to get into NATO and even into the European Union… are now being stopped by the United States and by their friends!' He would laugh of course, he would joke, but I thought that there was something there."

Power even clarifies that, "My guess was that he wanted Russia to expose the fact that when those countries put forward candidates, the United States and Europe didn't root for them. He wanted to make a political statement out of it. In a sense, it seemed, they had this separate interest in putting some distance between us and Eastern Europe, in pulling Serbia into Russia's orbit, in publicly interfering with a lot of elections. It was a time where it was part of Russia's strategy to, basically, create a rift between the US and a number of Eastern European countries. So, this seemed in their strategic interest, right? To make us publicly own a lack of support for whomever the Eastern European candidates might have been."

They needed to wait until October, when Georgieva became part of the equation, for this theory to come crashing down.

Russia's declared opposition to the name sponsored by the European right wing was majorly interpreted as the harbinger of a veto to come. And the now gathering strength was that Guterres might just be the candidate of consensus that everybody would be able to get along with.

There was only one piece left in the puzzle.

To put the missing piece into the right place, the Portuguese candidate had to wait until the final moment. Only then could he play his trump card, and this was definitely a move that could not be made as part of any bluff.

"I knew that Russia was not opposing António Guterres," reveals Hollande. "Nor was the America of Obama. China, who had negotiated Macau with him, would also give preference to Guterres, and the United Kingdom was the only state missing."

The time for emissaries, for ambiguities and diplomatic subtleties was over. It was time to call in the big guns. Thus, on the eve of the scheduled vote, the French President called the British Prime Minister.

In London, Theresa May was increasingly buried under internal and external pressures in negotiating the UK's departure from the European Union, when she took the call.

"I wanted to convince Theresa May how important it was to avoid another division among us Europeans and that it made no sense to enter into a process of vetoes," explains Hollande.

On the telephone, the President told May, "We know that you are voting against António Guterres. So, we want to tell you that if you veto him in the next round, then we shall veto Georgieva." At that moment, the line went dead.

Five minutes went by in total silence. Until finally May returned the call.

It all turned out to be a misunderstanding—as if it could be anything else.

"The United Kingdom already had too many problems with Brexit," emphasises Hollande, "and, furthermore, Chancellor Merkel, who was supporting Georgieva, never wanted any direct confrontation with France. Hence, there were no motives for London to veto Guterres."

Guterres himself had had doubts about the different positions and motives of the British representatives throughout the entire process, especially as "Boris Johnson swore that they always supported me." According to Mark Malloch-Brown, the former deputy to Secretary-General Kofi Annan and minister under Tony Blair, the wish to get a woman elected to run the United Nations might explain this ambiguity: "Many of us, despite great personal affection for António Guterres and respect for him, were actually of the view that it was time for a woman. But I think there were a lot of countries which were very disappointed by the female candidates in the early stages. So I believe there might have been people who hoped that by holding back their vote they would encourage more women to enter the race."

The key to unblocking the election was not to be found in the midst of the geostrategic tensions that divided Washington and Moscow. But rather in the small axis spanning the 350 kilometres between London and Paris.

6th Round

5 October 2016. The Security Council was meeting for the sixth time to vote for the next Secretary-General of the United Nations. This was the first round in which Georgieva was on the ballot paper.

"Had she been a candidate since the first days, would the results be any different?" wonders Delattre. "It's a fair question, but I don't have an answer to that." The then French Ambassador to the UN says that, "By the time Kristalina came, there was already too much steam, too much traction for António Guterres. The move was perceived by many members of the Council as too late, and you know… it was not well received by some."

Georgieva's result reflected the reactions of the member states to the way in which she had entered the race, running roughshod over all the work they had engaged in over the preceding months: eight discouragement votes, only five in favour, and two abstentions. She was the third-worst ranked candidate, well below Bokova, who ended as the best classified female candidate.

"I had, all through the process, the impression that if Kristalina Georgieva had been put forward before, at the first round, she would have been the Eastern European woman that could have really had the chance of being elected," recognises Lykketoft. According to the President of the General Assembly, "In the old system it would not necessarily have been a disadvantage to come late, but in this new procedure it was a very important disadvantage because most of the countries had made up their mind already."

At this time, Miroslav Lajčák was the one causing greatest concern to Guterres, especially since he did not have any opposition from Moscow. And, furthermore, according to the information gathered in Lisbon, should the straw polls drag on, the Russians would not hesitate in vetoing Georgieva.

In regards to the US position, no one in Guterres' team expected Washington to change its views with the arrival of Georgieva. Robert Sherman explains how, "We were not so married to the position of finding a woman that we would overlook what was clearly an attempt to hijack the process from there. So, it never even became part of a serious conversation at all, I think it was just recognised that it was not the right thing to do."

The leader board in this latest straw poll, which already expressed the vetoes of the permanent members, was topped entirely by men. Jeremić and Lajčák were tied, each receiving six votes against and seven in favour.

And in first place was Guterres, who got an even better result than in the previous round. Having spent the entire race with no less that eleven votes in favour, in this sixth round he picked up 13 encouragements.

Just two abstentions: New Zealand, which still had its own candidate on the ballot paper, and Russia, which, as promised, maintained its "No Opinion" vote in all of the straw polls.

No country voted against.

Guterres recalls that, already close to the end of the process, "The Russians told us formally that they would abstain. There was a formal communication from the Russian government to the Ambassador of Portugal to Moscow and also from the Ambassador of Russia in Lisbon. And that reflects correctly the results, it adds up."

We Have a Clear Favourite

"It's over! They're coming out!"

Freitas Ferraz was a bag of nerves. Glued to his computer screen, which had survived the passage of many years, the Portuguese diplomat accompanied every movement broadcast by the UN Web TV live streaming service.

Guterres was right there by his side, at the round table where the veteran ambassador directed the operational side of his campaign. Not once did he look at the screen; he simply remained seated, awaiting the results.

In Lisbon, the clock was five hours ahead of New York, but the room, which appeared more like a small library with its walls lined with packed bookshelves, was still lit by the warm light of early autumn.

Courtesy of outdated technological resources, the sound coming out of the primitive speakers was practically inaudible. Nevertheless, the image distinctly depicted all those present: Churkin, Power, Delattre, and the remaining twelve ambassadors making up the Security Council.

Today, Delattre insists that, "It was not planned. My colleague Vitaly said at the end of the poll that we should do a joint initiative: 'Why don't we all go out there and announce the outcome together, like in a group?' and everyone agreed, 'Oh yes, good idea!' So it was very spontaneous."

Churkin took up his position at the speaker's podium, which depicts the UN symbol at its centre. To his right stood Power, and Delattre was standing immediately to his left. The scene was completed by the other diplomats, whether behind or alongside the Russian.

In Portugal, 5 October fell on a public holiday, so Guterres was dressed accordingly. Without tie or jacket, wearing just a white weekend shirt and beige trousers, he kept his gaze fixed on the secular book collection that lined the office.

At the same time, Freitas Ferraz continued to be entranced by the streaming.

"Well, ladies and gentlemen, you are witnessing a historic scene. I don't think it has ever been done this way, in the history of the United Nations,"[11] began Churkin, with a smile.

The grey monitor, all the fashion in the 1990s, occupied almost half the desk. But even hunched up close to the computer, Ferraz was hardly able to make out what was being said: "Today, after th… sixt… straw po… we have a clear favour… name of An… Gu…er…s" "You're elected!" "I'm what?" "You've been elected!" "What's that?" "YOU'VE BEEN ELECTED!"

Freitas Ferraz remembers that, "I had to scream at him. He continued sitting at the table and the sound on that rubbish was so low! Then a few minutes later, the Minister [of Foreign Affairs] turned up, followed by the Prime Minister and after that his telephone just didn't stop ringing."

Guterres smiled and accepted the congratulations. He exchanged embraces and conversed with the leaders of the government who, twenty years earlier, had been his ministers. He responded to some messages out of the avalanche that flooded his phone, and only took the most important calls.

Revisiting the internal game of chess, Guterres' assessment is that he was probably elected because the five permanent members of the Security Council were to a greater or lesser extent at loggerheads: "For the first time in history, there was no meeting of the five due to the tensions that already existed. And as they never talked, nobody could know for certain what the others were doing, and this was ongoing. I kept on passing because I had a lot of support in the General Assembly and among the non-permanents. In other circumstances, I admit that the permanent members might have reached an agreement around Georgieva and vetoed the others afterwards. But, in fact, they did not speak with each other."

22

THE 45TH PRESIDENT

Guterres closed the door behind him, took half a dozen steps to the left and called the elevator. Behind him, a peaceful line of trees watched over the condominium. The pink coloured building, his home in Portugal, was divided into two wings of apartments, one in front of the other, that opened onto verandas over the central patio that led to the swimming pool.

Since his election on the previous day, the world did not seem to have changed that much. And since the recommendation of the United Nations General Assembly would only be made in a few hours, Guterres was planning his morning as he would any other, going about the commitments already on his agenda.

All by himself, he went down to the garage and got into his Skoda wagon, which he continued to drive in Lisbon, carefully moving out of his parking space before continuing on his way, equally carefully, up the steep and twisting roads in this old part of the city.

The board of the Calouste Gulbenkian Foundation, where he held the position of non-executive board member, was meeting that morning and the man who was officially nominated as the next Secretary-General of the United Nations saw no reason to skip the occasion. After all, this organisation dedicated to culture, and financed by an oil-industry-generated legacy, had already invited him to serve as its next president, if the UN plan had not worked out.

Guterres arrived at the meeting with the topics duly prepared and participated in the meeting as if nothing had happened the previous day. The only difference was that he answered one or two of the many calls he kept receiving.

At the same time, on the other side of the city, the task force phones were also incessantly ringing. The candidate chosen by the Security Council had not issued any public declaration since the Russian Ambassador announced his name, and journalists around the world were now clamouring for a reaction, a message, a promise from the next UN leader. And there was no shortage of pressing topics.

With the sharp-tongue style of the French press, *Le Monde* newspaper would portray the position handed onto the Portuguese politician with a cartoon in which Ban Ki-moon bids him farewell while saying, "Well, I'll be off; it's all been taken care of! … Except for Syria, Iraq, Afghanistan, Daesh, the climate, the migrants, et cetera."

After a decade in Geneva and a year living on aeroplanes, Guterres once again packed his bags to take up residence in New York. Until he formally takes office, he would work in a UN building located a block away from the Secretariat.

In the final months of 2016, his transition team would be studying the dossiers announced as priorities by his campaign, preparing the first reforms and intensifying his contacts with the member states, especially on the new structure for the Secretariat and the choices for the key positions.

However, by a rare coincidence in the calendar, attentions were necessarily and overwhelmingly turned towards the US elections.

Not since 1961 had a new US President and a new UN Secretary-General taken office in the same year. Guterres' predecessors had taken office with the US head of state fully installed in the White House, having had time to study their style of leadership, strategy for foreign policy, and executive priorities.

The good news, for the meantime, was that the opinion polls continued to point to a victory by his friend of over two decades,

Hillary Clinton. And the widely expected triumph of the Democrat became especially relevant given that, as the campaign lengthened, the positions of the Republican candidate—who Guterres had never met—emerged as entirely incompatible with those of the next Secretary-General of the United Nations.

Election Night

Guterres decided to break with protocol. His own protocol. Despite already having gone to bed in his New York hotel room, on that night of 8 November he would not be opening any book. The political agenda forced him to exchange the silent written words of historians for the shrill, excited voices of the journalists on television.

After all, there was history in the making.

To no surprise, the first forecasts from all news channels confirmed Hillary Clinton as the front runner. In addition to being the only result admissible to the liberal media, this was the outcome many believed in, even within the Republican campaign. Resigned, the other candidate was following the numbers from Trump Tower in Manhattan, reportedly even admitting to his wife that he had been defeated.

And yet, at 10.40 pm in New York, Donald Trump picked up the first swing state. Ohio had got it right with every American presidential election since 1964.

Guterres began to get suspicious.

Not even fifteen minutes later, the results from Florida were in. The state which had voted for Obama, George W. Bush, Clinton and George H. W. Bush delivered its twenty-nine electoral votes... to Trump.

"Florida is a must-win today. You can't win without it," CNN was reporting.

At 11.15 pm, it would be the turn of North Carolina to go red. This was followed by Utah.

And Iowa.

"Well, this is in the bag," thought Guterres.

It was already past 1 am when the very last hope for Hillary Clinton was announced. The Democrat had even chosen

Pennsylvania as the destination for one of her final rallies and had brought out her heavy weaponry for the occasion: none other than Barack Obama.

But it had been in vain.

Having attained 264 electoral college votes, Trump had the White House all but guaranteed.

An official winner, however, would only be declared after the announcement of the results from Wisconsin. Despite having lost the popular vote, Trump's 304 electoral votes to Clinton's 227 meant Trump had won the race and became the 45th President of the United States in an outcome that was surprising to such an extent that the Democrat team had not even prepared a concession speech.

Alone in his room in New York, Guterres, who would be taking office in five weeks, could only think about what this result would mean for his plans, for the United Nations, and for the world: "I said to myself right then: the terms of reference for all this are going to change dramatically."

EPILOGUE

THE PEACE BELL

The familiar notes of "Ode to Joy" spread throughout the garden. It was the last rehearsal before the ceremony began. Around the small orchestra, the staff rushed over some final preparations: the two microphones on the podium still needed to be aligned at the exact same height. Somebody would still have to distribute the guests around the Asian-looking temple, located amid the trees. Even the cameraman was still zooming in and out before settling on the desired frame to record all the speeches.

> "We are here because we are determined
> And we don't give up."

A group of young musicians stood in the background. They were all children, teenagers at most, all dressed in white, all of different ethnicities.

None of them had any memory of the conflict that had led, seventy years before, to the construction of the two buildings surrounding them. None of them, of course, could have lived the story of war and peace that had taken place there, right there in front of the discreet corner where they were tucked in, that enormous Japanese bell.

> "We know that human rights are violated in so many parts of the world. We even know that the human rights agenda is losing ground. But we don't give up."

341

Summoned by Beethoven's 9th Symphony, the Deputy Secretary-General, Amina J. Mohammed, and the *chef de cabinet*, Maria Luiza Viotti, the two most powerful women in the United Nations, finally arrived. They were followed by the President of the General-Assembly and by the Ambassador of Japan, accompanied by his wife. The group was completed when Guterres entered.

In this discreet garden, hidden away between the General Assembly and the Secretariat buildings, a concerned assistant, with his credentials impeccably on display over his tie, set about aligning the dignitaries in their respective positions. They were to wait while standing in a line, each placed according to the importance the in-house protocol attributed them. Such hierarchy constituted the UN's dogma and, given the symbolism of this particular occasion, the order of precedence had to be tightly observed.

The 2018 International Day of Peace was being celebrated, just as the diplomatic traditions of the UN demanded, next to the bell that Japan had donated to the United Nations headquarters. Ever since 1954, this bell had sounded the warning, to New York and to the world, of the timeless story of a prosperous and thriving nation that succumbed to nationalist temptations.

Convinced that destiny had reserved its right to a leading place in the race for global supremacy, this proud empire was crushed by the military, economic and technological prowess of its chosen enemy. But the Japanese Bell also told a story of reconciliation: of a people devastated by the only two nuclear bombs ever dropped by one state on another and the choice that this nation was subsequently confronted with—to remain isolated on the world stage, out of anger at the bombings, or to commit to the new system of state relations emerging from the ashes and carnage of World War II.

At the heart of this system, operating through patient cooperation and common ground for seeking dialogue, there would stand the Organization of the United Nations.

> "We know that when we appeal for combatants to have a pause,
> to respect this Day, we know many will not respect it.
> But we don't give up."

Guterres was about to take the stage, but just as the diligent assistant took the first step towards the podium to lay there the printed speech that had been so carefully prepared by the UN services, someone raised a hand in front of him.

The man responsible for the whole operation was so concentrated on making sure that there were no flaws whatsoever during the boss' address, that he didn't even notice the Secretary-General's gesture. It was Guterres himself who was trying to stop him, nudging him once, twice, three times on the arm. He wanted to speak without any papers.

As soon as the man grasped what was happening, he tilted his whole body and head forward, to confirm that the Secretary-General was sure about improvising on such an occasion, then exchanged a confused glance with somebody on the other side of the garden, and finally backed down, shrugging his shoulders, as if apologising for his obvious powerlessness to go against the wishes of his boss.

Guterres proceeded slowly towards the podium.

"We see conflicts multiplying everywhere in the world.
We see links between conflicts and terrorism.
We see insecurity prevailing.
But we don't give up."

Guterres is the 9th Secretary-General of the United Nations. The position, which President Roosevelt once suggested ought to be titled "Moderator", is described in just over 300 words in the organisation's founding Charter, reflecting how the governments that created and still maintain the UN to this day never wanted to endow the position with any real power.

In fact, the main description of the role only appears in Chapter 15 of the Charter: the Secretary-General is the "chief administrative officer of the Organization". The priority for this position is therefore the working of its many bureaucratic processes. It exists because it would always have to exist, in this organisation like any other.

However, further along, in Article 99, the administrative officer finally gains some strength: "The Secretary-General may bring to the attention of the Security Council any matter which in his opinion may threaten the maintenance of international peace and security." Now, this prerogative comes interlinked with a political facet: "bring to the attention" presumes making judgements and having the autonomy to do so regarding "any matter" implies a choice. Based on which criteria? The "opinion" of the Secretary-General.

Guterres' opinions reflect, of course, his personal assessment of international politics and the role the UN should play in our uncertain and fragmented era, but especially the lessons he accumulated throughout his political and personal life.

This is what this biography is about. This is the story of the decisions, experiences and values that shaped Guterres' political persona. Our goal as authors was to help understand how the United Nations Secretary-General thinks and operates in today's chaotic global order, by revealing the most important events, ideas and people on his journey to the top of the UN. Our hope is that this book can serve as a lens through which readers can interpret his recent actions and predict the issues he chooses to overlook as the most influential diplomat in the world.

During his first mandate as Secretary-General, Guterres deliberately chose to put his time and efforts into the un-newsworthy recipe he had already tested at the UNHCR and that had proven successful: internal reforms. Besides, that had been one of his campaign promises and one for which he did not need the approval of the deadlocked Security Council. Above all, he knew that reforms were the one topic where he would find common ground with US President Donald Trump, in order to avoid a major rupture between the UN and its main donor.

But for his second term, which will end in 2026, we can see in this book's political and personal history some of the issues he is likely to tackle—and those he is likely to pass over.

He will not, for instance, name and shame China on the Uyghur issue and he kept valuing his personal connection with Vladimir Putin, with whom he has been dealing since the 1990s.

He will also continue to ignore most of the papers that come from the Department of Political Affairs, as he will always prefer to engage directly with the people in the field and brainstorm with his most trusted advisers.

He will keep friendly ties with both Israeli authorities and Arab leaders, since he has decades-long friendships on both sides.

He will continue to answer all his personal emails in a matter of minutes, only to delete them afterwards, keeping his inbox immaculately empty.

He will feel the same genuine distress when confronted with the victims of abuses of power, catastrophes and poverty that led him to do volunteer work in the slums of Lisbon sixty years ago.

Due to his reputation and acquaintances in Africa, since the days of the Socialist International, this is a region where he will be dedicating his talents and good offices. Many present-day African leaders still call him "Prime Minister".

He will not, however, be in a position to implement his long-standing vision for the rehabilitation of the international order: dividing the Security Council into two organs, one political and one economical, or reforming the post-war financial order known as the Bretton Woods system, which he always considered ineffective and unable to deal with, or even understand, the root causes of the Global South's development issues.

By telling those stories from Guterres' past that reveal the intricate nuances of his personality, we aimed to contribute to more insightful analyses of the obstacles and bottlenecks that the UN— our most fundamental and irreplaceable multilateral organisation—and its leader face today. Such substance, we believe, has not been duly provided by international media, least of all social networks, and this biography was designed to fill this gap.

Indeed, it is our understanding that for all the limitations and powerlessness of the Secretary-General, he continues to be the closest representation we have of a moral conscience of humanity.

For as much as his actions might be—or have to be—hidden from the cameras, for as much as his public condemnations seem to have—or do have—little impact on the actions and decisions of the ones being targeted, global citizenship still perceive this as the highest political office we have, the anointed leader of the international order. The UN Secretary-General can and should be the beacon of righteousness and justice they have to look up to when humankind is faced with cruelty and suffering, and need someone to look up to.

It is also a fact that no Secretary-General ever had an easy mandate, but Guterres' path has been an especially lonely one.

Since 2017, when he first took office, the world has seemingly been sinking into a sort of global swamp that questions the very utility of the United Nations as our best safety net against unmanaged competition and war.

Even in liberal democracies, the commitment to multilateralism is being questioned, especially inside the country that most helped shape and most benefitted from the liberal international order, the United States of America.

Confrontations between states continue to intensify, shaping a new bipolar competition between Washington and Beijing that expands to unregulated arenas like cyberspace and social media.

In addition to the threat of self-destruction by nuclear weapons, we face the risk of extinction due to the overheating of the planet. In this context, Guterres is presented with the challenges from an array of nations where people tend to choose myth over fact and faith over science that hinder his efforts to respond to such threats.

The Covid pandemic has amplified the fracture between the Global North and South, making the vaccine distribution process a striking picture of our present asymmetries, but has especially evidenced the rich world leaders' short-sightedness, nationalism and lack of political will to level the playing field.

Impunity is on the rise among autocracies and illiberal regimes that work more and more as an international network that safeguards its members from paying a price for their criminal activities and human rights violations.

The perpetuation of violent conflicts has thrown the number of displaced people to its highest level, precisely since World War II.

This biography deliberately does not cover Guterres' term as the United Nations Secretary-General. He is only halfway through his ten-year tenure, and we have no doubt it is too soon to write that story with adequate depth and distancing, especially due to the complexity and number of interconnected problems on his desk. That would have to be another book. But we hope that this one will inform those who do come to write that story, the story of Guterres' leadership of the UN, and of the precarious world he is trying to steer in this first quarter of the twenty-first century.

EPILOGUE

Back on 21 September 2018, while hosting his second International Day of Peace in the small Manhattan garden, Guterres finished his speech by recognising:

> "Peace is the unifying concept that brings us together at the United Nations. That peace is now at risk."

NOTES

1. SOCIAL ENGINEER

1. The International and Defence State Police (PIDE) was created in 1945 to repress all forms of political and social opposition to the Portuguese dictatorship.

2. To know more about the evolution of US policy in Africa, see Metz, Steven, "American Attitudes Towards Decolonization in Africa", *Political Science Quarterly*, no 3 (Fall 1984), pp. 515–533.

3. In 1946, the USSR vetoed in the UN Security Council the requests for membership of Portugal and Ireland. Portugal was only able to become a UN member state in 1955.

4. FFMS, "Taxa de analfabetismo segundo os censos: total e por sexo", Pordata, 2015.

5. "Lamento a tragédia e, na medida do possível, tudo farei para minorar o sofrimento das pessoas que necessitarem dos nossos socorros", *Diário de Notícias*, 26 November 1967, p. 1.

6. Prata, R. "Memórias do CASU", *Revista Povos e Culturas*, Special number "Os Católicos e o 25 de Abril", 2014, p. 318.

7. "Welcome Dag Hammarskjöld to the most impossible job on this earth". On 9 April 1953, Trygve Lie, the first Secretary-General of the United Nations, greeted his successor at Idlewild airport (now JFK) in New York, with these encouraging words.

8. "Até ao Topo do Mundo", *Expresso*, 22 October 2016.

9. Cunha, Adelino, *Os Segredos do Poder*, Lisbon: Alêtheia Editores, 2013, pp. 63–72.

10. Swedish Prime Minister between 1982 and 1986 considered one of the main figures of European social democracy.

11. The Yugoslavian model proposed a political and economic alternative to communism and socialism. It defended that property and the means of production should not be in the hands of the state, but under direct administration of the workers.

12. Rafael Prata, private memoirs, unpublished, 14 August 2014.

2. A WATCHMAKER'S WORK

1. Due to the illegality of opposing political parties during the dictatorship, the Portuguese Socialist Party was founded in Bad Münstereifel, in Germany, in 1973, under the auspices of the Friedrich Ebert Foundation and the SPD (Germany's Social Democratic Party).
2. The three figures were, respectively, Otelo Saraiva de Carvalho, President Francisco da Costa Gomes, and Prime Minister Vasco Gonçalves.
3. Carlucci, Frank, "The View from the US Embassy", in Hans Binnendijk, ed., with Peggy Nalle and Diane Bendahmane, *Authoritarian Regimes in Transition*, Washington, D.C.: U.S. Department of State, Foreign Service Institute, Center for the Study of Foreign Affairs, 1987, p. 210.
4. Huntington, Samuel P., "Democracy's Third Wave", *Journal of Democracy*, Spring 1991, p. 13.
5. Telegram sent by the US Embassy in Lisbon to the State Department on 1 October 1979.
6. Internet access is blocked in North Korea for all but the highest-level officials; all traditional media outlets are state-owned and controlled.
7. Guterres, António, *A Pensar em Portugal*, Lisbon: Editorial Presença, 1999, p. 156.
8. "A ascensão de Guterres no PS: uma história de conspiração, intriga, vingança e traição", *Sábado*, 13 October 2016.
9. Official Gazette of the General Assembly (Diário da Assembleia da República), 8 February 1991, V Legislature 4th Legislative Session, I Series—Number 40, p. 1312.

3. ESTATES-GENERAL

1. "The Diary of Anatoly Chernyaev", 10 November 1989.
2. The foundations of the organisation based in London, created in 1951, trace back to the International Workers' Association, founded in 1864 by Karl Marx; to the Second International established in 1889 by Friedrich Engels, where 1st May was declared as International Workers' Day in homage to the workers' rally in Haymarket Square, in Chicago; and to the Labour and Socialist International—created in opposition to the Third International, or Comintern, led by Lenin—established in 1923, that ended after the beginning of fascist regimes in Europe.
3. The Treaty of Maastricht was signed on 7 September 1992, and it is a fundamental document of the European Project. It legally created the European Union. France, Ireland and Denmark only ratified the Treaty after popular referendums.
4. Guterres, António, *A Pensar em Portugal*, Lisbon: Editorial Presença, 1999, p. 25.
5. Interview to RTP1, 19 July 1995.
6. "Uma Nova Maioria—Estados Gerais—Contracto de Legislatura", Partido Socialista, 1995.
7. Ibid.

8. Ibid.
9. Ibid.
10. Ibid.
11. Ibid.
12. Ibid.
13. "António Guterres: 'é fazer a conta'", YouTube. Uploaded on 12 December 2015.
14. The Congress of Vienna (1814–15) established the German Confederation, a group of states that met in Assembly, called Diet, in the city of Frankfurt, presided by Austria. One of the aims was to re-establish the absolutist regime that ended with the Napoleonic Wars. German unification was only achieved in 1871, with the constitution of the German Empire, led by Prussia.
15. Interview to RTP1, 19 July 1995.
16. Ibid.
17. Ibid.

4. ORDER AND PROGRESS

1. Between 1808 and 1821, to flee the Napoleonic invasion and maintain national sovereignty, the Prince Regent of Portugal, future King João VI, officially declared Rio de Janeiro his capital, taking with him his court and a library of over 60,000 books. Portugal became the only country in history to have its capital in a colony.
2. "Meeting of the President of the Republic with a Foreign Authority—Key Contents for the Interview". Available at: http://acervo.ifhc.org.br/
3. Ibid.

5. A NATO-RUSSIA ALLIANCE?

1. Boutros-Ghali, Boutros, Unvanquished, London: Random House, 1999, p. 6.
2. Albright, Madeleine, Madam Secretary: A Memoir, New York: Harper Perennial, 2013, p. 208.
3. Guterres, António, A Pensar em Portugal, Lisbon: Editorial Presença, 1999, pp. 132–137.
4. The United Nations member states are divided into five regional groups—Africa, Latin America and the Caribbean, Asia-Pacific, West Europe and East Europe—and mutually divide among themselves the non-permanent seats on the Security Council in accordance with unwritten rules.
5. Official Records of the United Nations General Assembly, 51st Session, 39th plenary meeting, 21 October 1996, New York, p. 3. Available at: https://undocs.org/A/51/PV.39
6. António Guterres: "Grande Vitória", Público, 22 October 1996.
7. Paixão, João Quintela, "A candidatura de Portugal ao Conselho de Segurança das Nações Unidas", Política Internacional, No. 14, 1997, p. 80. Available at: http://

www.ipris.org/files/14/G_14_A_candidatura_de_Portugal_ao_Conselho_
de.pdf

8. Lake, Antony, "National Security Council, Schedule Proposal sent to Stephanie
S. Streett, director of scheduling to the President", 7 December 1996, Clinton
Presidential Records (Obtained from the U.S. Information Agency under the
Freedom of Information Act).

9. "Remarks Prior to Discussions with Prime Minister Antonio Guterres of
Portugal and an Exchange with Reporters", Office of the Press Secretary, The
White House, 3 April 1997.

10. Ibid.

11. Clinton, Hillary Rodham, "Letter to the Prime Minister of Portugal and Mrs.
Guterres", 23 August 1997, Clinton Presidential Records (Obtained from the
U.S. Information Agency under the Freedom of Information Act).

6. THE BRUSSELS JOB

1. Gibraltar is an enclave under British administration, located on the continental
mainland of Spain over which the two states maintain a dispute over sovereignty.

2. The Northern Dimension is a political mechanism involving four partners—the
European Union, Russia, Norway and Iceland—to deal especially with issues
interrelated to questions over the Baltic Sea, the area north-west of Russia and
the Artic region.

7. THE PEBBLE IN THE SHOE

1. "Não vou calar a minha voz", *Público*, 28 February 1996.

2. Alatas, Ali, *The Pebble in the Shoe: The Diplomatic Struggle for East Timor*, Jakarta:
Aksara Karunia, 2006.

3. Ibid. p. 81.

4. Annan, Kofi, *Interventions: A Life in War and Peace*, London: Penguin Books, 2012,
p. 102.

5. *Public Papers of the Presidents of the United States: William J. Clinton*, 1997, p. 383.

6. Alatas, Ali, *The Pebble in the Shoe: The Diplomatic Struggle for East Timor*, Jakarta:
Aksara Karunia, 2006.

7. "Timorese face uncertain future", BBC, 11 March 1999. Available at: http://
news.bbc.co.uk/2/hi/asia-pacific/264717.stm

8. Annan, Kofi, *Interventions: A Life in War and Peace*, London: Penguin Books, 2012,
p. 82.

9. Ibid. p. 83.

10. "U.S. Priority Is to Maintain Good Ties with Indonesia, Officials Indicate", *The
New York Times*, 8 September 1999. Available at: https://archive.nytimes.com/
www.nytimes.com/library/world/asia/090999timor-policy.html

11. "Arrepio de mãos dadas em Lisboa", *Público*, 9 September 1999.

12. *Public Papers of the Presidents of the United States: William J. Clinton*, 1999, p. 1518.
13. Clinton, William J., *Letter to the Prime Minister of Portugal*, 8 November 1999, Clinton Presidential Records (Obtained from the U.S. Information Agency under the Freedom of Information Act).

8. THE PEOPLE SPEAK

1. "A Semana", SIC, 16 September 1995.
2. Draft Law no. 451/VII, Diário da República II Series A, No. 27/VII/3, 29 January 1998, pp. 478–480, "On the exclusion of illegality in cases of voluntary interruption of pregnancy".
3. "Referendum for the decriminalization of abortion", RTP, 28 June 1998.

9. BETWEEN THE SWORD AND THE WALL

1. Minutes of the Portuguese Parliament "Diário da Assembleia da República", Plenary Session on 4 November 1999.
2. Ibid.
3. Article "EU Is Unmoved by Resignation of Haider", *Washington Post*, 1 March 2000.
4. Guterres, António, *Letter to the President of the United States Bill Clinton*, 14 December 1998, Clinton Presidential Records (Obtained from the U.S. Information Agency under the Freedom of Information Act).
5. Transcription of the telephone calls between President Bill Clinton and Prime Minister Tony Blair. William J. Clinton Presidential Library.
6. Ibid.
7. *Public Papers of the Presidents of the United States: William J. Clinton*, 2000, p. 1054.

10. OUT OF THE QUAGMIRE

1. Esteves, Fernando "Jorge Coelho o Todo-Poderoso", Lisbon: A Esfera dos Livros, p. 193.
2. "Jorge Coelho demite-se", *Público*, 5 March 2001.
3. "Projectos têm de ser repensados", *Público*, 19 June 2001.
4. "Guterres garante apoio a Arafat", *Público*, 2 July 1999.
5. "Arafat e Peres aprovam resolução a favor da paz", *Público*, 1 July 2001.
6. Lagos, Ricardo, "Guterres, la ONU y los tiempos inciertos", *Clarín*, Argentina, 15 January 2017.
7. 1971 Convention on Psychotropic Substances.

11. THE NETWORK

1. The "Bolsa Família", or "Family Allowance", resulted in the broadening and streamlining of a range of programmes already in place in Brazil. Notwithstanding

the frequent criticisms and problems, the "Family Allowance" is still in effect in Brazil, presently benefitting around 14 million families. Praised in important forums within the United Nations, the programme has been exported and adapted to many other countries and communities. For example, it was a great influence for "Opportunity NYC", launched in 2007 in New York City by Mayor Michael R. Bloomberg.

2. Lula da Silva, opening speech before the Congress of the Socialist International in the city of São Paulo, 27 October 2003. Available at: http://www.socialistinternational.org/viewArticle.cfm?ArticleID=186&ArticlePageID=925&ModuleID=18

3. "António Guterres defende coligação para uma nova ordem mundial", *Público*, 28 October 2003.

4. Ibid.

5. "António Guterres: Blair ficou ensanduichado", *Público*, 31 March 2003.

6. "António Guterres: resultados das eleições espanholas também condenam política de Bush", *Público*, 18 March 2004.

7. "António Guterres", *Diário de Notícias*, 10 October 2003.

8. "António Guterres: Blair ficou ensanduichado", *Público*, 31 March 2003.

9. From the Steering Committee of "Building Global Alliances for the 21st Century". On the American side were also Lee H. Hamilton (former US Congressman and Vice Chair of the 9/11 Commission), Morton H. Halperin (at the time, Senior Vice President of the Center for American Progress) and John Sweeney (former President of the American Federation of Labor and Congress of Industrial Organizations). On the European side were Robin Cook (former British Foreign Secretary), John Monks (former General Secretary of the European Trade Union Confederation), Poul Nyrup Rasmussen (former Danish Prime Minister) and Maria João Rodrigues (former minister in Guterres' government).

10. In his State of the Union speech given on 29 January 2002, President George W. Bush, in reference to North Korea, Iran and Iraq, alleged that, "States like these and their terrorist allies constitute an axis of evil, arming to threaten the peace of the world."

11. "A Nuclear Nonproliferation Strategy for the 21st Century", working paper, Building Global Alliances for the 21st Century, June 2004.

12. "Advancing the Progressive Foreign Policy Agenda: An International Perspective", transcript, Center for American Progress, 30 November 2004.

13. Ibid., p. 12.

14. Ibid., p. 12.

15. The International Commission on Intervention and State Sovereignty, "The Responsibility to Protect", International Development Research Centre, Ottawa, December 2001. The commission responsible for the report was set up by the Canadian government in 2000, after Secretary-General Kofi Annan had raised the following question in the General Assembly earlier that year: "If

humanitarian intervention is, indeed, an unacceptable assault on sovereignty, how *should* we respond to a Rwanda, to a Srebrenica—to gross and systematic violations of human rights that offend every precept of our common humanity?"

16. "Advancing the Progressive Foreign Policy Agenda: An International Perspective," transcript, Center for American Progress, 30 November 2004, p. 12.

17. Ibid., p. 32.

18. Ibid., p. 33.

19. Ibid., p. 33.

20. Ibid., p. 53.

21. Ibid., p. 53. The document refers to Resolution 337(V) of the General Assembly of the United Nations, adopted in 1950 during the Korean War, according to which: "If the Security Council, because of a lack of unanimity of the permanent members, fails to exercise its primary responsibility for the maintenance of international peace and security in any case where there appears to be a threat to the peace, breach of the peace, or act of aggression, the General Assembly shall consider the matter immediately with a view to making appropriate recommendations to Members for collective measures, including in the case of a breach of the peace or act of aggression the use of armed force when necessary, to maintain or restore international peace and security."

22. Ibid., p. 53.

23. Ibid., p. 53.

24. Annan, Kofi, *Interventions: A Life in War and Peace*, London: Penguin Books, 2012, p. 319.

25. Coleman, Norm, "Kofi Annan Must Go", *The Wall Street Journal*, 1 December 2004.

26. Holbrooke, Richard, "UN appoints Briton as new chief of staff", *The Guardian*, 4 January 2005.

27. Founded in 2002, the Club de Madrid is dedicated to the promotion of democratic values in the international community.

28. Evans, Gareth, *Incorrigible Optimist: A Political Memoir*, Melbourne: Melbourne University Press, 2017, p. 139.

29. At the request of Jorge Sampaio, then President of Portugal, the heads of state of the Community of the Portuguese-Speaking Countries wrote a letter to the United Nations Secretary-General to express their support for the candidacy of António Guterres.

30. UN General Assembly, "In larger freedom: Towards development, security and human rights for all", 2005; UN General Assembly, "A More Secure World: Our Shared Responsibility"—Report of the High-level Panel on Threats Challenges and Change, 2004.

31. Socialist International, "Reforming the United Nations for a new global agenda", position paper, May 2005. More than an original study, the document is above all a critical review of the existing literature. On the creation of the Economic,

Social and Environmental Security Council, see: Carlsson, Ingvar and Ramphal, Shridath, *Our Global Neighborhood: The Report of the Commission on Global Governance*, November 1994; Dervis, Kemal, *A Better Globalization: Legitimacy, Reform and Global Governance*, with Ceren Ozer, Washington, D.C.: Center for Global Development, Brookings Press, 2004.

32. Ibid., p. 22.
33. Ibid., p. 22.
34. Ibid., p. 2
35. Ibid., p. 23.
36. The proposal to limit the direct veto only to matters that fall under Chapter VII of the United Nations Charter, entitled "Action with respect to threats to the peace, breaches of the peace, and acts of aggression", was presented in 1999 by the Non-Aligned Movement. Letter from the Permanent Representative of Egypt, 28 July 1999, UN Doc. A/53/47, Annex X.

12. THE DIRT, THE MUD AND THE DUST

1. "Global Report 2007", United Nations High Commissioner for Refugees, p. 233.
2. "UNHCR's global refugee figure lowest since 1980, internal displacement, statelessness remain high", United Nations High Commissioner for Refugees, 17 June 2005.
3. Remarks by Mr. António Guterres, United Nations High Commissioner for Refugees, to the Informal Meeting of the Executive Committee of the High Commissioner's Programme (ExCom)", United Nations High Commissioner for Refugees, 17 June 2005.
4. "Funding UNHCR's Programs", The Global Report 2005, United Nations High Commissioner for Refugees, 2005.
5. Ibid., p. 22.
6. Ibid., p. 67.
7. "A Tragedy of Failures and False Expectations—Report on the Events Surrounding the Three-month Sit-in and Forced Removal of Sudanese Refugees in Cairo, September–December 2005", The American University in Cairo Forced Migration and Refugee Studies Program, June 2006, p. 5.
8. "12 Egyptian Rights Groups Demand International Fact-Finding Team on Killing of Sudanese Protestors", Egyptian Initiative for Personal Rights, 9 January 2006.
9. Ibid.
10. Ibid.
11. "UNHCR shocked, saddened over Cairo deaths", United Nations High Commissioner for Refugees, 30 December 2005.
12. *Note verbale* from the Permanent Mission of the Arab Republic of Egypt to the United Nations Office & International Organizations in Geneva to the United Nations High Commissioner for Refugees, 1 January 2006.

13. Ibid.
14. *Note verbale* from United Nations High Commissioner for Refugees to the Permanent Mission of the Arab Republic of Egypt to the United Nations Office & International Organizations in Geneva, 4 January 2006.
15. Ibid.
16. Ibid.
17. "Statement to the media by Mr. António Guterres, United Nations High Commissioner for Refugees, on the conclusion of his Mission to the People's Republic of China", United Nations High Commissioner for Refugees, 23 March 2006.

13. THE NURSE AND THE SURGEON

1. "Preparations for UNHCR's Global Service Centre in Budapest are well under way", United Nations High Commissioner for Refugees, 4 October 2007.
2. "UNHCR—Outposting Feasibility Study", PricewaterhouseCoopers, 16 April 2007, p. 14.
3. Ibid.
4. CNN *Larry King Live*, interview with Perez Musharraf, broadcast on 22 October 2001.
5. In May 2018, the National Assembly of Pakistan approved a constitutional amendment to integrate these tribal areas—known as the Federally Administrative Tribal Areas (FATA)—in the border province of Khyber Pakhtunkhwa.
6. Peter Nicolaus in "Afghan refugee strategy a 'big mistake'", Agence France-Presse, 27 December 2011.
7. Ibid.
8. Ibid.
9. Ibid.
10. The Department of Political Affairs was held by the UK representatives between 1993 and 2005, when Kieran Prendergast retired and was replaced by the Nigerian Ibrahim Gambari.
11. Holmes, John, *Politics of Humanity: The Reality of Relief Aid*, Head of Zeus, 2013, p. 2.
12. Ibid.
13. In the mausoleum lay the tombs of Ali al-Hadi and Hassan al-Askari, the 10th and 11th Imams of the Twelver Shiite tradition—considered the successors of the Prophet Muhammad.
14. Socialist International Conference, "Building Democracy in Iraq—Working for Peace in the Middle East", Rome, 18–19 July 2003.
15. "Guterres urges Arab League to play greater role in UNHCR's work", United Nations High Commissioner for Refugees, 5 March 2007.
16. "Statement by Mr. António Guterres, United Nations High Commissioner for

Refugees, to the Conference on Addressing the Humanitarian Needs of Refugees and Internationally Displaced Persons inside Iraq and in Neighbouring Countries", 17 April 2007.

17. "UNHCR Syria update on Iraqi refugees", United Nations High Commissioner for Refugees, February 2008.

18. Georgia's position was that they were defending themselves against aggressions perpetrated by militias from South Ossetia. On the other hand, Russia claimed to act in protection of their peace forces in the territory. This led to the start of a violent conflict on August 2008. This region in the Caucasus had been at war in the 1990s, when South Ossetia self-proclaimed their independence from Georgia, which was never recognised by the international community.

14. SPRING TIDE

1. "Remarks of President Barack Obama—Responsibly Ending the War in Iraq", Obama White House Archives, 27 February 2009.

2. Duby, Georges, "Ano 1000, Ano 2000. Na Pista dos Nossos Medos", UNESP, 1998, pp. 30–31.

3. Ibid.

4. Braudel, Fernand, *Civilização Material, Economia e Capitalismo Séculos XV-XVIII*, Part I, Lisbon: Teorema, 1992, p. 79.

5. Ibid.

6. Taylor, A. J. P., *The Course of German History: A Survey of the Development of German History since 1815*, London: Routledge, 2001, p. 243.

7. Ibid. p. 243.

8. Convention Relating to the Status of Refugees, 1951.

9. Ibid.

10. According to the UNHCR, there were "ten specific areas of humanitarian intervention by 'clusters' of UN agencies, NGOs and other organizations" and "within this system, at the global level, UNHCR accepted leadership of the Protection Cluster, as well as of the Camp Coordination and Camp Management, and Emergency Shelter Clusters for situations of conflict-generated internal displacement"; "UNHCR Global Report 2010", United Nations High Commissioner for Refugees, June 2006, pp. 40–43.

11. "Internal Displacement—Global Overview of Trends and Developments in 2009", Internal Displacement Monitoring Centre, Norwegian Refugee Council, March 2011.

12. African Union Convention for the Protection and Assistance of Internally Displaced Persons in Africa, 2009.

13. UN Mission in the Democratic Republic of the Congo (MONUSCO) deployed 20,000 soldiers.

14. "Mortality in the Democratic Republic of the Congo—An Ongoing Crisis", International Rescue Committee, Burnet Institute, 2007.

15. The expression was first used by Margot Wallström, the Special Representative of the Secretary-General on Sexual Violence in Conflict, during a Security Council session, in April 2010.

16. "New displacement due to unrest, displacement due to Sa'ada conflict continues", Internal Displacement Monitoring Centre, October 2011.

17. "Arab Human Development Report 2002: Creating Opportunities for Future Generations", United Nations Development Programme, Arab Fund for Economic and Social Development, 2002, p. 27.

18. "Arab Human Development Report 2003: Building a Knowledgeable Society", United Nations Development Programme, Arab Fund for Economic and Social Development, 2003, p. 3.

19. "Arab Human Development Report 2004: Towards Freedom in the Arab World", United Nations Development Programme, Arab Fund for Economic and Social Development, 2004, p. 9.

20. "Arab Human Development Report 2005: Towards the Rise of Women in the Arab World", United Nations Development Programme, Arab Fund for Economic and Social Development, 2005, p. 3.

21. "Arab Human Development Report 2009: Challenges to Human Security in the Arab Countries", United Nations Development Programme, Arab Fund for Economic and Social Development, 2009, p. 2.

22. "Riots reported in Tunisian city", Al Jazeera, 20 December 2010.

23. Ibid.

24. Security Council, Security Council Resolution 1973 (2011) on the situation in the Libyan Arab Jamahiriya, 17 March 2011, UN Doc. S/RES/1973(2011).

25. "Humanitarian Emergency Response to the Libyan Crisis. 28 February 2011—27 September 2011: Seven-month Report on IOM's Response", International Organization for Migration, 2011.

15. AT EUROPE'S DOOR

1. "António Guterres, United Nations High Commissioner for Refugees: Remarks at the opening of the judicial year of the European Court of Human Rights", United Nations High Commissioner for Refugees, Strasbourg, 28 January 2011.

2. Ibid.

3. Ibid.

4. "Increased influx of migrants in Lampedusa, Italy", Joint Report from the Ministry of Health, Italy and the WHO Regional Office for Europe Mission of 28–29 March 2011, World Health Organization.

5. "UNHCR Global Report 2011", United Nations High Commissioner for Refugees, June 2011.

6. "UN urges refugee 'solidarity' within European Union", BBC, 19 June 2011.

7. Ibid.

8. "Draft Resolution / France Germany, Portugal, United Kingdom and Northern Ireland, and United States of America", 4 October 2011, UN Doc. S/2011/612.

9. Ibid.
10. Ibid.

16. FAITH AND PROTECTION

1. "Aid Worker Security Report 2012: Host states and their impact on security for humanitarian operations", Humanitarian Outcomes, December 2012.
2. "Human Resources Issues", Presentation by the Director, Division of Human Resources Management, to the Standing Committee, United Nations High Commissioner for Refugees, September 2012.
3. "Hardship Classification", Consolidated List of Entitlements Circular, International Civil Service Commission, ICSC/CRIC/HC/7, April 2011.
4. "Three UN refugee agency staff killed in Afghan suicide attack", UN News, 31 October 2011.
5. El-Wafa, Abou, "The Right to Asylum between Islamic Shari'ah and International Refugee Law: A Comparative Study", United Nations High Commissioner for Refugees, Organisation of the Islamic Conference and Naif Arab University for Security Sciences, 2009, p. 5.
6. Ibid. p. 30.
7. Ibid. p. 71.
8. Ibid.
9. Ibid. p. 45.
10. "2009 Global Trends Refugees, Asylum-seekers, Returnees, Internally Displaced and Stateless Persons", United Nations High Commissioner for Refugees, 15 June 2010.
11. "Alto Comisionado lanza libro sobre contribuciones del Islam a la protección de los refugiados", United Nations High Commissioner for Refugees, 24 June 2009.
12. "The rather dangerous Monsieur Hollande", The Economist, 28 April 2012.
13. See "Partnering with Religious Communities for Children", UNICEF, January 2009.
14. "High Commissioner's Dialogue on Protection Challenges, Theme: Faith and Protection; Opening remarks by Mr. António Guterres", United Nations High Commissioner for Refugees, 12 December 2012.
15. Ibid.
16. Ibid.
17. Ibid.
18. "Welcoming the Stanger: Affirmations for Faith Leaders", United Nations High Commissioner for Refugees, 2013.

17. THE GREAT MARCH

1. Cross-line operations require delivery of humanitarian aid to both sides of a conflict, i.e. to areas controlled by the government and areas under the rebels' control.

2. "Breaking the Stalemate: The Military Dynamics of the Syrian Civil War and Options for Limited U.S. Intervention", Centre for Middle East Policy, Brookings Institution, August 2012.
3. "UNHCR Global Report 2013", United Nations High Commissioner for Refugees, June 2013.
4. António Guterres, United Nations High Commissioner for Refugees and Yoka Brandt, UNICEF Deputy Executive Director Press Conference, Geneva, 23 August 2013, United Nations Webcast.
5. See the reports of the Independent International Commission of Inquiry on the Syrian Arab Republic, United Nations Human Rights Council.
6. "Obama issues Syria a 'red line' warning on chemical weapons", *Washington Post*, 20 August 2012.
7. "Obama warns Syria over chemical weapons", Al Jazeera, 4 December 2012.
8. "US sees evidence of chemical arms in Syria", Al Jazeera, 1 May 2013.
9. "Remarks by the President in Address to the Nation of Syria", The White House Office of the Press Secretary, 10 September 2013.
10. "Popularité: Hollande baisse de 9 points", *Le Figaro*, 11 November 2012.
11. "One Year On: Jordan's Za'atari Refugee Camp mushrooms into major urban centre", United Nations High Commissioner for Refugees, 29 July 2013.
12. "From slow boil to breaking point: A real time evaluation on UNHCR's response to the Syrian refugee emergency", United Nations High Commissioner for Refugees, July 2014, p. 10.
13. "A million children are now refugees from Syria crisis", United Nations High Commissioner for Refugees, 23 August 2013.
14. "UNHCR Global Report 2013", United Nations High Commissioner for Refugees, June 2013.
15. "Remarks by António Guterres, United Nations Commissioner for Refugees, Second International Humanitarian Pledging Conference for Syria", United Nations High Commissioner for Refugees, 15 January 2014.
16. Ibid.
17. "UNHCR: Syria 'biggest displacement crisis of all time'", BBC, 2 September 2013.
18. "From slow boil to breaking point: A real time evaluation on UNHCR's response to the Syrian refugee emergency", United Nations High Commissioner for Refugees, July 2014, p. 7.
19. "Independent Programme Evaluation (IPE) on UNHCR's Response to the refugee influx in Lebanon and Jordan", United Nations High Commissioner for Refugees, January 2015, p. 7.
20. "Second International Humanitarian Pledging Conference for Syria", United Nations Office for the Coordination of Humanitarian Affairs, 15 January 2014.
21. Ibid.
22. "Central African Republic Sub-regional Crisis Factsheet—November 2014", UNICEF, 30 November 2014.

23. See "The Dadaab Dilemma—A Study on Livelihood Activities and Opportunities for Dadaab Refugees", Danish Refugee Council and United Nations High Commissioner for Refugees, August 2013.
24. "UNHCR Global Trends 2013", United Nations High Commissioner for Refugees, 20 June 2014.
25. Ibid.
26. Ibid.
27. Ibid.
28. "Arc of instability" was a concept first used at the end of the 20th century by Australian external policy. East-Timor, Indonesia, Papua New-Guinea, Salomon Islands were among the arc. Since 9/11, the concept has been adapted to other geopolitical contexts.
29. "Remarks to the 65th Session of the Executive Committee of the High Commissioner's Programme", United Nations Secretary-General, 1 October 2014.
30. "Migrant arrivals by sea in Italy top 170,000 in 2014", International Organization for Migration, 16 January 2015.
31. "Visit to Lampedusa, Homily of Holy Father Francis", The Holy See, 8 July 2013.
32. "Fatal Journeys—Tracking Lives Lost During Migration", International Organization for Migration, 2014.
33. "Total number of Syrian refugees exceeds four million for first time", United Nations High Commissioner for Refugees, 9 July 2015.
34. "Hungary raids Norway-backed NGOs", *EUobserver*, 10 September 2014.
35. "Illegal migration clearly linked with terror threat: Hungary PM", Reuters, 25 July 2015.
36. "Orban demonises immigrants at Paris march", *EUobserver*, 12 January 2015.
37. Ibid.
38. "Hungary summons U.S. envoy over McCain's 'neo-fascist' comments", Reuters, 3 December 2014.
39. The Tunisian National Dialogue Quartet is formed by the Tunisian General Labour Union, the Tunisian Confederation of Industry, Trade and Handicrafts, the Tunisian Human Rights League, and the Tunisian Order of Lawyers.
40. "The Nobel Peace Prize for 2015", The Norwegian Nobel Committee, 10 October 2015.
41. "Paris attacks: What happened on the night", BBC, 9 December 2015.
42. "UNHCR chief says it is 'absolute nonsense' to blame refugees for terror", United Nations High Commissioner for Refugees, 17 November 2015.
43. "The CBS Democratic debate transcript, annotated", *Washington Post*, 15 November 2015.
44. "Trump: Paris massacre would have been 'much different' if people had guns", CNN, 14 November 2015.
45. "Remarks to the United Nations Security Council by António Guterres, United

Nations High Commissioner for Refugees", United Nations High Commissioner for Refugees, 18 April 2013.

46. United Nations Security Council, Seventieth year, 7592nd meeting, 21 December 2015, New York.

18. AFTER MALAYSIA

1. Excerpt from the letter A/70/623–S/2015/988, sent on 17 December by the President of the General Assembly, Mogens Lykketoft, and by the President of the Security Council, Samantha Power, to all the member states of the United Nations.
2. "A Better Process, a Stronger UN Secretary-General: How Historic Change Was Forged and What Comes Next", *Ethics and International Affairs*, 9 June 2017.
3. Letter from the President of the UN General Assembly, Mogens Lykketoft, and the Permanent Representative of the United States and the pro-tempore President of the Security Council, Samantha Power, 15 December 2015.
4. Ibid.
5. Official page of the first candidacy of António Guterres for Secretary-General of the United Nations: https://www.antonioguterres.gov.pt/candidacy-antonio-guterres/
6. Ibid.
7. Ibid.
8. Ibid.
9. Lykketoft, Mogens and Mette Holm, *Serving the World: 15 Months for the UN*, Copenhagen: Rosinante, 2017.
10. Ibid.

19. BACK TO CAMPAIGNING

1. Sherman, Robert, "Dez Milhões e Um—Uma visão sobre os portugueses do embaixador de Obama no nosso país", Coimbra: Actual Editora, 2018.
2. The Treaty of Windsor established the obligation for mutual assistance in case of enemy attack, or the need for military assistance and diplomatic support.
3. "Nudging the decision on UN Secretary General from the Security Council", *The Huffington Post*, 1 October 2017.
4. "Informal dialogue with the General Assembly of the United Nations of the candidate António Guterres for the position of Secretary-General", UN Web TV, 12 April 2016.
5. Originally said in French: "Quand les causes profondes des problèmes deviennent de plus en plus interreliés, la primauté de la prévention demande une vision holistique. Il faut comprendre les méga tendances globales de notre temps et il faut trouver les stratégies et les politiques qui puissent s'adresser ensemble et simultanément aux trois piliers de l'action des Nations Unies."

6. Originally said in Spanish: "Incumbe al Secretario General movilizar todo el sistema de la ONU—en cooperación con las otras organizaciones regionales y internacionales, la sociedad civil y el sector privado—para apoyar a los Estados, que son los protagonistas del proceso. Un apoyo total que garantice el éxito de la implementación de la agenda 2030."
7. "UN Sec-Gen candidates' debate", United Nations Association—UK (UNA-UK), 3 June 2016.
8. "The Cambridge Analytica Files", *The Guardian*, 2018.
9. "Nigel Farage EU poster reported to police for 'inciting racial hatred' as it's compared to Nazi propaganda", *The Mirror*, 17 June 2016.
10. "The UN debate", Al Jazeera English, 18 July 2016.
11. Ibid.
12. Ibid.
13. Ibid.

20. THE STRAW POLLS

1. "Strengthening the United Nations in the 21st century—a Platform for Impact and Action", Vuk Jeremić, Candidate for Secretary General of the United Nations, 2016.
2. "Identical letters dated 1 February 2017 from the Permanent Representative of Japan to the United Nations addressed to the Secretary-General and the President of the Security Council", A/71/774, 2 February 2017.
3. UN GA President, "#UNSC should communicate results of 1st informal straw polls on #NextSG to #UNGA to live up to transparency. Letter: http://ow.ly/ThJn302trXg", 21 July 2016, Tweet.
4. Letter from the President of the General Assembly to all Permanent Representatives and Permanent Observers to the United Nations New York, 21 July 2016.
5. Shortly after the Carnation Revolution, in 1974, Portugal accepted that its former colonies would be fully sovereign states, ruled without interference from the former metropole.
6. "Portugal's Guterres eyed ahead of second poll for next U.N. chief", Reuters, 3 August 2016.
7. Ibid.
8. "Hollande's Approval Rating Returns to All-Time Low: Elabe Poll", Bloomberg, 8 September 2016.
9. "Read Donald Trump's Speech to AIPAC", *Time*, 21 March 2016.
10. "'President Trump?' Here's How He Says It Would Look", *The New York Times*, 4 May 2016.
11. "UN aid worker suspended for leaking report on child abuse by French troops", *The Guardian*, 29 April 2015.
12. Complete documents and correspondence available at: http://www.codeblue-campaign.com/spotlight-car/#documents

13. "We've got to avert this looming disaster at the UN—The dire UNESCO boss can't be allowed to wreck the UN too", *The Times*, 25 August 2016.

21. CHECKMATE

1. Selmayr, Martin, "Would be great loss for @EU_Commission. But Kristalina would make strong UNSG, and many Europeans proud. + strong signal for gender equality", 10 September 2016, Tweet.
2. "Martin Selmayr, l'euro fort", Coulisse de Bruxelles, 4 February 2018.
3. "Who Will Run the U.N.? The best choice for reform at Turtle Bay is Serbia's Vuk Jeremic", *The Wall Street Journal*, 23 September 2016.
4. Ibid.
5. "Rift brewing between Putin and Merkel over UN nomination", EURACTIV, 12 September 2016.
6. "Identical letters dated 1 February 2017 from the Permanent Representative of Japan to the United Nations addressed to the Secretary-General and the President of the Security Council", A/71/774, 2 February 2017.
7. "A Better Process, a Stronger UN Secretary-General: How Historic Change Was Forged and What Comes Next", *Ethics & International Affairs*, June 2017.
8. "Bulgaria announces new candidate Georgieva for U.N. leadership race", Reuters, 28 September 2016.
9. Leviev-Sawyer, Clive, "Bulgaria's dumping of Bokova for Georgieva in UN race sparks political row", *The Sofia Globe*, 28 September 2016.
10. "Assembly Holds Informal Dialogue with Candidate for Next Secretary-General, Kristalina Gerogieva", UN Audiovisual Library, 3 October 2016.
11. "SC President, Vitaly Churkin (Russian Federation) on the selection process for the position of the next UN Secretary-General", Security Council Media Stakeout, 5 October 2016.

BIBLIOGRAPHY

In English:

Abbas, Hassan, *The Taliban Revival: Violence and Extremism on the Pakistan-Afghanistan Frontier*, New Haven: Yale University Press, 2014.

Abouzeid, Rania, *No Turning Back: Life, Loss, and Hope in Wartime Syria*, New York: W. W. Norton & Company, 2018.

Alatas, Ali, *The Pebble in the Shoe: The Diplomatic Struggle for East Timor*, Jakarta: Aksara Karunia, 2006.

Albright, Madeleine, *Madam Secretary: A Memoir*, New York: Harper Perennial, 2013.

Al-Khalidi, Ashraf, S. Hoffman, and V. Tanner, "Iraqi Refugees in the Syrian Arab Republic: A Field-Based Snapshot", Washington, D.C.: Brookings-Bern Project on Internal Displacement, 2007.

Annan, Kofi, *Interventions: A Life in War and Peace*, London: Penguin Books, 2012.

Betts, Alexander, G. Loescher, J. Milner, *UNHCR: The Politics and Practice of Refugee Protection*, London: Routledge, 2012.

Boutros-Ghali, Boutros, *Unvanquished*, London: Random House, 1999.

Chesterman, Simon, *Secretary or General? The UN Secretary-General in World Politics*, Cambridge: Cambridge University Press, 2007.

El-Wafa, Abou, *The Right to Asylum between Islamic Shari'ah and International Refugee Law: A Comparative Study*, United Nations High Commissioner for Refugees, Organization of the Islamic Conference, and Naif Arab University for Security Sciences, 2009.

Evans, Gareth, *Incorrigible Optimist: A Political Memoir*, Melbourne: Melbourne University Press, 2017.

Hall, Nina, *Displacement, Development, and Climate Change: International Organizations Moving Beyond Their Mandates*, London: Routledge, 2016.

Holmes, John, *Politics of Humanity: The Reality of Relief Aid*, London: Head of Zeus, 2013.

BIBLIOGRAPHY

Lykketoft, Mogens and M. Holm, *Serving the World: 15 Months for the UN*, Copenhagen: Rosinante, 2017.

Makdisi, Karim, *Land of Blue Helmets: The United Nations and the Arab World*, Oakland: University of California Press, 2016.

Martin, Ian, *Self-Determination in East Timor. The United Nations, the Ballot, and International Intervention*, Boulder: Lynne Rienner Publishers, 2001.

Maxwell, Kenneth, *The Making of Portuguese Democracy*, Cambridge: Cambridge University Press, 1997.

Rawlence, Ben, *City of Thorns: Nine Lives in the World's Largest Refugee Camp*, New York: Picador, 2016.

"Report of the Secretary-General on the situation of children and armed conflict affected by the Lord's Resistance Army", United Nations Security Council, 25 May 2012.

Rhodes, Ben, *The World as It Is: A Memoir of the Obama White House*, London: Random House, 2018.

Rice, Condoleezza, *No Higher Honor: A Memoir of My Years in Washington*, New York: Broadway Paperbacks, 2012.

Sahnoun, Mohamed, *Somalia: The Missed Opportunities*, Washington, D.C.: United States Institute of Peace Press, 1994.

Taylor, A. J. P., *The Course of German History: A Survey of the Development of German History since 1815*, London: Routledge, 2001.

The International Commission on Intervention and State Sovereignty, "The Responsibility to Protect", International Development Research Centre, Ottowa, December 2001.

Vlaardingerbroek, Pieter (editor), *The Portuguese Synagogue in Amsterdam*, Cultural Heritage Agency of the Netherlands, Zwolle: W Books, 2013.

Weiss, Michael and H. Hassan, *ISIS: Inside the Army of Terror*, New York: Regan Arts, 2016.

In Portuguese:

Adamopoulos, Sarah and Vasconcellos, José Luís de, "Liceu Camões 100 anos 100 testemunhos", Lisbon: Quimera Editores, 2009.

Antunes, José Freire, "Kennedy e Salazar—o leão e a raposa", 1ª Edição, Lisbon: Dom Quixote, 2013.

Branco, J. F., "Visões do Técnico no centenário 1911–2011", Lisbon: Centro em Rede de Investigação em Antropologia, 2013.

Braudel, Fernand, "Civilização Material, Economia e Capitalismo Séculos XV-XVIII", Tomo I: As Estruturas do Quotidiano, Lisbon: Editorial Teorema, 1992.

BIBLIOGRAPHY

"Estados Gerais para Uma Nova Maioria: Contrato de Legislatura", Lisbon: Gabinete de Estudos do Partido Socialista, 1995.

Duby, Georges, "Ano 1000, Ano 2000. Na Pista dos Nossos Medos", São Paulo: Editora UNESP, 1998.

Gomes, A., "A JUC, o Jornal Encontro e os primeiros inquéritos à Juventude Universitária. Contributos para a história das modernas ciências sociais em Portugal", Sociologia, Problemas e Práticas, 2005.

Guterres, António, "A pensar em Portugal", Lisbon: Editorial Presença, 1999.

Marker, Jamsheed, "Timor-Leste—Relato das Negociações para a Independência", Lisbon: Ministério dos Negócios Estrangeiros de Portugal, 2009.

Meneses, Filipe Ribeiro de, "Salazar: uma biografia política", 4ª Edição, Lisbon: Dom Quixote, 2010.

Pereira, Bernardo Futscher, "O Crepúsculo do Colonialismo", 1ª Edição, Lisbon: Dom Quixote, 2017.

Salazar, António de Oliveira, "Discursos e Notas Políticas 1928–1966", Coimbra: Coimbra Editora, 2016.

Silva, Cavaco, "Autobiografia Política II", Lisboa: Temas e Debates, 2004.

Sherman, Robert, "Dez Milhões e Um—Uma visão sobre os portugueses do embaixador de Obama no nosso país", Coimbra: Actual Editora, 2018.

Vieira, Joaquim, *Mário Soares—Uma Vida*", Lisboa: Esfera dos Livros, 2013.

In Spanish:

"Portugal responde en las Naciones Unidas", Ministerio de los Negocios Extranjeros. Imprensa Nacional, 1970.

INDEX

Note: Page numbers in italics refer to *n* denotes endnotes or *t* denotes tables

INDEX

INDEX

INDEX

INDEX

Moura, Joaquim Pina, 53, 68
Moya, 136
Mozambique, 8, 10, 293
Muallem, Walid, 204
Mugabe, Robert, 168–9, 280
Muhammad, Prophet, 190, 223, 357n13 (ch.13)
Muller, Sophie, 192–3
Muslim Council of Liberia, 200
Muslims, 188, 215
Mustafa Mahmoud Park, 140–2
Myanmar, 194, 306

Naif University, 190
Nairobi, 217
"National Candidacy", 246
National Democratic Institute (NDI), 124, 156
NATO (North Atlantic Treaty Organization), 7, 40, 305
Portugal departure from, 87
NDI. See National Democratic Institute (NDI)
Netanyahu, Benjamin, 280
The Netherlands, 226
"New Electoral Majority", 40
"New Majority Caravan", 41
New York Times, The (newspaper), 87, 246
New York, 1, 58, 83, 112
Guterres arrival in, 288
9/11 attack, 113–14, 124
New Zealand, 88, 249, 292, 323
Nicolaus, Peter, 155
Nigeria, 181
1951 Convention, 147
9/11 (attack), 113–14, 124
Non-Aligned Movement, 253, 356n36
North Africa, 172
2011 uprisings in, 178
North Americans, 301

North Carolina, 339
North Kivu, 170
North Korea, 32–3, 125, 350n6 (ch.2)
refugees, 145
North London, 76
Northern Dimension, 352n2 (ch.6)
Northern Uganda, 135
Norway, 299–300
Nossa Senhora da Luz, 17
Nouicer, Radhouane, 140, 142–3
Nyanzale, 170

Obama, Barack, 2, 124, 164
air strikes against Islamic State, authorization of, 221
reacts to chemical weapon usage in Syria, 206–7
See also White House
Observer, The (newspaper), 19
"Ode to Joy", 341
Ohio, 339
Okoth-Obbo, George, 167–8
Opium Wars, 55
Opus Dei, 129
Orbán, Viktor, 150
Organic Law, 36
Organisation of Islamic Cooperation, 242
Orthodox Church of Greece, 200
Os Lusíadas (poem), 8
Ottoman Empire, 14
Oval Office, 63
Oxford (university), 71

P5, 1, 229, 244
Pacem in Terris ("Peace on Earth"), 16–17
Pakistan, 152, 357n5

INDEX

Pakistanis, 153, 154

Palácio do Planalto, 50

Palais de Bourgogne, 71

Palais des Nations Assembly Hall, 218

Palais des Nations, 157, 198–9

Palestine/Palestinians, 112–13

Palestinian Question, 218

Palme, Olof, 20

"The Parable of the Talents", 18, 19–20, 199

Paris, 2, 83, 101
   divergences between Moscow and, 314
   Socialist International Congress in, 112
   terror attack in, 228

Path to Peace Foundation award, 238–9

pathos, 45

Patrão, Luís, 47, 48, 76
   moved out of São Bento, 99

peace agreement (Khartoum, 2005), 136–7

Peace and Security, 277–8

Pearl Harbour, 114

"The Pearl of Africa", 136

Pennsylvania, 340

Peres, Shimon, 38, 112

perestroika, 29

Persian Gulf state, 175

Pervez, Musharraf, 152–3, 154

Philippines, 28, 79

Pimentel, João Lima, 43, 50, 64
   views on rise of Guterres, 72–3
   visit to Vienna, 75

Pinochet, Augusto, 22, 113–14

Podesta, John, 125

Podesta's Center, 125

Poland, 28, 30, 68

Pope Francis, 220–1

Portas, Paulo, 109, 299

Portugal, 351*n*1, 364*n*5
   alliance between US and, 7–8
   analysis on members of Security Council, 265–8
   bonds with the US and NATO, 50
   bridge accident, 110
   Colonial War, 10, 21
   departure from NATO, 87
   European project, accession to, 33
   financial assistance to Palestine, 113
   Lisbon floods, 11–12
   1974 revolution, 35
   victory in Security Council election, 60
   See also Guterres; Portuguese Socialist Party (PS)

Portuguese (language), 82

Portuguese Central Bank, 111

Portuguese government, 83, 112, 299
   Alpha Plan, 67–8

Portuguese Parliament, 30–1, 93

Portuguese political police, 5

Portuguese Socialist Party (PS), 25, 26, 91, 350*n*1
   Conference in 1992, 36
   defeat of, 115–16
   failed to gain absolute majority, 99
   rise of Guterres in, 27
   victory in first democratic election, 28
   See also Guterres; Portugal

Portuguese Communist Party (PCP), 92

"Positive Candidacy" rule, 244

Pourmohammadi, Mostafa, 151, 188

381

INDEX

Obama left, 2
Obama speech in, 206
Winter Palace (Tsars), 29
Wisconsin, 83, 340
Workers' Party (Brazil), 122
World Assembly of Muslim
  Youth, 199
World Bank, 31, 59, 88, 241
World Council of Churches,
  199, 200
World Evangelical Alliance, 200
World Food Programme (WFP),
  170, 285
World Health Organization
  (WHO), 114, 241
World Refugee Day, 135, 137,
  208
World Summit (2005), 130
World Trade Organization, 130,
  305

World War I, 14
World War II, 1, 28, 134, 166,
  169, 273
WSJ. *See The Wall Street Journal*
  (WSJ)

Yemen, 289, 306
  Houthi insurgency, 170–1
Yemeni government, 171
YouTube, 174
Yugoslavia, 20

Za'atari, 208–10
Zaydi rebels, 171
Zebari, Hoshyar, 156, 157
Zenha, Francisco Salgado, 34
Zhao Ziyang, 145
Zhu Rongji, 55
Zimbabwe, 280
Zizas. *See* Melo, Luísa